Harold Pinter

Methuen Drama Engage offers original reflections about key practitioners, movements and genres in the fields of modern theatre and performance. Each volume in the series seeks to challenge mainstream critical thought through original and interdisciplinary perspectives on the body of work under examination. By questioning existing critical paradigms, it is hoped that each volume will open up fresh approaches and suggest avenues for further exploration.

Series Editors
Mark Taylor-Batty
University of Leeds, UK
Enoch Brater
University of Michigan, USA

Titles

Brecht and Post-1990s British Drama
Anja Hartl
ISBN 978-1-3501-7278-4

Drag Histories, Herstories and Hairstories: Drag in a Changing Scene Volume 2
Edited by Mark Edward and Stephen Farrier
ISBN 978-1-3501-0436-5

Contemporary Drag Practices and Performers: Drag in a Changing Scene Volume 1
Edited by Mark Edward and Stephen Farrier
ISBN 978-1-3500-8294-6

Performing the Unstageable: Success, Imagination, Failure
Karen Quigley
ISBN 978-1-3500-5545-2

Drama and Digital Arts Cultures
David Cameron, Michael Anderson and Rebecca Wotzko
ISBN 978-1-472-59219-4

Social and Political Theatre in 21st-Century Britain: Staging Crisis
Vicky Angelaki
ISBN 978-1-474-21316-5

Watching War on the Twenty-First-Century Stage: Spectacles of Conflict
Clare Finburgh
ISBN 978-1-472-59866-0

Fiery Temporalities in Theatre and Performance: The Initiation of History
Maurya Wickstrom
ISBN 978-1-4742-8169-0

For a complete listing, please visit
https://www.bloomsbury.com/series/methuen-drama-engage/

Harold Pinter

Stages, Networks, Collaborations

Edited by Basil Chiasson
and Catriona Fallow

Series Editors:
Mark Taylor-Batty and Enoch Brater

methuen | drama
LONDON • NEW YORK • OXFORD • NEW DELHI • SYDNEY

METHUEN DRAMA
Bloomsbury Publishing Plc
50 Bedford Square, London, WC1B 3DP, UK
1385 Broadway, New York, NY 10018, USA
29 Earlsfort Terrace, Dublin 2, Ireland

BLOOMSBURY, METHUEN DRAMA and the Methuen Drama logo
are trademarks of Bloomsbury Publishing Plc

First published in Great Britain 2021
This paperback edition published 2022

Copyright © Basil Chiasson and Catriona Fallow and contributors, 2021

Basil Chiasson and Catriona Fallow have asserted their right under the Copyright, Designs and Patents Act, 1988, to be identified as editors of this work.

For legal purposes the Acknowledgements on pp. xii–xiii constitute an extension of this copyright page.

Series design by Louise Dugdale
Cover image: Harold Pinter, 1983 (© Express Newspapers / Stringer / Getty Images)

All rights reserved. No part of this publication may be reproduced or transmitted in any form or by any means, electronic or mechanical, including photocopying, recording, or any information storage or retrieval system, without prior permission in writing from the publishers.

Bloomsbury Publishing Plc does not have any control over, or responsibility for, any third-party websites referred to or in this book. All internet addresses given in this book were correct at the time of going to press. The author and publisher regret any inconvenience caused if addresses have changed or sites have ceased to exist, but can accept no responsibility for any such changes.

A catalogue record for this book is available from the British Library.

Library of Congress Control Number: 2020949666

ISBN: HB: 978-1-3501-3362-4
PB: 978-1-3502-1194-0
ePDF: 978-1-3501-3364-8
eBook: 978-1-3501-3365-5

Series: Methuen Drama Engage

Typeset by Integra Software Services Pvt. Ltd.

To find out more about our authors and books visit www.bloomsbury.com and sign up for our newsletters.

Contents

List of Contributors ix
Acknowledgements xii
Notes on the Text xiv

Introduction *Basil Chiasson and Catriona Fallow* 1

Part One (Re)situating Pinter, Critical Orientations

1 Pinter's Modernism(s) Revisited: A Drama Reliant upon Prose
  Basil Chiasson 15

2 The Theatre of the Absurd as Professional Network in
  Harold Pinter's Early Career *Harry Derbyshire* 36

3 The Elite Pinter and the Pinter Elite *James Hudson* 53

4 'Too Much of a Modern?': Pinter's Jew*ish*ness *Eckart Voigts* 71

5 Pinter's Connections with the Middle East *Ibrahim Yerebakan* 88

Part Two Pinter as Playwright, Playwrights and Pinter

6 'An insistence in my mind': Pinter's Writing Ethic *Steve Waters* 107

7 Beyond the Mainstage: Harold Pinter at the Royal Shakespeare
  Company *Catriona Fallow* 121

8 Theatre's Dark Matter: Pinter's 'Staging' of Systemic Violence and
  Its Influence in Contemporary British Theatre *Alex Watson* 139

9 Faith, Telos and Failure: Pinter, Butterworth, Kelly *David Pattie* 157

10 The Crimpesque: Pinter's Legacy in the Theatre of Martin Crimp
   Maria Elena Capitani 174

Part Three Conversations with Collaborators

    Chinonyerem Odimba   197

    Nancy Meckler   201

    Douglas Hodge   203

    Jamie Lloyd   205

    Soutra Gilmour   210

Index   217

List of Contributors

Maria Elena Capitani teaches at the University of Parma, Italy, and was a visiting scholar at the Universities of Barcelona, Spain and Reading, UK, for 2014 and 2015. Her research interests are in twentieth- and twenty-first-century British literature and culture, with a special focus on drama, fiction, intertextuality, identity and translation for the stage. She has presented at international conferences across Europe and has published articles on contemporary British dramatists such as Martin Crimp, Sarah Kane, Tony Harrison, David Greig and Liz Lochhead. She is currently working on her first monograph, provisionally entitled *Contemporary British Appropriations of Greek and Roman Tragedies: The Politics of Rewriting*.

Basil Chiasson is Assistant Professor in the Faculty of Information and Media Studies and the Creative Arts Program at Western University, Canada. His publications on Harold Pinter include articles, book chapters, book reviews and one monograph, *The Late Harold Pinter: Political Dramatist, Poet and Activist* (2017). Other research and publications include articles and book chapters on neoliberalism and performance in contemporary British drama. From 2017 to 2019 he was a Research Fellow on the Arts and Humanities Research Council-funded project, Harold Pinter: Histories and Legacies, where he worked on an open-access database which captures the British production history of Pinter's works for stage, screen and radio.

Harry Derbyshire is Principal Lecturer in English Literature and Drama at the University of Greenwich, UK. His doctoral thesis, completed in 2000 at King's College, London, was entitled 'Harold Pinter: Production, Reception, Reputation 1984–1999'. He has since published on Pinter as celebrity, Pinter and style, Pinter and London, and the reception of Pinter's *Moonlight*; in other work he has considered theatre and human rights and the work of Edward Bond, Caryl Churchill, debbie tucker green, Arnold Wesker and Roy Williams. He is currently working on a history of the Theatre of the Absurd on the British stage.

Catriona Fallow is Lecturer in Drama, Theatre and Performance Studies in the Department of Drama at Queen Mary University of London, UK. Between 2017 and 2019 she was a Research Fellow on the Arts and Humanities Research Council-funded project, Harold Pinter: Histories and Legacies, based at the University of Birmingham. She is currently contributing to collections on the #MeToo movement (*Performing #MeToo: How Not to Look Away*, 2021) and the playwright Dennis Kelly (2021). Catriona's work has been published in *Studies in Theatre and Performance* and presented at various conferences and symposia nationally and internationally.

James Hudson is Lecturer in Drama at the University of Lincoln, UK. He has published on Edward Bond, Sarah Kane, David Greig and Howard Barker. He is currently conducting research on Simon Stephens, the British Council's support for touring drama and the relationship between theatre and right-wing politics. He wrote the programme note for the Derby Theatre production of Pinter's *Betrayal*. His special issue on performance and the right is forthcoming in *Studies of Theatre and Performance* (2021) and he is currently working on a monograph on populism, right-wing politics and British drama.

David Pattie is Senior Lecturer in Drama and Theatre Arts at the University of Birmingham, UK. He researches and publishes in a number of fields including contemporary British theatre, Scottish theatre, Samuel Beckett, popular performance and performance in popular music. His publications include *Modern British Playwriting the 1950s: Voices, Documents, New Interpretations* (2012), *Rock Music and Performance* (2007) and *Samuel Beckett* (2004) as well as edited collections on Kraftwerk and Brian Eno and numerous journal articles.

Eckart Voigts is Professor of English Literature at TU Braunschweig, Germany. He has written, edited and co-edited numerous books and articles, such as *Reflecting on Darwin* (2014), *Dystopia, Science Fiction, Post-Apocalypse* (2015) and *The Routledge Companion to Adaptation* (2018). He was President of the German Society for Theatre and Drama in English (CDE) from 2010 to 2016 and serves on the board of numerous journals. As a member of the research group 'Cultures of Participation' (Oldenburg), between 2016 and 2019 he led a research project on 'British-Jewish Theatre' (VW Foundation) with Jeanette Malkin. He is co-editor of *A Companion to British-Jewish Theatre since the 1950s*, for Methuen Drama's Engage series.

Steve Waters is a playwright and Professor of Scriptwriting in the School of Literature, Drama and Creative Writing at the University of East Anglia, UK. His recent works include *Limehouse* (2017), *Temple* (2015) and *World Music* (2004) at the Donmar Warehouse. Other works include *Why Can't We Live Together?* (Menagerie Theatre Company/UK Tour/Soho Theatre/Theatre

503), *Europa*, co-authored (Birmingham Rep/Dresden Staatspielhouse/ Teater Polski/Zagreb Youth Theatre), *Ignorance/Jahiliyyah*, *English Journeys* and *After the Gods* (Hampstead), *Capernaum in Sixty-Six Books*, *Little Platoons*, *The Contingency Plan* and *In a Vulnerable Place* (Bush), *Fast Labour* (Hampstead/West Yorkshire Playhouse) and *Habitats* (Gate and Tron Theatre Glasgow). Steve has also written extensively for radio and screen and is the author of *The Secret Life of Plays* (2010).

Alex Watson is a Visiting Lecturer and PhD candidate at Royal Holloway, University of London, UK. His research primarily explores 2010s British theatre and the concepts of violence and performativity. He has presented at various national and international conferences on topics including issues of protest, environmental damage, neoliberalism, European-British identities and gendered and racial violence. He is currently the book and performance reviews editor for *Platform*, Royal Holloway's journal for theatre and performance studies.

Ibrahim Yerebakan is Professor of English Dramatic Literature and Theatre Arts in the Department of English Language and Literature at Recep Tayyip Erdogan University, Rize, Turkey. He earned his PhD in contemporary English theatre from the University of Hull, UK. His research and publishing interests lie primarily in the theoretical, historical and practical investigation of the theatre, especially British political theatre in the twentieth century. His publications include *The Question of Class in Post-War British Theatre: Reassessing the New Wave Movement 1956–1965* (2011) and a number of articles published in international refereed and indexed journals.

Acknowledgements

It is fitting that a book that takes 'stages', 'networks' and 'collaborations' as its touchstones is the product of many rewarding collaborations, networks of support and stages of development.

Our collaboration as editors was initiated during the Arts and Humanities Research Council-funded project Harold Pinter: Histories and Legacies (grant number AH/P005039/1, http://pinterlegacies.com/). Between 2017 and 2019, we had the opportunity to immerse ourselves in the scholarly and archival materials pertaining to Pinter's stage work across the UK, to talk to some of Pinter's closest friends, collaborators, inheritors and fans, and to engage with Pinter scholars internationally. As well as enabling our own research, which has shaped our individual contributions to this collection, this book as a whole would not have been possible without the time, resources and access afforded by the Harold Pinter: Histories and Legacies project. We are grateful to its principal investigator, Mark Taylor-Batty, and the rest of the research team (Graham Saunders, Jonathan Bignell, William Davies, Billy Smart and Amanda Wrigley) for their shared enthusiasm for all things Pinter.

Our sincerest thanks to all our authors – whose chapters initially began as contributions to the Harold Pinter: Histories and Legacies project's first international conference, Staging Pinter: Networks, Collaborators, Legacies, in April 2018 at the University of Birmingham – for bringing fresh perspectives, approaches and insights to Pinter. We would like to thank Chinonyerem Odimba, Nancy Meckler, Douglas Hodge, Jamie Lloyd and Soutra Gilmour for their time and generosity in sharing their insights and experiences with us and for allowing us to reproduce them here. We are very grateful to Anna Brewer, Meredith Benson and all of the team at Bloomsbury, including the Engage Series Editors, Enoch Brater and Mark Taylor-Batty, for their feedback and enthusiasm for the collection.

We have both had the immense privilege of working with staff at various libraries and collections both in the UK and internationally. Basil would particularly like to thank the staff at the British Library, the New York Public Library and the Lilly Library at Indiana University. Catriona would like to thank the staff at the Shakespeare Birthplace Trust Library and Archives, particularly Jim Ranahan, Paul Edmondson and Paul Taylor, for their assistance and permission to quote materials from the RSC collections in her chapter.

Our final thanks to colleagues at the Universities of Leeds, Birmingham and Queen Mary University of London, and our friends and family for their support and encouragement over the course of developing this work. Particular thanks to our nearest and dearest – Joanna, Atticus and Ida, and Luke, Ann and David – for their endless patience and care.

Notes on the Text

Throughout this collection, the year indicated for Pinter's plays refers to the year the work in question premiered for stage, radio or television as relevant unless otherwise indicated.

Across all chapters, quotations from Pinter's plays are taken from the following Faber and Faber editions:

Pinter, H. (1996), *Harold Pinter: Plays 1*, London: Faber and Faber.
Pinter, H. (1996), *Harold Pinter: Plays 2*, London: Faber and Faber.
Pinter, H. (1997), *Harold Pinter: Plays 3*, London: Faber and Faber.
Pinter, H. (2011), *Harold Pinter: Plays 4*, London: Faber and Faber.

In some exceptional cases, a specific single edition has been cited because it contains contextual or introductory material that is specific to that edition.

Within the quotations from Pinter's plays, three dots in parentheses (…) correspond to Pinter's original convention; three dots in square brackets […] indicate an omission.

Introduction

Basil Chiasson and Catriona Fallow

It is difficult, perhaps, to conceive of a time when Harold Pinter, often said to be one of Britain's greatest playwrights, was not afforded the status, prestige or level of critical and artistic engagement that his life and work have inspired. By the 2000s, for example, Pinter's hegemony was such that it was possible to assert that his 'very name [had] become a cultural commodity, a phantom value attending the individual reception of his works' (Begley 2004: 87). This cultural status and attendant value were evident in 2018, ten years after Pinter's death, when the Jamie Lloyd Company occupied London's Harold Pinter Theatre for an entire season devoted to Pinter's shorter works. Part of *Pinter 10*, a partnership between the British Film Institute (BFI), the Harold Pinter Estate, and Faber and Faber publishers to mark the tenth anniversary of Pinter's passing, the *Pinter at the Pinter* season comprised more than thirty different pieces including one-act plays originally written for the stage, radio and television alongside revue sketches, poetry and prose. Rather than moving chronologically through these works, the season juxtaposed different texts from across the Pinter canon, assembling them into seven different instalments.[1] Throughout the season, the theatre's fire curtain appeared adorned with only the surname – PINTER – in sizeable block letters appearing as if chiselled into stone. A design choice such as this is perhaps ambivalent, given how its affirmation of Pinter's stature and permanence could be understood, for many in attendance, as a reminder of how a playwright undergoes a second death in becoming canonical and a third one still '[i]f then his or her work is regarded as untouchable' (Devine 2012: 42). At the same time, the Jamie Lloyd Company's casting of new talent alongside well-established actors now considered synonymous with Pinter and the season's innovative treatment of a range of works – across the seven instalments and in a stand-alone production of *Betrayal* (1978) which followed after – demonstrated how much collaboration was an intrinsic part of Pinter's career, the collaborative effort it takes to stage such a season and how the Pinter canon remains open to fresh perspectives, new interpretations and a multiplicity of creative voices.

Alongside examples of Pinter's work in performance, there is a by now well-established body of Pinter scholarship and criticism that similarly seeks to interrogate and celebrate, memorialize and enliven the legacies of the playwright's life and work. In the 2001 *Cambridge Companion to Harold Pinter*, Peter Raby describes how '[p]utting together a collection of essays about a living writer carries a special sense of excitement, even danger' (2001: 1). Writing in 2020, more than a decade after Pinter's death, this 'danger' or frisson of excitement that Raby identifies has shifted. While there is no longer the 'danger' of Pinter, for example, reacting unfavourably to academic discussion of his works, other challenges present themselves when the playwright in question is no longer responding to the world in real time and when their status has, if anything, increased and concretized. Now, more than ever, to write about or to stage Pinter is to engage with the monolithic entity PINTER.

Putting together a collection of essays about a writer of Pinter's stature, then, is as much a process of reassessment of what is known or held to be true as it is an attempt to showcase and generate new knowledge. In the context of renewed interest in Pinter's writing for contemporary audiences and a wave of fresh approaches to staging Pinter, this collection seeks to contribute to and expand current critical understandings of Pinter's significance by reappraising a number of the various stages, networks and collaborations that were endemic to Pinter's career and that continue to define his legacy. The chapters in this collection therefore engage with examples of the expansive range of influences, locations, institutions, collaborators and inheritors that have shaped and, in turn, have been shaped by Pinter's life and work.

After five decades of Pinter scholarship, the terrain has become vast. Because this collection emerges more than a decade after Pinter's death and since the last edited collection dedicated to Pinter appeared in 2009, it is important to account for the key themes, ideas and foci which have emerged in the intervening years and which resonate with this book's foci and orientations.[2] From the outset, studies of Pinter's plays were overwhelmingly concerned with the playwright's style and dramatic language, and this strand of scholarship continues at a pace. Scholars remain interested, for example, in the nature of the characters' dialogue; the use, function and meaning of Pinter's pauses and silences; and the mixture of lyrical and popular idioms in his writing. Studies of how Pinter's plays are variously aligned with Realism and Naturalism, Expressionism, Surrealism, Absurdism, Modernism and Postmodernism have generated their own critical shorthand that includes – and continually rethinks – terms and categories such as the Pinteresque, comedy of menace and Pinter's so-called memory plays.

Biographical approaches, while rarer, remain key touchstones in Pinter discourse. The most comprehensive is unquestionably Michael Billington's authorized biography, *Harold Pinter* (2007 [1996]). In tracing Pinter's life and career, Billington's depiction of nearly all of Pinter's work as political inaugurated a predominant way of interpreting Pinter in the late twentieth century. What also remains evident, more than twenty years since its publication, is how valuable the use of interviews and personal insights are to the study of Pinter. Ian Smith's *Pinter in the Theatre* (2005) and Mark Taylor-Batty's *About Pinter: The Playwright and the Work* (2005) followed Billington's lead by gathering and publishing original interviews with both Pinter and his close collaborators. Lady Antonia Fraser's published diaries, *Must You Go?* (2010) and *Our Israeli Diary* (2017), and Henry Woolf's *Barcelona Is in Trouble* (2017) offer more intimate biographical readings of Pinter. William Baker's most recent publication, *Pinter's World* (2018), represents a continued interest in biographical readings of Pinter, explicitly foregrounding Pinter's personal and professional relationships and interests.

Billington's focus on Pinter's politics and, crucially, how they manifest across the Pinter canon set the stage for scholars to focus more on Pinter's later, overtly political dramas, poetry and activism and to rethink how other works might be read as political. Charles Grime's *Harold Pinter's Politics* (2005) and Basil Chiasson's *The Late Harold Pinter* (2017) consider at length the scope and nature of Pinter's representation of political realities as an artist and a citizen, the political implications of his work in both arenas, and the various ways they inform each other. Related to this discursive focus on Pinter's politics are studies which seek to politicize Pinter by adopting a particular critical approach to the plays' modes of representation. Elizabeth Sakellaridou's *Pinter's Female Portraits* (1988) and Drew Milne's 'Pinter's Sexual Politics' (2001) are key examples given their essential interrogations of Pinter's representation of women and gendered power relations. Critical approaches to Pinter also include studies which de-centre Pinter from exclusively British and North American contexts. More recently, perspectives on Pinter have become increasingly global, with important work being done on Pinter in translation and performance beyond the English-speaking West, such as Tomaž Onič's 'Perspectives on Pinter Abroad' (2012) and more specific studies such as Łukasz Borowiec's 'Harold Pinter on Polish Radio and Television: Between Tradition and Innovation' (2020).

Another key strand of scholarship consists of studies that consider Pinter's influences and those he might be said to have influenced. Critical work in this area began early, with Martin Esslin's *Theatre of the Absurd* (1961) followed by *The Peopled Wound: The Work of Harold Pinter* (1970), as well as a range of journal articles and chapters in edited collections which offered comparative readings of Pinter and writers such as Samuel Beckett, Franz Kafka, Marcel Proust, Eugene O'Neill, August Strindberg, Anton Chekhov, T. S. Eliot, Ernest Hemingway and William Shakespeare. More recently, comparative approaches have begun to look beyond the usual figures to consider Pinter in relation to the likes of George Bernard Shaw (Grimes 2005), Noël Coward (Eltis 2008; Wixon 2009), Sarah Kane (Taylor-Batty 2009, 2014) and Philip Ridley (Wyllie 2009) and in ways that complicate the relationship between Pinter's texts and practice and those of others in order to go beyond a strictly comparative approach.

Over time, Pinter scholarship has increasingly looked beyond textual readings of his plays by focusing on Pinter's work as it unfolds in performance and in other forms such as his screenplays, writing for radio, poetry and prose fiction and non-fiction, and his directing and acting. Sustained interest in the range of Pinter's activity and variety of the works themselves has also resulted in studies which attend specifically to the transmedial nature of Pinter's work and career, evident across the essays featured in 'Harold Pinter's Transmedial Histories' (Bignell and Davies 2020).

A great deal of the existing discourses on Pinter flourished in parallel to his own growing body of works. From a contemporary vantage point, the authors in this collection are writing at a time where there is arguably less concern for ascertaining what Pinter's plays *mean* in and of themselves, particularly at the moment of their production. Instead, trends in Pinter scholarship suggest increasing interest in enlarging understandings of how Pinter's work is positioned and what it signifies in different sociopolitical, geographical and cultural contexts and from different, new critical and conceptual perspectives. Divided into three parts, this book offers readers a collection of chapters which re-contextualize and resituate Pinter as a cultural figure, explore and interrogate Pinter's influence on contemporary British playwriting, and offer a series of original interviews with theatre makers engaged in the staging of Pinter's work today. Collectively, these chapters demonstrate the different ways that Pinter's praxis and influence extended – and continue to extend – beyond individual plays or seminal productions to connect with and contribute to wider networks of people, places and practices.

This collection is concerned primarily with Pinter as a dramatist, who began his career performing and writing for stages across Britain. This is not to elide the significance of Pinter's work as a writer, director and performer in other contexts; as reflected in the critical trends outlined above, over five decades, Pinter's work traversed various forms and genres across theatre, film, television and radio drama, poetry, prose and political activism and intersected with the work of other writers and artists across a series of institutions and production companies. However, by focusing specifically on Pinter's writing for the stage, this collection establishes important groundwork for further reappraisals of his work in other media and by scholars outside of the fields of theatre and performance studies, while also generating new insights and material related to British drama and Pinter studies specifically.

Central to the applicability of the concepts and points of departure explored in this collection to other areas of scholarship is a collective endeavour by all the authors to think of Pinter as both a playwright and, more broadly, a cultural figure whose creative practice, personal politics and enduring significance have evolved over time. While textual and performance analysis of specific Pinter plays appear across most of the chapters, it is often secondary to or illustrative of the broader critical concerns, concepts and questions that each author proposes and interrogates. Pinter's plays and playwrighting, then, are not positioned as stable or having a fixed end point, nor as the work of a sole creative figure. Rather, this collection positions Pinter and his stage works as part of a series of wider cultural, political and social networks and evolving scholarly discourse by focusing on Pinter's relationships to different institutions and individuals throughout his career.

The subtitle of this collection – *Stages, Networks, Collaborations* – speaks to the plurality that we are trying to capture. Rather than focusing on a single 'stage', for example, the chapters in this collection are interested in multiple *stages* both in terms of the evolution of Pinter's career and the myriad of stages that his work has appeared on. *Networks* are understood and explored in these chapters as an exchange of ideas, practices and influence, as well as systems of interconnected people, places or works. Across the collection, chapters explore the broader series of networks that Pinter produced and engaged with, both as an artist and as a citizen, and demonstrate how these networks offer us fresh insights into Pinter's activity and influence while he was alive and how they continue to reverberate to define his legacy. *Collaborations* are often at the heart of these networks, particularly during Pinter's lifetime. They are also evident in the way his work engages with previous literary and theatrical movements and how, in turn, his works have been taken up and evolved by subsequent playwrights, practitioners and scholars. In approaching these various stages, networks and collaborations from Pinter's past and the contemporary present, this collection ultimately hopes to shape future interventions in Pinter scholarship and performance.

Taking up this tripartite division of past, present and future, Part One, '(Re)situating Pinter, Critical Orientations', is concerned with the 'past', that is, with reappraising key strands in Pinter scholarship and, in some instances, excavating and evolving overlooked or forgotten moments. Collectively, these first five chapters traverse a number of significant artistic, conceptual, geopolitical and biographical contexts that shaped Pinter's life and work while engaging critically with ubiquitous or even taken-for granted ways of seeing, discussing and understanding Pinter's practice. The first two chapters return to and interrogate two major artistic and aesthetic movements that remain at the forefront of Pinter scholarship – modernism and the Theatre of the Absurd – by considering how the former facilitated Pinter's originality as a playwright and how the latter was both useful and a hindrance to Pinter's early identity and growth as a writer. Basil Chiasson's 'Pinter's Modernism(s) Revisited: A Drama Reliant upon Prose' offers a comparative and intertextual reading of Pinter's plays and key moments in modernist fiction as a way to interrogate and evolve the discourse of influence. In so doing, Chiasson represents Pinter's modernist influences and the originality of his plays as inextricably linked. In 'The Theatre of the Absurd as Professional Network in the Early Career of Harold Pinter', Harry Derbyshire circumvents the tendency in Pinter scholarship to focus on identifying whether or not Pinter is an Absurdist (and if so, how) to instead rearticulate the role of the Theatre of the Absurd in Pinter's early career in terms of expediency. By examining the role the Theatre of the Absurd played in fostering collaborative relationships and professional networks, Derbyshire shifts the critical focus away from questions of genre and adherence to cultural trends to focus instead on how the Absurd, as a literary and theatrical phenomenon, functioned and circulated practically, and the possibilities and constraints it presented Pinter as a result.

The subsequent three chapters in Part One each add significant detail to key areas of discussion within Pinter scholarship while re-interrogating aspects of Pinter's biography, particularly notions of elitism and class, cultural heritage and identity and political activism. James Hudson's 'The Elite Pinter and the Pinter Elite' redresses the paucity of studies on Pinter and class by turning to C. W. Mills and Pierre Bourdieu for a theoretical discourse on the sociology of elites in order to offer a dual perspective on elitism as it relates to Pinter: both the way that elites are represented in plays such as *The Homecoming* (1965), *Betrayal, One for the Road* (1984) and *Party Time* (1991) and the dimensions of Pinter's own elite status as an artist and public figure. Eckart Voigts's chapter, '"Too Much of a Modern?": Pinter's Jew*ish*ness', intersects with Hudson's enquiry by also introducing a new discursive construct into Pinter studies, the concept of 'Jew*ish*ness', enabling him to return to and evolve the contentious subject of what Jew*ish*ness has to do with Pinter's plays and the playwright himself. Voigts's critical engagement with assertions about Pinter and his work's relation to cultural heritage, religion, spirituality and the politics of being Jewish locates

Pinter and plays like *The Birthday Party* (1958) and *Ashes to Ashes* (1996) beyond essentializing discourses. Ibrahim Yerebakan's 'Pinter's Connections with the Middle East' focuses on Pinter's identity as a political activist by foregrounding his concern with minorities who suffer under political conflict. Yerebakan reappraises the history of Pinter's first-hand experiences of the Middle East and subsequent critique of its governments, specifically Turkey, by elaborating on the relevant sociopolitical context and introducing, for the first time into Pinter scholarship, contrasting perspectives evident in Turkish-language media coverage. By offering new, granular details drawn from primary material in dialogue with the extensive volume of existing Pinter scholarship in these areas, the chapters in Part One both nuance and complicate Pinter's status as an individual, celebrity and historical figure, as well as Pinter's relationship to American and European literary traditions, their authors and the wider world.

If Part One's chief concern is with reappraising and evolving 'past' or established discursive trends and critical orientations, Part Two, 'Pinter as Playwright, Playwrights and Pinter', centres on Pinter's legacies and influence in the present, specifically for contemporary British playwrights. To establish this dialogue between Pinter's playwrighting and subsequent generations of writers, Part Two opens with Steve Waters's '"An insistence in my mind": Pinter's Writing Ethic', a playwright's attempt to identify the specific power and singularity of Pinter's achievement by looking closely at Pinter's scattered yet telling accounts of his own writing process. By tracking how Pinter's process and aesthetic run counter to the main currents of British new writing from the 1950s to the 1970s alongside his own experiences of Pinter's work, Waters explores the allegorical possibilities of two Pinter dramas specifically, *Old Times* (1971) and *No Man's Land* (1975). Building on the reappraisal of Pinter's writing ethic that Waters offers, in 'Beyond the Mainstage: Harold Pinter at the Royal Shakespeare Company', Catriona Fallow explores the versatility of Pinter's writing within the wider structures of a theatrical institution that played a key role in his career: the Royal Shakespeare Company (RSC). Looking beyond the mainstage successes of premieres like *The Homecoming* or widely cited collaborations with director Peter Hall, Fallow focuses on two lesser-known, small-scale instances of Pinter's work at the RSC during the company's first decade in order to reflect on the institution's role in shaping public perceptions of the accessibility of Pinter's work, while simultaneously consolidating and validating the writer's canonical status.

Following these recalibrations of popular perceptions of Pinter's writing practice and institutional affiliations, the final three chapters in Part Two each illuminate Pinter's impact on British playwriting's vernacular both generally and in the work of several key contemporary playwrights. In 'Theatre's Dark Matter: Pinter's "Staging" of Systemic Violence and Its Influence in Contemporary British Theatre', Alex Watson identifies a pervasive, ongoing interest with staging sociocultural violence in the work of contemporary British dramatists, tracing this aesthetic and political preoccupation back to Pinter's early stage works. Drawing on the theories of Slavoj Žižek and Étienne Balibar, Watson's chapter places the work of debbie tucker green (*ear for eye*, 2018) and Mark Ravenhill (*The Cane*, 2018) in dialogue with Pinter's *The Caretaker* (1960) and *Party Time*, respectively, focusing on how dialogue and absence are central to capturing a sense of the often invisible, intangible but nevertheless pernicious machinations of systemic violence. David Pattie's chapter, 'Faith, Telos and Failure: Pinter, Butterworth, Kelly', also explicates Pinter's influence on two other contemporary playwrights, Jez Butterworth and Dennis Kelly, via a specific thematic turn in contemporary British drama: the metaphysical. Arguing that Pinter's influence on both writers is discernible not simply in the dialogue and the structure of plays like Butterworth's *The River* (2012) or Kelly's *Orphans* (2009), Pattie explores how all three writers create play worlds that are fundamentally unstable, in which the power relations between characters are prone to sudden, unpredictable shifts and characters are subject to external power structures that in some ways actively resist the process of dramatization. The final chapter in Part Two explores the connections between Pinter and one other contemporary writer: Martin Crimp. Where writers such as Butterworth and Kelly have referenced the formative impact of Pinter's work upon them, Maria Elena Capitani's 'The Crimpesque: Pinter's Legacy in the Theatre of Martin Crimp' interrogates Crimp's ambivalence towards – or even contestation of – Pinter's influence. Here, Capitani offers a close reading of the defamiliarizing texture and structure of a selection of Crimp's plays, and *The Country* (2000) specifically, demonstrating how the Pinteresque permeates, to a greater or lesser extent, Crimp's entire output.

Part Three, 'Conversations with Collaborators', looks towards the future by offering a selection of interviews with contemporary theatre and performance practitioners who are or have been engaged in the staging and continued circulation of Pinter's work in performance. Taking up the questions pertaining to influence raised in both Parts One and Two, these conversations explore how each interviewee has navigated Pinter's continued influence in their own work throughout the late twentieth and twenty-first centuries, in some cases when collaborating with Pinter directly. Insights from established, long-standing friends and collaborators of Pinter, such as director Nancy Meckler and actor and director Douglas Hodge, sit alongside perspectives from practitioners most recently engaged with directing and designing Pinter's work for UK stages. These include playwright, poet and director Chinonyerem Odimba, assistant director on *The Caretaker* at the Bristol Old Vic and Northampton Royal and Derngate Theatres in 2017, director Jamie Lloyd, and designer Soutra Gilmour who – thanks in part to their work on the *Pinter at the Pinter* season as well as multiple other productions of Pinter's plays – have, respectively, directed or designed more of Pinter's work for the stage than anyone else. These conversations affirm, nuance and, in some cases, contest well-established truisms and approaches to staging Pinter; they rearticulate and demonstrate what makes Pinter's work and the artist himself distinctive, both in his own time and for subsequent generations, and critically reflect on a worldwide Pinter industry concerned with maintaining Pinter's legacy.

Notes

1 *Pinter One* included *Press Conference* (2002), *Precisely* (1983), *The New World Order* (1991), scenes from *Mountain Language* (1988), *American Football* (written in 1991), *The Pres and Officer* (2017), *Death* (written 1997), scenes from *One for the Road* (1984), all directed by Jamie Lloyd, and *Ashes to Ashes* (1996), directed by Lia Williams. *Pinter Two* included *The Lover* (1963) and *The Collection* (1961), both directed by Lloyd. *Pinter Three* comprised *Landscape* (1968), *Apart from That* (2006), *Girls* (written in 1995), *That's All* (1960), *God's District* (1997), *Monologue* (1973), *That's Your Trouble* (1959), *Special Offer* (1959), *Trouble in the Works* (1959), *Night* (1969) and *A Kind of Alaska* (1982), all directed by Lloyd. *Pinter Four* included *Moonlight* (1993), directed by Lyndsey Turner, and *Night School* (1960), directed by Ed Stambollouian. *Pinter Five* included *The Room* (1957), *Victoria Station* (1982) and *Family Voices* (1981), all directed by Patrick Marber. *Pinter Six* included *Party Time* (1991) and *Celebration* (2000), directed by Lloyd. Finally, *Pinter Seven* included *The Dumb Waiter* (1959) and *A Slight Ache* (1959), both directed by Lloyd. Alongside these seven programmes, there were several one-off or limited-run events including two performances of Pinter's Nobel Prize acceptance speech, *Art, Truth and Politics* (2005), performed by Mark Rylance and directed by Harry Burton, and a gala evening event, *Happy Birthday, Harold*, that consisted of a further thirty-nine pieces of work including scenes from Pinter's full-length plays such as *The Birthday Party* (1958), *The Caretaker* (1960), *The Hothouse* (written in 1958, premiered in 1980) and *The Homecoming* (1965) alongside poetry, sketches and prose. Collectively, then, the *Pinter at the Pinter* season represents the most extensive programme of Pinter's work ever staged.

2   Notable collections to emerge in 2009 include *Pinter Et Cetera*, edited by Craig N. Owens; *Harold Pinter's The Dumb Waiter*, edited by Mary F. Brewer (which, despite the title's focus, offers a range of critical approaches to Pinter beyond that play); and *Viva Pinter: Harold Pinter's Spirit of Resistance*, edited by Brigitte Gauthier.

Works Cited

Baker, W. (2018), *Pinter's World: Relationships, Obsessions, and Artistic Endeavors*, Madison, WIS and Teaneck, NJ: Fairleigh Dickinson University Press.

Batty, M. (2005), *About Pinter: The Playwright and the Work*, London: Faber and Faber.

Begley, V. (2004), 'The Modernist as Populist: Pinter's Betrayal and Mass Culture', in F. Gillen and S. Gale (eds), *The Pinter Review: Collected Essays 2003 and 2004*, 83–102, Tampa: University of Tampa Press.

Bignell, J., and W. Davies (2020), 'Introduction: Harold Pinter's Transmedial Histories', *Historical Journal of Film, Radio and Television*, 40 (3): 481–98.

Billington, M. (2007), *Harold Pinter*, 2nd edn, London: Faber and Faber.

Borowiec, Ł. (2020), 'Harold Pinter on Polish Radio and Television: Between Tradition and Innovation', *Historical Journal of Film, Radio and Television*, 40 (3): 584–601.

Brewer, M., ed. (2009), *Harold Pinter's The Dumb Waiter*, Amsterdam: Rodopi.

Chiasson, B. (2017), *The Late Harold Pinter: Political Dramatist, Poet and Activist*, London: Palgrave.

Devine, M. (2012), 'Returning to Roots: Pinter as Alternative Theatre Playwright', *ELOPE*, 9 (1): 41–9.

Eltis, S. (2008), 'Bringing Out the Acid: Noël Coward, Harold Pinter, Ivy Compton-Burnett and the Uses of Camp', *Modern Drama*, 51 (2): 211–33.

Esslin, M. (1961), *The Theatre of the Absurd*, Garden City, NY: Anchor.

Esslin, M. (1970), *The Peopled Wound: The Plays of Harold Pinter*, London: Methuen.

Fraser, A. (2011), *Must You Go? My Life with Harold Pinter*, London: Phoenix.

Fraser, A. (2017), *Our Israeli Diary, 1978: Of That Time, of That Place*, London: Oneworld.

Gauthier, B., ed. (2009), *Viva Pinter: Harold Pinter's Spirit of Resistance*, Bern: Peter Lang.

Grimes, C. (2005), *Harold Pinter's Politics: A Silence beyond Echo*, Madison, WIS and Teaneck, NJ: Fairleigh Dickinson University Press.

Milne, D. (2001), 'Pinter's Sexual Politics', in P. Raby (ed.), *The Cambridge Companion to Harold Pinter*, 195–211, Cambridge: Cambridge University Press.

Onič, T. (2012), 'Pinter Abroad', *ELOPE*, 9 (1): 5–9.

Raby, P., ed. (2001), *The Cambridge Companion to Harold Pinter*, Cambridge: Cambridge University Press.
Sakellaridou, E. (1988), *Pinter's Female Portraits: A Study of Female Characters in the Plays of Harold Pinter*, Totowa, NJ: Barnes and Noble.
Smith, I. (2005), *Pinter in the Theatre*, London: Nick Hern Books.
Taylor-Batty, M. (2009), 'What Remains? *Ashes to Ashes*, Popular Culture, Memory and Atrocity', in C. N. Owens (ed.), *Pinter Et Cetera*, 99–116, Newcastle upon Tyne: Cambridge Scholars.
Taylor-Batty, M. (2014), 'How to Mourn: Kane, Pinter and Theatre as Monument to Loss in the 1990s', in M. Aragay and E. Monforte (eds), Aleks Sierz (Foreword), *Ethical Speculations in Contemporary British Theatre*, 59–75, Basingstoke and New York: Palgrave Macmillan.
Wixon, C. (2009), 'That Was the Play: Harold Pinter and Noël Coward', in C. N. Owens (ed.), *Pinter Et Cetera*, 31–42, Newcastle upon Tyne: Cambridge Scholars.
Woolf, H. (2017), *Barcelona Is in Trouble*, Warwick: Greville Press.
Wyllie, A. (2009), 'The Politics of Violence after In-Yer-Face: Harold Pinter and Philip Ridley', in C. N. Owens (ed.), *Pinter Et Cetera*, 63–77, Newcastle upon Tyne: Cambridge Scholars.

Part One

(Re)situating Pinter, Critical Orientations

1

Pinter's Modernism(s) Revisited: A Drama Reliant upon Prose

Basil Chiasson

Since *The Birthday Party*'s journey from the English provinces to misadventure and near-complete failure in London in 1958, theatre critics have compared Harold Pinter to other writers as a way of making sense of Pinter's plays. Writing for the *Jewish Observer* in 1960, Charles Marowitz observed how '[m]any critics have noted Pinter's resemblance to [Samuel] Beckett and [Eugène] Ionesco, and [...] the more deductive have uncovered links with [Franz] Kafka and the symbolists' (1960). Comparing Pinter to other writers – and thereby attaching him to examples of artistic genius and venerable aesthetic traditions – was one way for theatre critics and scholars to celebrate Pinter's plays. What is also apparent is a desire to affirm Pinter's originality by depicting it as existing apart from his influences. Hence, Marowitz claims that '[a]ll of these *influences* exist to an extent, but only as embellishments to a talent which is Pinter's own' (ibid.; emphasis in original). Claims to any author's or artist's originality seem always to be informed by the notion of creating 'something that marks a significant departure from the norms of the cultural matrix within which it is produced and received' (Attridge 2017: 51–2). The latter part of Marowitz's assertion exemplifies a desire, in Pinter scholarship and in the study of literature more broadly, to place distance between the matter of Pinter's influences – his relationship to the past and tradition – and his originality. What if, however, one refused to see influence as an embellishment and endeavoured instead to locate Pinter's originality specifically in his response to other writers' originality? What if, as Harold Bloom has suggested, 'poetic influence need not make poets less original; as often it makes them more original' (Bloom 1975[1973]: 7)?

In order to make Pinter's influences the locus of his originality as a playwright, this chapter looks at the period and cultural phenomenon with which Pinter was arguably most engaged: modernism. The subject of Pinter and modernism forms a significant dimension within Pinter scholarship

(Stevenson 1984; Knowles 2001; Begley 2004, 2005; Taylor-Batty 2007: 2; Gordon 2012: 6; Billington 2017; Baker 2018: 185–7, 192–208), so much so that already in the late 1990s it was suggested that the subject had run its course and that it was time to think more seriously about Pinter in terms of postmodernism (Watt 1998: 91). Curiously, just as interest in Pinter's postmodernism was developing and scholars were focused on Pinter's shift to political drama and activism, Randall Stevenson initiated an important, and arguably still-open, mode of enquiry when he posited that Pinter's writing for stage and his plays are influenced most by the modernist novel (1984: 29). Others have elaborated his thesis by comparing select moments and features of Pinter's dramas to prose works by the likes of Kafka (Armstrong 1999), Ernest Hemingway (Hays and Tucker 1985; Luyat 2009) and Ford Maddox Ford (Wrenn 2007). The tendency of such approaches, however, has been to draw parallels or 'spot differences' between Pinter and any number of his modernist precursors on the basis of content, themes, and symbols and structure. Meanwhile, the interpretive possibilities – particularly where method is concerned – invite further attention. In addition to the importance modernism held for Pinter's approach to drama and his plays, much has arguably been taken for granted about the meaning and nature of influence, with the relationship between modernism, influence and originality still yet to be explored in any significant way.

This chapter's exploration of how Pinter's originality derives in large part from modernism's influence hybridizes the discourses of influence and intertextuality, emphasizing a literary text's capacity to be influential by '[changing] the components of the intertext and their relative weighting' (Clayton and Rothstein 1991: 30). Thinking about modernism's influence upon Pinter from the standpoint of the latter's alteration and transformation of devices, conventions and styles which are characteristic of the former enables a clearer articulation of how influence can catalyse originality. In this chapter, I elaborate on the dimension of intertextuality which involves Pinter's alteration of what came before by proposing the concept of *transmutation*. Thinking of intertextuality as transmutation enables a form of comparative analysis which accounts for the immanence of influence and originality. Pinter's originality derives from the changes that take place when literary conventions are interpolated from one form into another. This process of recycling and displacing of modernisms is made more complex by the fact that modernist works were already considered original thanks to their engagement in overturning cultural norms, aesthetic traditions and identifiable styles.

Scholarship locating Pinter in relation to modernism typically proceeds by scrutinizing the conventions employed by Pinter's plays such as the mixture of high and popular modernist forms which Pinter's writing draws upon (Scott 1986: 13; Begley 2004, 2005; Rees 2009; Patterson 2009) and/or by considering the political and epistemological implications of Pinter's representation of language, perception, truth and identity (Aragay 2001: 285; Quigley 2001: 13). I want to proceed by fusing both approaches in order to show how Pinter extends and reimagines modernism's own innovative approach to certain conventions. The second section of this chapter, then, locates Pinter in relation to strategies, conventions and innovations in the medium of prose fiction that were germane to modernism, particularly stream-of-consciousness narrative and dialogue and a minimalist approach to plot, action, character and subtext.

Originality from Influence

Critics' and scholars' desire to separate Pinter's influences from his originality channels the discourse of influence from the eighteenth century, particularly the tendency within Romanticism to see originality, along with genius, as existing in tension with influence (Clayton and Rothstein 1991: 4–5). Uncoupling influence and originality, therefore, may prevent one from fully appreciating how creativity 'requires a close engagement with the circumambient cultural matrix' (Attridge 2017: 53). Insisting on the connection between influence and originality should enhance our understanding that Pinter exists within a network of authors and texts, how influence begets originality, and how Pinter was always and already responding to conventions and styles in ways that appear to produce something entirely new.

Ronald Knowles's comparative reading of Pinter's plays and a selection of modernist playwrights is a useful starting point for considering Pinter's influences as something deeper than an embellishment and without sundering influence and originality: '[W]e can see the likely influence of Beckett, and the direct *influence* of Eliot and Joyce, on the genesis of specific plays, and the indirect influence of realist and experimental dramatic traditions. In some cases, Pinter's technique bears a fascinating resemblance to his predecessors' (2001: 85; emphasis in original). Knowles's invocation of a language of genesis, his nuanced distinction between direct and indirect influence, his emphasis of Pinter's 'technique' and his observation of a 'fascinating resemblance' to others are all useful starting points for further critical thinking about how to posit influence in the context of Pinter and, moreover, how to interrogate the discourse of influence along the way. As Knowles concludes his essay, however, a key tension appears as his affirmation of Pinter's various intersections with Anton Chekhov, August Strindberg, Luigi Pirandello, Eliot and Joyce slides into an affirmation of Pinter's originality which might be read as at odds with the general argument for influence: '[O]n closer analysis we find that each of Pinter's plays has its own character and accomplishment, and the totality of his drama, over nearly half a century, is of unique, unrivalled distinction' (2001: 85).

In an earlier comparative study of Pinter's *Betrayal* (1978) and Joyce's only stage play *Exiles* (1919), Knowles claims in passing that 'Pinter absorbed all of Joyce in adolescence and as a consequence he derived an aesthetic, subsequently adapted to drama, that draws on Stephen Hero and *A Portrait of the Artist as a Young Man* [1916]' (1998: 184). Written three years prior to his comparison of Pinter to a raft of modernist playwrights, it is here that one finds the sharpest articulation of the intimate relationship between Pinter's influences and his originality as a playwright. This earlier work also evidences Knowles's understanding that something more than a standard comparative reading is required for characterizing the relationship between Pinter and modernism. Knowles's claim that Pinter fashioned an aesthetic for drama from 'all of' a particular modernist author who worked predominantly as a novelist and short story writer opens a space for thinking simultaneously about (a) the local details of the works, (b) the writers' approaches to convention and representation, (c) their styles and, crucially, (d) what seems to have happened in the exchange.

The Trouble with Influence

While comparative studies and the discourse of influence are conspicuous in Pinter scholarship, Pinter scholars have rarely engaged critically with the concept of influence, acknowledging, for example, the widespread perception of its weakness, the suspicion that it carries unwanted implications and more generally the widespread 'belief in its outright tendentiousness as a concept' (Clayton and Rothstein 1991: 12). When the concept of influence began to 'fall into decline' in the 1970s (12), Arlene Sykes was already addressing 'these unprovable "derivations"' whose only proof is 'that Harold Pinter, like most young writers, was impressionable, influenced perhaps unconsciously by a style he admired, while his own was evolving' (1972: 59). More recently, Judith Roof has engaged more rigorously with the concept, observing that '[t]heories of influence are premised on imagined author psychology, fashioned upon an oedipal economy operating in a uni-directional, linear manner' (2009: 9). Roof emphasizes the difficulty of empirically verifying where Pinter is responding to precursors while more specifically identifying two problematic areas: that claims about influence too easily begin to psychologize lineage and thereby come with the weighty baggage of an empirically elusive authorial intention and agency (Clayton and Rothstein 1991: 7) and that they unrealistically 'refer to relations built on dyads of transmission from one unity (author, work, tradition) to another' (3).

When influence is depicted as flowing unidirectionally down through literary history, political implications arise. These can appear in the form of a literary canon undergirded by thinking which 'values individual creativity but continues to rely on the powerful *traditum*, that which is handed down [...] It smacks of the system of earned rule that supplanted lineage, the capitalism of bold, oblivious robber barons' (ibid. 12). Making the same observation but framing it in psychoanalytic terms, Roof speaks of 'an oedipal model of influence', offering a brief discussion of modernism before reaching the crux of her argument and reading of Pinter that offers another 'model of artistic relation' which is Foucauldian in its constitution and which contends that the plays of Pinter and Beckett under discussion 'play out a model of exchange' that is 'circular, multidirectional, indirect, and unconscious' and betray 'resonances, echoes, mutual practices, and divergences' (2009: 10–11). Even though Pinter's and Beckett's plays do not, Roof contends, 'respond directly to one another nor provide any locus for previous address', 'they do enact a species of exchange that addresses absence as presence and presence as absence' (11).

Despite Roof's abstract language of absence/presence, it is evident that she is resorting to intertextuality as a means of navigating the problems inherent to theories of influence. In what follows, I retain a number of the predicates found in Roof's analysis: her observation, shared with Sykes, that a traditional conception of influence is not good enough; her criticism of the assumptions embedded in traditional conceptions of influence which place the author 'and more or less conscious authorial intentions and skills' at the centre of analyses of the text (Clayton and Rothstein 1991: 3–4); and her complication of the direction in which influence is widely thought to flow between authors (and texts) in the creative process. I also explore the notion that influence runs from certain modernist writers to Pinter, but to complicate such a view of influence by situating the analysis in 'a much more impersonal field of crossing texts' (ibid. 4) and therein focusing on the significance of Pinter's mediation of the strategies, conventions and styles of modernists, all of which enabled Pinter's precursors to make their own key interventions into the history of literature.

Modernism's Influence: Passion, Anxiety, Tentative Acceptance

Pinter's passion for modernism is evident in a number of his plays that contain allusions and references to it. Deeley in *Old Times* (1971) claims to be Orson Welles (Pinter 1997a: 280). Man, the lone character in *Monologue* (1973), reminds his absent friend of yore how he introduced him to modernists Tristan Tzara, André Breton, Alberto Giacometti, Louis Ferdinand Céline and John Dos Passos (Pinter 2011: 122–3). *No Man's Land* (1975) is replete with allusions to and quotations from the history of literature, many to do with modernist figures and works.[1] Robert and Jerry bond in *Betrayal* over a conversation about their love for W. B. Yeats's poetry. In *Celebration* (2000), the Waiter makes an entrance by claiming to have overheard a conversation about T. S. Eliot and then praises his grandfather in a speech that turns out to be an ode to modernism.

In interviews Pinter spoke with relish about formative encounters with Joyce's *Ulysses* (1922), an excerpt of Beckett's *Watt* (1953) followed by a copy of *Murphy* (1938) pilfered from the local library and hours spent reading all of Kafka. Pinter's childhood friend and colleague, Henry Woolf, and his official biographer Michael Billington added to this list: T. S. Eliot, Virginia Woolf, D. H. Lawrence, Dylan Thomas, Henry Miller and John Dos Passos (Billington 2007: 12; 2017; Woolf 2007). While Thomas's and Eliot's poetry has been identified as an influence on both Pinter's own verse and his plays (Billington 2007: 29), Yeats has been pinpointed as an inspiration for Pinter's dramas (see Dohmen 1986: 198; Prentice 1994: 234). A range of modernist poets have figured prominently in the poetry readings Pinter gave over the course of his career[2] alongside the support and friendship he offered late modernists such as Stephen Spender, George Granville Barker, W. S. Graham and Robert Lowell (Baker 2018: 208–13).[3] Modernist film has also been said to have had considerable influence upon Pinter's writing for both stage and film (Taylor-Batty 2007: 2) and it has been noted how Pinter often 'returned to classic modernist texts' in his prolific career as a screenwriter (Grimes 2005: 144).

Despite these obvious connections, Pinter was outwardly resistant to the notion of influence. At most, he spoke in terms of admiration and affect: Shakespeare was a key figure and John Webster's *The White Devil* (1612) and the aforementioned *Ulysses* were formative texts. On one notable occasion, however, Pinter admitted:[4]

> If Beckett's influence shows in my work that's all right with me. You don't write in a vacuum; you're bound to absorb and digest other writing; and I admire Beckett's work so much that something of its texture might

appear in my own. I myself have no idea whether this is so, but if it is, then I am grateful for it. However, I do think that I have succeeded in expressing something of myself.

(qtd. in Thompson 1961: 8–9)

As with any writer, Pinter would have been both conscious and unconscious to varying degrees of the impact other writers had upon his own creative process and work. In adducing this passage, however, my intention is not to pursue a biographical reading but to instead borrow Pinter's own language to begin thinking critically about how modernism and influence enable deeper reflection on the notion of originality. I want to stress and reconcile the tensions at play in Pinter's statements about the act of digesting other writers' styles and work, how that input manifests as a *texture* in the playwright's own work and, within this matrix of activity, his desire to express something that is 'himself'. Pinter's affirmation and absorption of Beckett's writing as a kind of renewal recalls T. S. Eliot's 1919 essay 'Tradition and the Individual Talent', where an engagement with tradition produces a new moment in the history of the arts while still reaffirming and enabling new encounters with that tradition (Bell 1999: 16).

Passages That Enable New Articulations

In defining intertextuality, Julia Kristeva identifies how utterances are transferred 'from one textual space […] into another' (1980: 46) and sign systems are transposed from one into another (2002: 48), but most important is her focus upon the retention, deviation, displacement and permutation of semiotic 'matter', which she also identifies as key features of the exchange and passage (ibid.). The changes that influential utterances, sign systems and texts are subjected to catalyse and define a 'new articulation' (Clayton and Rothstein 1991: 59–60), that is, an original identity which emerges and is expedient for conceptualizing Pinter's originality and how modernism figures in the production of that originality and its meaning. Furthermore, because Pinter's reliance upon modernist prose fiction to make unorthodox drama entails a movement across media, exchanging the prefix 'inter' in intertextuality with the prefix 'trans' emphasizes not only the movement 'across' at the heart of the definition but also the prepositions 'through' and 'beyond' and the verb phrase 'changing thoroughly' – all of which are key to its meaning. To enrich reflection upon various kinds of intertextuality in Pinter's plays and to enhance the ongoing discussion of Pinter's embellishment and reimagining of elements of modernist prose into the medium of drama, I want to propose the concept of *transmutation*.

The earliest usage of the term in relation to Pinter appears in an early appraisal of realism in Pinter's plays where the author, F. J. Bernhard, suggests that 'beneath the realistic prose of Pinter's plays lurks the spirit of a poet, transmuting the same drab material into something more like poetry than anything else for which we have a name' (1965: 185). Nicholas De Jongh used the term in his *Evening Standard* review of Pinter and Di Trevis's *Remembrance of Things Past* (2000), stating that 'Proust's vast novel, his reminiscence of childhood, love and desire in high French society, has been triumphantly compressed, distilled and transmuted for performance on stage' (qtd. in Baker 2018: 200). Pinter also used the term while reflecting upon the autobiographical component of his play *Betrayal* (1978), specifically in the form of the experience of his and Joan Bakewell's extramarital affair: 'I got this original image of the pub and I thought, I know where I am in this ... I knew I was going to go into something related to my own past, but not literally my own past ... because that was not the case. The experience was transmuted into something else' (qtd. in Billington 2007: 266; ellipses in original).

Etymologically, 'transmutation' is closely linked to physics, alchemy specifically, and denotes '[t]he (supposed or alleged) conversion of one element or substance into another, esp. of a baser metal into gold or silver' ('Transmutation, n.'). Additional meanings include a '[c]hange of condition; mutation; sometimes implying alternation or exchange [Obsolete or archaic]'; the '[c]hange of one thing into another; conversion into something different; alteration, transformation'; in the legal realm a transmutation of possession means the 'transfer or change of ownership'; and in biology a '[c]onversion or transformation of one species into another' (ibid.). The concept seems particularly apt for identifying and elaborating upon the process whereby Pinter's plays rely upon facets of modernist prose in order to fashion a drama which may ultimately carry very little trace of the influences involved. Thinking in terms of transmutation enables a movement away from similarity and/or difference analyses (false dilemmas) to apprehend the complexities of Pinter's achievement of originality by means of creative departures which return to, recycle and reimagine modernisms that were, already in their own right, engaging with cultural norms and aesthetic tradition to create something new.

Transmuting Modernisms

Although Pinter's plays can be read as offering a critique of issues afflicting Britain in the time in which they are set and staged,[5] their investment in the circumstances and experiences of the marginalized and dispossessed characters it occasionally featured was always ambivalent and partial. As Alex Fox notes, Pinter was not quite exploring, 'as the social realists were, the "dialectic between an individual's subjectivity and objective reality"' (2015: 12). Pinter was more evidently a (neo)modernist given his interest in psychology and interiority (Rufford 2009: 91) and the extent to which his characters appear withdrawn and socially atomized (Simard 1984: 33; Sakellaridou 1988: 139; Inan 2000: vi, 31). Pinter was extending modernism's 'revolt against the traditional relation of the subject to the outside world' (Eysteinsson 1990: 28), and investments and features such as these provide a starting point for interrogating the texture of modernism's 'radical "inward turn" in literature' within Pinter's plays and examining how they mediate modernism's foregrounding of 'human consciousness (as opposed to a mimetic concern with the human environment and social conditions)' and its rupture of 'the conventional ties between the individual and society' (26). The tangential, episodic, associative, imagistic and rhythmic character of Pinter's stage dialogue set him apart from his post-war contemporaries and resulted in his association with the Theatre of the Absurd. These qualities, however, are equally characteristic of the stream-of-consciousness narrative and dialogue one finds in a number of late-nineteenth- and twentieth-century novels and short stories. Rather than framing Pinter as an Absurdist, I want to posit that his characteristic stage dialogue drew upon and reworked the stream-of-consciousness narrative convention which emerged under modernism and which is now regarded as one of its most remarkable inventions.

Developed initially by Dorothy Richardson and taken up by Joyce, Woolf, Dos Passos and others, the convention often takes the form of verbal and mental reportage which '[supersedes] conventional narrative structure' (Gillies 1996: 162) by blurring the boundary between a character's inner mind and the external world – between characters' own narrative voices and points of view and those belonging to omniscient narrators and by juxtaposing and associating images, recollections, impressions, sense perceptions, ideas, confessions, anecdotes, objects and people. As a form of monologue which complicates the relationship between the self and the wider world, stream of consciousness can render subjectivity as something of a 'vanishing point' (Levenson 2008: 206). The convention sought to deviate from previous narrative traditions by capturing the peripatetic and often disordered disposition of mental activity and internal narrative as it is often experienced in life beyond fiction. Dorothy Richardson's thirteen-volume novel sequence *Pilgrimage* (1915), for example, 'manipulates the narration so frequently that the reader is often in [the protagonist] Miriam's mind in one passage and outside it in the next' (Gillies 1996: 162).

Part of what constitutes Pinter's intervention into stage dialogue's tendency towards Naturalist idioms or verse was the way he endowed conversation and dialogue with features that might be attributed to stream-of-consciousness narrative. Early on in *The Room* (1957), for example, when Mr Kidd and Rose Hudd conduct a conversation about the room she and her husband, Bert, are letting from Kidd, the contents and features of the habitat appear to affect Kidd, mostly triggering memories, such that it becomes difficult to ascertain when and if he is fully present in the conversation or in his mind, and thus when and whether or not he is actively speaking to Rose or to himself:

Mr Kidd   This was my bedroom […] When I lived here.

[…]

Rose   When was that then?

Mr Kidd   Eh?

[…]

Rose   I was telling Bert I was telling you how he could drive.

Mr Kidd   Mr Hudd?

[…]

Rose   How many floors you got in this house?

Mr Kidd   Floors. (*He laughs*). Ah, we had a good few of them in the old days.

[…]

Rose   What about your sister, Mr Kidd?

Mr Kidd   What about her?

[…]

Rose   What did she die of?

Mr Kidd   Who?

Rose   Your sister.

Pause.

Mr Kidd   I've made ends meet.

Pause. (Pinter 1996a: 91–3)

The suggestion of instantaneous and random movement of the character's ego between interiority and the more evidently social world of conversation and relations of power, and then the final change of subject which sends Kidd in an altogether different direction, replicates the logic of stream-of-consciousness narration. Kidd's repetition of some of what Rose says to him seems initially like a symptom of deafness or perhaps resistance to Rose's engagement, yet the scene develops in a way that suggests the boundaries between present and past, self and other are porous. If read this way, it's possible to appreciate how this feature of Pinter's stage language simultaneously distinguishes his dialogue and representation of subjectivity and character relations from his contemporaries and reveals an originality derived from modernism's experimentation with representing movements and shifts between egological positionings.

As is typical of modernist stream-of-consciousness narrative, Pinter's dialogue also juxtaposes a character's thoughts, observations and sensory perceptions in ways that require spectators or readers to interpret by looking for associations between assertions and parts of the narrative, over and above the content. Pinter's *Landscape* (1968), as has been observed, 'work[s] through monologues' (Hinchliffe 1974: 139), and it remains unclear whether the only characters, Beth and Duff, are even addressing or hearing one another. As they touch upon different moments in their life together in a more or less tandem fashion, with Beth ultimately spiralling off into an altogether different life shared with an anonymous lover, the play's juxtaposition of their lines throughout and the interplay of monologues requires the audience to infer the relationship between each character's statements and make sense of how they relate. Furthermore, the dialogue in *Landscape* and its companion piece, *Silence* (1969), is organized such that each character's quasi-monologues appear to be inspired by something the other has said, whether that be a topic, event or a single word. This aesthetic arrangement pushes Joseph Conrad's and Ford Maddox Ford's understanding that in real life people almost always don't listen because 'they are always preparing their own next speeches' to its limit, confirming both authors' 'unalterable rule' for depicting 'genuine conversions', that 'no speech of one character should ever answer the speech that goes before it' (Ford 1924: 200–1).

Pinter's beloved Joyce and *Ulysses* are also key touchstones here, particularly the way Leopold Bloom recounts his day and then asks Molly for breakfast in bed after she has declined his sexual advances and before he settles down to sleep. Something he says in this equation then becomes the stimulus for Molly's extended monologue which ranges over her entire life (Gillies 1996: 147). This arrangement whereby '[e]ach memory-image provokes another, which holds centre stage until it is replaced by another which it again has provoked' (147) takes on another form throughout Pinter's *Landscape* in the interlacing of Duff's and Beth's respective recollections of past events. Where stream of consciousness suggests – if it doesn't always entail – a steady flow of verbal and mental activity, Pinter's transmutation of features of modernist prose also entailed minimalism. As way of further defining his transmutation of modernism and demonstrating its role in his originality, for the remainder of this chapter I want to explore Pinter's minimalism, particularly his approach to plot, action and character and his use of subtext.

Scholars have used the phrase minimalism to describe aspects of Pinter's plays and refer to the spare and economical approach to writing (Erickson 1993; Gussow 1994: 75; Chaudhuri 1997: 98; Angel-Perez 2009: 139). Part of this aesthetic concerns how Pinter pares away and even omits features which spectators and readers are acculturated to expect to find in a play that is ostensibly naturalistic. Pinter's minimalism is evident, for example, in his austere approach to plot and action (Simard 1984: 30; Innes 2002: 328). Although this terrain has been covered, new insights are possible if we locate this feature of Pinter's plays and style in relation to the modernist novel, regarding it as a reworking of, say, Joseph Conrad's tendency in *The Secret Agent: A Simple Tale* (1907) or *Under Western Eyes* (1911) to include 'a number of dramatic events' only to depict the characters' actions as nothing more than 'futile gestures' and to ensure that action 'never really amounts to much' and certainly never results in any social change (Gillies 1996: 182–3). This approach to writing character and action might aptly describe any number of Pinter's characters, their arcs and the overall progression of events in the play. Despite being one of the most significant dramatic events and plot developments in *The Birthday Party*, Stanley's abduction by Goldberg and McCann is met with a more or less non-response by the characters: Meg and Petey breakfast in a way that is suggestive of the play's opening scene, almost as though the action has yet to begin. In *The Homecoming* (1965), Teddy lingers at the margins of the sitting room, as if paralyzed, while Ruth negotiates a new life with his brothers and father, and Max, Lenny and Joey's attempts to define the terms of their proposal for Ruth to become their sex worker are ultimately ineffectual. Pinter's redefinition of what constitutes plot and action and his use of the strategies of reduction, omission and truncation to do so begin from conditions that Conrad established in his approach to the novel.

Pinter's minimalism also came to bear on the plays' unorthodox approach to 'central elements in the construction of theatrical characterisation' (Lacey 1995: 145). Pinter's widely cited discovery that '[m]y characters tell me so much and no more, with reference to their experience, their aspirations, their motives, their history' (Pinter 1996b: xii) is effectively a declaration of Pinter's embrace of a minimalist approach to character that reworks the narrator's warning in F. Scott Fitzgerald's story 'The Rich Boy' that if when writing you 'begin with a type, […] you find that you have created – nothing' (1926: 1). Pinter's commitment to this discovery inspired him to jettison a range of features that would hitherto have been considered necessary: backstory, motivation, intention and so on.

The upshot of Pinter's simplification of the devices of plot, action and character and his re-imagination of their nature and function is that characters do not, and cannot, experience revelation and change. This aspect of Pinter's plays embodies the modernist novel's response to the tendency of nineteenth-century novels to stage 'moments of revelation [and] recognition scenes' which in turn enable the renewal or completion of identity (Trotter 1999: 94). Hemingway pushes the critical approach to epiphany and revelation along with the possibility of change to their limits by writing characters who cannot experience personal revelation, and then grow and change, precisely because they somehow cannot confront their problems and struggles. The protagonist in the short story 'Soldier's Home' (1925), Harold Krebs, returns to his parents' home in Oklahoma years after the First World War has ended. Failing to readapt to life in his community and to take up employment, he sits stolidly on the front porch watching the world until his circumstances, which go unarticulated, drive him to plan to leave home, which he may or may not do as the story concludes: 'He wanted his life to go smoothly. […] He would go over to the schoolyard and watch Helen play indoor baseball' (Hemingway 1995a: 93). Krebs's post-traumatic stress disorder (PTSD) causes his stasis, preventing the story from moving forward at the level of plot and action. However, the stasis and lack of progression were a way for Hemingway to call into question readers' acculturated expectations surrounding the conventions which facilitate development and change, at both individual and societal levels.

Pinter would seem to have relied heavily on Hemingway given how his characters are never subject to change in the way of personal and social growth. Stasis rules the day, they are frozen and nothing changes, as Hirst laments in *No Man's Land* (1975). At the end of *The Birthday Party*, Meg and Petey resume their routines as if Stanley's abduction never even happened, with Meg behaving as naively as ever as she waits for Stanley to come down to breakfast. One could argue that by the end of *The Homecoming* Ruth, Lenny and Max all transform from family members into sex trade workers and that, in tandem, Ruth and Teddy's marital relation undergoes a change. Reflection upon that still shocking outcome might suggest, however, that Ruth and her in-laws (as with Meg, Petey and Stanley) all end up where they, and perhaps we, knew they would, and to search for revelations and epiphanies in effort to discover what they learn along the way would be to get the wrong end of the interpretive stick. While remarking on the silences which exist in language, Pinter has identified a form of speech that is 'speaking of a language locked beneath it [...] a necessary avoidance, a violent, sly, anguished or mocking smokescreen which keeps the other in its place' (1996b: xiii). This underscores the importance of subtext in his work, another form of minimalism but also another vantage from which to explore Pinter's transmutation of modernism and Hemingway specifically. While many writers employ the convention, Pinter's subtext is unique given the way his use of implication and suggestion, his characters' suppression of information and thoughts, feelings and motivations, and the specific ways they mediate and displace what they really think and feel function to engender specific kinds of affects. However, Pinter's subtext only becomes unique by drawing upon previous traditions but somehow differing the convention and sign system. Beyond the obvious connections to Chekhov, whose own plays and prose make extensive use of the convention, Hemingway is arguably the more consonant influence here (Luyat 2009: 238). This is most evident in Hemingway's 'technique of cutting out any reference to the real subject matter of a story' (Fenton 1995: xx), how his characters engage in small talk as a way of masking what is actually going on in their hearts, minds and relationships, and how characters and/or narrators engage with the objective environment as a means of avoiding their problems and of navigating conflict with others.

In 'Hills Like White Elephants', a man referred to by the narrator as 'the American' and a woman he calls 'Jig' wait for a train at a table under a blazing Spanish sun. While they appear exposed to the elements and readers are offered detailed descriptions of the landscape and features of the station, throughout the story the couple refrain from openly discussing the abortion Jig has had, or is planning, and relatedly their failing relationship. They enact their avoidance by engaging in banal conversation:

> 'It's pretty hot,' the man said.
> 'Let's drink beer.' (Hemingway 1995b: 199)

And then a little later:

> 'We want two Anis del Toro.'
> 'With water?'
> 'Do you want it with water?'
> 'I don't know,' the girl said. 'Is it good with water?'
> 'It's all right.' (199)

In addition to the protracted discussion of alcoholic beverage quoted here, the narration reveals how the clouds become of interest to the woman –

they look like white elephants, she submits, thus invoking the story's title and its reference to the idiomatic expression denoting a refusal to address what is evident to all present – and the man's interest in the parts of the table and how he rises and travels, first, to the bar and, later, to the end of the platform. The lack of event and narrative progression can be painful; however, the minimalism, whose grammar is stasis and omission of expected information, works to imply that so much is happening in their minds and between them. The characters' avoidance of speaking explicitly about what it is that has fractured the relationship – a technique which has been called Hemingway's 'lexical riddle' (Barton 1994: 72) – is the point of the story, the drama. By employing various forms of suppression and repression while investing significant energy in producing a concrete and tangible world consisting of surface facts, the story compels readers to engage in a form of textual interpretation which can only ever be defined by inference and speculation (Fenton 1995: xx).

Pinter refashioned this prose formula in many of his plays in order to create similar effects for the medium of theatrical performance. In Act I of *The Homecoming*, when Lenny waits up for Ruth who is just returning from a late-night stroll, both characters engage in a lengthy, banal conversation wherein Lenny keeps, with the utmost discipline, from revealing what is bothering him about Ruth's presence in the family home. Ruth, in turn and with equal discipline, keeps from revealing how she feels about Lenny. The style of conversation Lenny employs occasionally resorts to politeness to suppress his feelings for Ruth – he asks her if she has finished using the ashtray and if he may relieve her of it, for example – and occasionally resorts to anecdotes which focus and vent desire and endeavour to menace her, recalling, for example, his own history of violence against women. The negotiation over the articles of furniture and the water glass replace the beer, Anis liqueur and the elephant-like clouds in Hemingway's story. Pinter's transmutation of what one finds in Hemingway's short story, however, is how these objects become a focal point and conductor for Lenny's negative feeling for Ruth and a tool for Ruth to break Lenny down and begin to gain the balance of power in his house. Lenny's final statement in the scene as he runs to the stair banister and shouts after Ruth who ascends and disappears – 'What was that supposed to be? Some kind of proposal?' (Pinter 1997b: 43) – is almost a meta nod to Pinter's commitment in the scene to making spectators resort to inference and speculation about the nature of Ruth and Lenny's encounter and what is transpiring between them and why.

Ultimately, the prose fiction strategies and conventions of certain modernists I have taken up and which have, I argue, undergone a transmutation in Pinter's process of writing for the stage all contributed to a feature of Pinter's plays that was both a convention Hemingway experimented with and decided upon as an objective for his prose: omissions that will strengthen 'the story and make people feel something more than they understood' (Hemingway qtd. in Fenton 1995: xxi). This appears to be an objective of Pinter's, even if the means he employed differed precisely because he did not replicate Hemingway's approaches but rather engaged in a transmutation of what Hemingway and others were experimenting with.

Conclusion

Locating Hemingway's reflection on his own writing process and objectives in the affective dimensions of Pinter's plays and accounting in more detail for the range of ways that Pinter transmuted a network of modernist prose conventions and styles enriches the perennial discussion of what the Pinteresque means, makes a case for articulating the relationship between influence and originality more fully, and explores the possibilities of refining existing concepts and approaches such as intertextuality. This chapter has endeavoured to demonstrate that the subject of Pinter's modernism is worth revisiting given how it might be evolved by interrogating extant discourses (influence), making connections between them (influence and originality) and refining existing approaches and concepts (framing intertextuality as transmutation). In order to attend to and critically engage with the problems with influence that have been raised over time, my study of Pinter's modernist influences is neither seeking to verify influence empirically nor to demonstrate psychological lineage. The aim is rather to posit a reading of Pinter which is mediated by modernist texts and discourses about modernism that will, ideally, change readers' perceptions of Pinter's originality. Appraising Pinter's originality by making analytical claims about the conditions of its emergence and its nature is perhaps one of the most elusive dimensions of Pinter studies. The work in this chapter, therefore, invites further scholarly work in this mode and proposes that a more formalized discourse for engaging with and appreciating Pinter's originality is in order. In using the concept of transmutation to refine an intertextual approach for educing Pinter's modernisms, I am committed to the idea of what Clayton and Rothstein call 'a renewed practice of literary history' where Pinter is concerned (28). This chapter's consideration of the passage of modernism into Pinter's work and, from that, Pinter's transmutation of it to an original outcome has sought to elaborate the notion that Pinter's writing for the stage entailed a certain kind of collaboration (Taylor-Batty 2007: 1–2) – with a network of authors, texts and approaches to tradition.

Notes

1. See, for example, Nancy Bogen's 'Report from the Front: The Meaning of Pinter's No Man's Land', unpublished, undated twenty-four-page typed document submitted for consideration to *The New York Review of Books*. Retrieved in The New York Public Library, Stephen A. Schwarzman Building, Manuscripts, Archives and Rare Books Division, New York Review of Books Records, Series 1: Robert B. Silvers files Mss Col 23385, box RBS208, RBS 208.17. File folder entitled 'Harold Pinter' and with 'manuscripts' handwritten on cover leaf.
2. While T. S. Eliot and Wilfred Owen appear consistently in records of such events, of interest is the earliest record I could find of Pinter giving a poetry reading, at the Poetry Center in New York City for the Young Men's and Young Women's Hebrew Association at the Theresa L. Kaufmann Concert Hall in NYC. Taking place on 5 February 1967 at 8:30 pm, David Harris played guitar during what were called 'musical interludes' and Pinter read selections by Thomas Hardy, W. B. Yeats, e. e. cummings, Edna St Vincent Millay and Stevie Smith (Lily Library, Indiana University Bloomington, Red Dust Mss, LMC 2350, Box 8, folder entitled 'Red Dust Mss, Correspondence: Pinter, Harold 1968', programme of event, no ff.).
3. Pinter's appointment diaries indicate meetings with all three: Spender and Barker and Lowell at the Mermaid Theatre in the run up to Pinter's production of *Exiles* (The British Library, The Harold Pinter Archive, Add MS 88880/12/004: Diary 1970, entry for 29 November). As William Baker observed recently, Pinter was a supporter of Barker's and Graham's verse in particular (2018: 208–13).
4. 'Harold Pinter,' Martin Esslin notes, 'acknowledges Beckett, together with Franz Kafka, as the main influence on his work' – Esslin presumes a scenario in which Pinter joins Beckett in writing plays that constitute a culturally defined reflection of 'the precariousness, the stark comfortlessness of the human condition' (Roof 2009: 12; qting. Esslin's 'Godot and His Children', 145).
5. The earlier work is set in working-class milieus and features socially marginalized minorities, for example the sightless, black character Riley in *The Room* and the homeless Davies in *The Caretaker*, both of whom suffer abuse at the hands of the white and working-class tenants.

Works Cited

Angel-Perez, E. (2009), 'Ashes to Ashes: Pinter's Dibbuks', in B. Gauthier (ed.), *Viva Pinter: Harold Pinter's Spirit of Resistance*, 139–60, New York: Peter Lang.

Aragay, M. (2001), 'Pinter, Politics and Postmodernism (2)', in P. Raby (ed.), *The Cambridge Companion to Harold Pinter*, 246–59, Cambridge: Cambridge University Press.

Armstrong, R. (1999), *Kafka and Pinter Shadow-Boxing: The Struggle between Father and Son*, Basingstoke and London: Macmillan Press.

Attridge, D. (2017), *The Singularity of Literature*, London and New York: Routledge.

Baker, W. (2018), *Pinter's World: Relationships, Obsessions, and Artistic Endeavors*, Madison, WIS and Teaneck, NJ: Fairleigh Dickinson University Press.

Barton, E. J. (1994), 'The Story as It Should Be: Epistemological Uncertainty in Hemingway's "Cat in the Rain" (Ernest Hemingway)', *The Hemingway Review*, 14 (1): 72–8.

Begley, V. (2002), 'The Aesthetics of Refusal: Pinter among the Radicals', *Modern Drama*, 45 (4): 628–45.

Begley, V. (2004), 'The Modernist as Populist: Pinter's *Betrayal* and Mass Culture', in F. Gillen and S. H. Gale (eds), *The Pinter Review, Collected Essays 2003 and 2004*, 83–102, Tampa, FL: University of Tampa Press.

Begley, V. (2005), *Harold Pinter and the Twilight of Modernism*, Toronto, Buffalo and London: University of Toronto Press.

Begley, V. (2009), 'Return of the Referent', in M. Brewer (ed.), *Harold Pinter's The Dumb Waiter*, 71–87, Amsterdam and New York: Rodopi.

Bell, M. (1999), 'The Metaphysics of Modernism', in M. Levenson (ed.), *The Cambridge Companion to Modernism*, 9–32, Cambridge: Cambridge University Press.

Bernhard, F. J. (1965), 'Beyond Realism: The Plays of Harold Pinter', *Modern Drama*, 8 (2): 185–91.

Billington, M. (2007), *Harold Pinter*, 2nd edn, London: Faber and Faber.

Billington, M. (2017), 'An Introduction to *The Homecoming*', *Discovering Literature: 20th Century*, 7 September. Available online: https://www.bl.uk/20th-century-literature/articles/an-introduction-to-the-homecoming (accessed 30 June 2020).

Bloom, H. (1975[1973]), *The Anxiety of Influence: A Theory of Poetry*, London, Oxford, New York: Oxford University Press.

Chaudhuri, U. (1997), *Staging Place: The Geography of Modern Drama*, Ann Arbor: University of Michigan Press.

Clayton, J., and E. Rothstein. (1991), 'Figures in the Corpus: Theories of Influence and Intertextuality', in J. Clayton and E. Rothstein (eds), *Influence and Intertextuality in Literary History*, 3–36, Wisconsin: University of Wisconsin Press.

Dohmen, W. F. (1986), 'Time after Time: Pinter Plays with Disjunctive Chronologies', in S. H. Gale (ed.), *Harold Pinter: Critical Approaches*, 187–200, London and Toronto: Associated University Presses.

Erickson, J. (1993), 'Pinter and the Ethos of Minimalism', in K. H. Burkman and J. L. Kundert-Gibbs (eds), *Pinter at Sixty*, 100–7, Bloomington and Indianapolis: Indiana University Press.

Esslin, M. (1961), *The Theatre of the Absurd*, Garden City, NY: Anchor.
Eysteinsson, A. (1990), *The Concept of Modernism*, Ithaca and London: Cornell University Press.
Fenton, J. (1995), '"Introduction"', in J. Fenton (ed.), *Ernest Hemingway the Collected Stories*, xiii–xxv, London: Everyman's Library.
Fitzgerald, F. S. (1926), 'The Rich Boy', in *All the Sad Young Men*, 1–56, New York: Charles Scribner's Sons.
Ford, F. M. (1924), *Joseph Conrad: A Personal Remembrance*, Boston: Little.
Fox, A. (2015), 'Self against Others: A Psychoanalytic Reading of Harold Pinter's Work', PhD diss., University of Dundee, UK.
Gillies, M. A. (1996), *Henri Bergson and British Modernism*, Montreal and Kingston: McGill-Queen's Press.
Gordon, R. (2012), *Harold Pinter: The Theater of Power*, Ann Arbor: University of Michigan Press.
Grimes, C. (2005), *Harold Pinter's Politics: A Silence beyond Echo*, Madison: Fairleigh Dickinson University Press.
Gussow, M. (1994), *Conversations with Pinter*, New York: Grove.
Hays, P. L., and S. Tucker. (1985), 'No Sanctuary: Hemingway's "The Killers" and Pinter's "The Birthday Party"', *Papers on Language and Literature*, 21 (4): 417–24.
Hemingway, E. (1995a), 'Soldier's Home', in J. Fenton (ed.), *Ernest Hemingway the Collected Stories*, 87–93, London: Everyman's Library.
Hemingway, E. (1995b), 'Hills Like White Elephants', in J. Fenton (ed.), *Ernest Hemingway the Collected Stories*, 199–203, London: Everyman's Library.
Hinchliffe, A. P. (1974), *British Theatre 1950–70*, Oxford: Basil Blackwell.
Inan, D. (2000), 'The City and Landscapes beyond Harold Pinter's Rooms', PhD diss., University of Warwick, UK.
Innes, C. (2002), *Modern British Drama: The Twentieth Century*, Cambridge and New York: Cambridge University Press.
Knowles, R. (1998), 'Joyce and Pinter: *Exiles* and *Betrayal*', *Bells: Barcelona English Language and Literature Studies* 9: 183–91.
Knowles, R. (2001), 'Pinter and Twentieth-Century Drama', in P. Raby (ed.), *The Cambridge Companion to Harold Pinter*, 73–86, Cambridge: Cambridge University Press.
Kristeva, J. (1980), *Desire in Language: A Semiotic Approach to Literature and Art*, L. S. Roudiez (ed.), T. Gora, A. Jardine and L. S. Roudiez (trans.), New York: Columbia University Press.
Kristeva, J. (2002), 'Excerpts from *Revolution in Poetic Language*', in K. Oliver (ed.), *The Portable Kristeva*, 27–92, New York: Columbia University Press.
Lacey, S. (1995), *British Realist Theatre: The New Wave in Its Context 1956–65*, London: Routledge.
Levenson, M. (2008), 'The Time-Mind of the Twenties', in L. Marcus and P. Nicholls (eds), *The Cambridge History of Twentieth-Century English Literature*, 197–217, Cambridge: Cambridge University Press.

Luyat, A. (2009), 'The First Last Look in the Shadows: Pinter and the Pinteresque', in M. Brewer (ed.), *Harold Pinter's The Dumb Waiter*, 231–45, Amsterdam and New York: Rodopi.

Marowitz, C. (1960), 'Harold Pinter: Assault from the Fringe', *Jewish Observer*, February. The British Library Modern Manuscripts Collection, The Harold Pinter Archive, Add MS 88880/8/1, ff. 121.

Patterson, M. (2009), 'Pinter's *The Dumb Waiter*: Negotiating the Boundary between "High" and "Low" Culture', in M. Brewer (ed.), *Harold Pinter's The Dumb Waiter*, 127–41, Amsterdam and New York: Rodopi.

Pinter, H. (1996a), 'The Room', in *Harold Pinter: Plays 1*, 85–110, London: Faber and Faber.

Pinter, H. (1996b), 'Introduction: Writing for the Theatre', in *Harold Pinter: Plays 1*, vii–xvi, London: Faber and Faber.

Pinter, H. (1997a), 'Old Times', in *Harold Pinter: Plays 3*, 243–313, London: Faber and Faber.

Pinter, H. (1997b), 'The Homecoming', in *Harold Pinter: Plays 3*, 13–90, London: Faber and Faber.

Pinter, H. (2011), 'Monologue', in *Harold Pinter: Plays 4*, 119–128, London: Faber and Faber.

Prentice, P. (1994), *The Pinter Ethic: The Erotic Aesthetic*, New York and London: Garland.

Quigley, A. E. (2001), 'Pinter, Politics and Postmodernism (1)', in P. Raby (ed.), *The Cambridge Companion to Harold Pinter*, 7–27, Cambridge: Cambridge University Press.

Rees, C. (2009), 'High Art or Popular Culture: Traumatic Conflicts of Representation and Postmodernism in Pinter's *The Dumb Waiter*', in M. Brewer (ed.), *Harold Pinter's The Dumb Waiter*, 111–25, Amsterdam and New York: Rodopi.

Roof, J. (2009), 'The Absent One: Harold Pinter's Influence on Samuel Beckett', in C. N. Owens (ed.), *Pinter Et Cetera*, 9–30, Newcastle upon Tyne: Cambridge Scholars Publishing.

Rufford, J. (2009), '"Disorder … in a Darkened Room": The Juridico-Political Space of *The Dumb Waiter*', in M. Brewer (ed.), *Harold Pinter's The Dumb Waiter*, 89–109, Amsterdam and New York: Rodopi.

Sakellaridou, E. (1988), *Pinter's Female Portraits: A Study of Female Characters in the Plays of Harold Pinter*, Totowa, NJ: Barnes and Noble.

Scott, M. (1986), '"Introduction"', in M. Scott (ed.), *Harold Pinter: The Birthday Party, The Caretaker and The Homecoming, A Casebook*, 9–22, London: Macmillan.

Simard, R. (1984), *Postmodern Drama: Contemporary Playwrights in America and Britain*, London and Maryland: University Press of America.

Stevenson, R. (1984), 'Harold Pinter–Innovator?', in A. Bold (ed.), *Harold Pinter: You Never Heard Such Silence*, 29–60, London: Vision.

Sykes, A. (1972), *Harold Pinter*, St. Lucia: University of Queensland Press.

Taylor-Batty, M. (2007), 'The Male Church: Pinter's Male Bonds', plenary speech for *Harold Pinter: Encontros* Conference at University of Lisbon.
Thompson, H. (1961), 'Harold Pinter Replies', *New Theatre Magazine* 2: 8–9.
'Transmutation, n'. *OED/Oxford English Dictionary: The Definitive Record of the English Language*. Available online: http://www.oed.com/view/Entry/204933?redirectedFrom=transmutation+#eid (accessed 30 June 2020).
Trotter, D. (1999), 'The Modernist Novel', in M. Levenson (ed.), *The Cambridge Companion to Modernism*, 70–99, Cambridge: Cambridge University Press.
Watt, S. (1998), *Postmodern/Drama: Reading the Contemporary Stage*, Ann Arbor: University of Michigan Press.
Watts, C. (2012), *Conrad's 'Heart of Darkness': A Critical and Contextual Discussion*, Amsterdam and New York: Rodopi.
Woolf, H. (2007), 'My 60 Years in Harold's Gang', *The Guardian*, 12 July. Available online: https://www.theguardian.com/stage/2007/jul/12/theatre.haroldpinter (accessed 30 June 2020).
Wrenn, A. (2007), '"Long Letters about Ford Maddox Ford": Ford's Afterlife in the Work of Harold Pinter', in P. Skinner (ed.), *Ford Maddox Ford's Literary Contacts*, 225–36, Amsterdam and New York: Rodopi.

2

The Theatre of the Absurd as Professional Network in Harold Pinter's Early Career

Harry Derbyshire

Harold Pinter's plays first gained recognition as part of a then-emergent strand of European and British drama which came to be called the Theatre of the Absurd, an early association which is now seen by some as unhelpful, a critical convenience that was soon outgrown.¹ This view reflects the many disputes about the nature, value and even the existence of the Theatre of the Absurd that have raged since the first publication of Martin Esslin's highly influential book of that title in 1961.² Such disputes reflect real critical difficulties, one of which lies in deciding what status to accord the Theatre of the Absurd: should it be referred to as a movement, a genre, a convention, a trend, a phenomenon? Or should only terms denoting scepticism, such as 'label' or 'critical construct', be used? In this chapter, I argue that one objectively verifiable manifestation of the Theatre of the Absurd was as a professional network which greatly aided Pinter's career in the late 1950s and early 1960s. Considering it in this way shines a new light on Pinter's early progress as a writer and on his career-long negotiations with the critical perceptions that defined him; it also suggests new and productive work that may be done with a critical term which has proved as persistent as it has been debatable.

Within contemporary business discourse there are thought to be two main kinds of professional network: 'expansive' and 'nodal'. According to *Flexjobs* writer Adrianne Bibby, an expansive network is 'a broad umbrella group of contacts' who 'can be present and former colleagues and industry contacts who can either speak specifically to your work experience and accomplishments, or offer a broader personal endorsement of you as a potential hire […] the group may include family members or friends' (2018). However, in a *Forbes* article entitled, 'You Need Two Types of Professional Networks to Get Super-Rich', Russ Alan Prince, President of R. A. Prince and Associates, adds that expansive networks are 'the type of network most professionals develop […] useful but often limited' (2017). Essential for serious success, it is suggested, is the development of a nodal network which, according to Bibby, 'typically [...] can be a more narrow subset of people, but also a more powerful group of "marquee" contacts who may wield influence in your industry' (2018). As Prince puts it, a nodal network comprises 'a few very powerful, highly targeted deep relationships that in turn have an array of similar relationships of their own' (2017).

An analysis of the contacts and connections through which Harold Pinter developed his career as a playwright, which was highly successful even if it did not make him 'super-rich', would seem to bear out the analysis offered by Bibby and Prince: initial opportunities came about via Pinter's expansive network, but real and lasting success was achieved through the development of a nodal network of influential critics and practitioners which included Harold Hobson, Donald McWhinnie, Barbara Bray, Martin Esslin, Peter Hall and Samuel Beckett. What I highlight in this chapter is how far Pinter, in making these crucial nodal connections, was joining a pre-existing network of like-minded professionals who were already engaged in producing and promoting a particular kind of avant-garde theatre with which his work shared identifiable affinities. Where previous studies have noted individual collaborations and points of connection, I will collate the evidence in such a way as to reveal an overall pattern of collective, though largely uncoordinated, endeavour. As Bibby notes, a node is 'the point in a system or network where different paths intersect or branch out' (2018), and one way to think about Pinter in these early years is as a significant node in the extensive network of artists and advocates whose cumulative efforts brought into being the Theatre of the Absurd.

The chapter is divided into three sections. In the first I establish the characteristics of the Theatre of the Absurd and the grounds that exist for considering Pinter a part of it. In the second I look in detail at Pinter's early career, identifying a network of significant contacts, each already connected to the Theatre of the Absurd, whose support helped him to establish himself as a playwright. The final section considers how fully Pinter was able to break his connection to the Absurd when it became unhelpful. Characterizing the Theatre of the Absurd as a network allows it to be seen anew, as a collective endeavour comprised not only of the innovative playwriting of Beckett, Eugène Ionesco, Pinter and others but of the numerous acts of encouragement, collaboration, patronage and advocacy that enabled the realization and acceptance of their work. It then becomes possible, without the need for rigid thematic interpretation, to regard the Theatre of the Absurd as a demonstrably real and culturally significant phenomenon, the impact, influence and meaning of which can be considered holistically. This account of Pinter's early career serves as a UK-focused case study offered in support of this suggested reconceptualization.

Pinter's Absurd Association

'The Theatre of the Absurd' is a term which has been used since the 1950s to refer to a body of post-war drama associated with Samuel Beckett, Eugène Ionesco and others. Its broad thematic concern, as it was defined by Martin Esslin, is a 'sense of metaphysical anguish at the absurdity of the human condition' (2001: 23–4), and this reflects the fact that, as Arnold P. Hinchcliffe notes, it 'derives its inspiration from an existential view of life' (1969: 92). Non-naturalistic and formally unconventional, it is characterized, in the words of Irving Wardle, by 'the substitution of an inner landscape for the outer world [and] the lack of any clear division between fantasy and fact' (1968: 15) so that, as Carl Lavery and Clare Finburgh write, 'significance in the absurdist text [...] is affective and allegorical: it expresses itself in rhythms, atmospheres and intensities' (2015: 17). While the dramatists connected with the Absurd did not comprise a unified movement, their plays, as Michael Y. Bennett has written, 'befuddled audiences in a similar manner' (2013: 1) and, as Dan Rebellato has shown, in London provoked hostility from those who feared that their 'refusal of vitality [...] would undermine the naïve realist strain of new British playwriting' epitomized by *Look Back in Anger* (1999: 146–7). Nonetheless, as John Bull has contended, by the time of Tom Stoppard's *Rosencrantz and Guildenstern Are Dead* in 1966, 'the strands of Absurdism that can be traced back to Beckett, and to Ionesco, had taken over as the model of British avantgarde theatre' (2000: 91).

While asserting the validity of his categorization, Esslin was careful not to claim too much:

> It must be stressed [...] that the dramatists whose work is here discussed do not form part of any self-proclaimed or self-conscious school or movement. On the contrary, each of the writers in question is an individual who regards himself as a lone outsider, cut off and isolated in his private world.
>
> (2001: 22)

There is some truth in this, but at the same time it is problematic to regard the writers of the Theatre of the Absurd as isolated outsiders when each was involved in making theatre, a collaborative enterprise necessitating the help of numerous facilitators and fellow practitioners. Pinter, in particular, having acted professionally since 1949, had acquired extensive experience and numerous contacts in the highly social world of the theatre – as William Baker's recent book *Pinter's World* shows in detail (see Baker 2018: 1–22). Moreover, almost as significant as their ties to other theatre workers was the encouragement and support which dramatists associated with the Absurd received from the many commentators and opinion formers – Esslin included – who saw value in their work. The Theatre of the Absurd was assuredly not a 'self-proclaimed or self-conscious school or movement', but neither was it a series of entirely unconnected one-person cottage industries. If the connections and collaborations that I will highlight below give one kind of justification for considering Pinter as part of the Theatre of the Absurd, another is provided by the fact that his early work was repeatedly likened to that of other writers associated with it. A representative example is reviewer Derek Granger's statement that *The Birthday Party* (1958) 'comes in the school of random dottiness deriving from Beckett and Ionesco' (qtd. in Billington 2007: 84), an assessment which was at least partly defensible, because Pinter acknowledged the influence of Beckett, though not that of Ionesco (see Batty 2005: 108 and Billington 2007: 94).[3] In keeping with such perceived affinities Pinter was included in Esslin's book, appearing in a chapter devoted to 'parallels and proselytes' (a suggestive title that leaves open how far those included are knowingly contributing to an identified trend). By the third edition of *The Theatre of the Absurd* in 1980, in accordance with his enhanced critical and commercial status, Pinter had been given his own chapter, signifying elevation in Esslin's hierarchy to the status of major Absurdist.

As we will see, Pinter was later to complain that the categorization of his work as Absurd had worked to foreclose and circumscribe interpretation, but its immediate effect in the 1950s and 1960s was as a means of promotion. In *The Theatrical Critic as Cultural Agent: Constructing Pinter, Orton and Stoppard as Absurdist Playwrights* (2001), Yael Zarhy-Levo has shown how conceiving Pinter's work as Absurd was a key step towards his acceptance by reviewers as a valid presence in British theatre. For her the most significant thing about the Theatre of the Absurd is the way it functioned to promote the writers associated with it:

> Constructing the group, and attaching a familiar label to it, can be perceived as Esslin's means for 'selling' the playwrights. Although Esslin's explicit claim is that he merely attempts to describe a new theatrical trend, the strategies he employs reveal his implicit motives of contributing to these playwrights' acceptance.
>
> (Zarhy-Levo 2001: 11)

As Zarhy-Levo shows, viewing Pinter's work as affiliated to the Absurd allowed critics to appreciate its avant-garde qualities, so that 'his "puzzling" style [was] evaluated anew and perceived as the attractive feature of his drama'

(24). As she also shows, the categorization facilitated Pinter's presentation as a British representative of an established continental trend. In both these ways, being linked to the Absurd was advantageous to Pinter as an emerging playwright.

This does not mean, of course, that he endorsed the connection. Artists often resist categorization and Pinter repeatedly expressed a dislike of theory, preferring to present himself as a practical man of the theatre. As he said, 'A rehearsal period that consists of philosophical discourse or political treatise does not get the curtain up at eight o'clock' (Pinter 1997). At the same time, Pinter did not explicitly refuse or refute the 'Absurd' label, for instance saying in a 1960 BBC interview that 'what I try to do in my plays is get to this recognizable reality of the absurdity of what we do and how we speak [...] There is a kind of horror about and I think that this horror and absurdity go together' (qtd. in Esslin 2001: 242).

While Pinter's willingness to use this language might be thought surprising given his later feelings about the Absurd, it can be accounted for in more than one way. First, because association with the Absurd had contributed to his acceptance by the critical establishment, distancing himself from it was not in his best interests, as he was more than likely aware. Second, debunking any particular interpretation would have seemed proscriptive from a playwright who preferred not to explain his work and consistently argued that 'a play has to speak for itself' (Pinter qtd. in Gussow 1994: 42). Finally, Pinter may have felt bound to the idea of the Theatre of the Absurd at the level of courtesy through his relationships with and indebtedness to a wide range of colleagues and supporters who were themselves associated with it, not least Esslin himself. Though these suggestions, especially the last, are speculative, they are consistent with the picture that emerges from an examination of the professional connections through which Pinter built his writing career.

Pinter's Absurd Connections

Harold Pinter's early career was enabled by the support of a number of powerful contacts, many of them already linked to the Theatre of the Absurd. Some were established practitioners through whose efforts his work was staged and broadcast; some were influential critics who helped to promote it through their public praise and support; one, Martin Esslin, was both. The many points of connection that can be identified between Pinter's various nodal contacts validate their designation as a network whose collective efforts to promote a particular kind of avant-garde drama resulted in the establishment of the Theatre of the Absurd in Britain.

Pinter's first introduction to the world of playwriting came via his expansive network – the 'Hackney gang' of his schooldays, with his old friend Henry Woolf, now at Bristol University, soliciting from him his first play, *The Room*, first performed in May 1957. It wasn't long, however, before he made, through that piece of writing, a more nodal connection, one which established the first of many direct and indirect links between Pinter and Samuel Beckett. In December 1957 *The Room*, having been entered into a student drama competition, brought Pinter to the attention of Harold Hobson, one of the judges and, as drama critic of the *Sunday Times*, one of the most influential people in the British theatre industry.

Hobson was quick to spot, and advertise, Pinter's talent, giving a glowing report on *The Room* in his column. The play was 'a revelation', Hobson told his readers, and he urged 'the directors of the London Arts Theatre and the English Stage Company [to] be after Mr. Pinter before they eat their lunch today' (Hobson 1958). In the event it was West End impresario Michael Codron who acted on Hobson's advice, contacting Pinter promptly and going on to produce *The Birthday Party* in May 1958 (see Billington 2007: 74). When this show was panned by the majority of his colleagues, Hobson became its champion, declaring himself 'willing to risk whatever reputation I have as a judge of plays' in its defence (qtd. in Esslin 2000: 9). This was in effect a reprise of his enthusiastic support for Beckett's *Waiting for Godot*, which most other critics had similarly disliked. He was to look back on this in 1984:

> One sometimes wonders mischievously how many of the university professors who now write books on the work of Beckett, and the PhD. candidates who now prepare theses on him would have recognized his greatness as a writer if Ken Tynan and I had not been in the audience that first night to recognize instantly his greatness and to proclaim it far and wide.
>
> (Hobson 1984: 188)

Hobson evidently relished his role as an almost uniquely perceptive evaluator of new and challenging drama and, in 1958, did not waste the opportunity to re-occupy centre stage in defence of *The Birthday Party*, writing a rave review that was to become one of the most celebrated in British theatre history. Pinter's first brush with British reviewers was therefore inescapably similar to Beckett's, and Hobson's outspoken championing of both gave them a common, and highly influential, ally.

The initial failure of *The Birthday Party* was discouraging for Pinter, who was to recall having been 'very depressed for about forty-eight hours' (qtd.

in Bensky 1977: 356). Before long, however, he was offered hope by BBC radio, which already had links to Beckett and also Ionesco. Both Donald McWhinnie, Assistant Head of Drama, and Barbara Bray, Script Editor for Sound Drama, were active supporters of Beckett, commissioning *All That Fall* (1957) and *Embers* (1959). Irving Wardle describes McWhinnie as acting as both 'director and [...] propagandist' for 'material he believed in' (Wardle 1968: 14), and Jennifer Birkett describes McWhinnie and Bray as determined 'to get Beckett's work before audiences, to explain it, and [...] to educate the public ear' (Birkett 2015: 166). Bray was to recall: 'We had the power to commission and Donald included Harold among a group of young writers to whom we extended patronage and help. After the failure of *The Birthday Party*, we were able to help Harold keep body and soul together' (qtd. in Billington 2007: 95).

Initially this help took the form of encouraging words, but eventually Pinter was commissioned by McWhinnie to write a radio play for a fee of 85 guineas. This became *A Slight Ache*, which was broadcast in July 1959 and which was followed by *A Night Out* in March 1960 and *The Dwarfs* in December of the same year; as Michael Billington comments, 'At this stage, BBC Radio and commercial television were Pinter's greatest champions' (Billington 2007: 111). During the same period Ionesco had also received exposure on BBC radio thanks to Sasha Moorsom, a producer in the features department who had recorded an introduction to his drama by the author himself; because he spoke almost no English, she 'translated his French, and got him to repeat it word for word on tape' ('D.R.' 1959). Moorsom's efforts to bring the theatrical avant-garde to the attention of British listeners complemented those of McWhinnie and Bray, who had become powerful additions to Pinter's nodal network as well as significant figures in the promotion of the Theatre of the Absurd.

Equally significantly, in 1961, McWhinnie was succeeded as assistant head of BBC radio drama by Martin Esslin, who had been with the BBC, mostly in the European Service, since 1940. Esslin worked at first under Bray, by then head of Radio Drama, and when she moved to Paris in 1963 he took over her post, which he would occupy until 1977 (see Calder 2002 and Birkett 2015: 178). Support for Pinter's work continued during this period: September 1962 saw the broadcast of the playwright reading his short story *The Examination*, in February and March 1964 nine short sketches written by Pinter were broadcast, and *Tea Party* followed in June (see Esslin 2000: 15, 16 and Billington 2007: 156, 158–9). Of Esslin's elevation to head of Radio Drama, Zarhy-Levo writes, 'One can suggest that Esslin's change of position [...] enhanced his authority as a drama "theorist"' (Zarhy-Levo 2001: 13), boosting the credibility of his conceptualization of the Theatre of the Absurd. This is no doubt true, but it might be added that his motivation to promote his ideas had likely been strengthened by his time as part of the proselytizing BBC radio drama team. Esslin's writing of *The Theatre of the Absurd*, in other words, can be seen as a continuation via different means of Bray and McWhinnie's patronage of Beckett and Pinter. Not only had Pinter profited from the support of three nodal contacts in significant institutional positions, in Esslin's case he benefited from support offered in more than one highly influential capacity.

Capitalizing on the connection in theatre as well as radio, Pinter nominated McWhinnie to direct *The Caretaker*, his first major stage success, in 1960 (see Billington 2007: 126).[4] This is one example of the way that, throughout this period, Pinter's work was presented to the public in ways that encouraged associations with the Theatre of the Absurd. Both *The Caretaker* and a 1963 double bill of *The Lover* and *The Dwarfs* were staged at the Arts Theatre which had, as Arnold P. Hinchcliffe observed, 'gained the reputation of being the home of the theatre of the Absurd' due to its earlier productions of Ionesco, Beckett and Jean Genet (Hinchcliffe 1974: 105). Also at the Arts, *A Slight Ache* played as part of a 1961 triple bill, *Three* (see Esslin 2000: 14), which also included a piece by 'South London Ionesco' N. F. Simpson ('Merlin' 1959). In the same month *The Caretaker* received its French premiere with Roger Blin, who had directed the premiere of *En Attendant Godot* in 1953 and created the role of Pozzo, playing Davies, and Jean Martin, the original Lucky, playing Aston and directing.[5] Such connections, associations and collaborations drew Pinter further into the dense and intricate network of professional contacts through which many of the plays associated with the Theatre of the Absurd were produced and promoted.

One of the most lasting and significant connections in Pinter's professional career, one that certainly could be called a 'deep relationship', provides another substantial link to the Theatre of the Absurd. In 1962, Pinter began his long-term association with Peter Hall who, as artistic director of first the Royal Shakespeare Company (RSC) and then the National Theatre (NT), was arguably the most influential individual in the British theatre during the 1960s and 1970s. As director of productions at the Arts between 1955 and 1957, Hall had directed the British premieres of Ionesco's *The Lesson* and Beckett's *Godot* (both in 1955), the latter engagement having had, as Sos Eltis has written, a profound impact on his career (see Eltis 2016: 91–4). Hall had been in Pinter's orbit since at least 1960, having been approached to direct *The Birthday Party* and *The Caretaker*, but having been too busy on each occasion (see Billington 2007: 141). He was also one of several who put up the money for the film of *The Caretaker* (1963) (see Esslin 2000: 16).

Hall and Pinter's first collaboration was to co-direct *The Collection* (1961) for the RSC in 1962, and in 1963 the playwright told Michael Codron that Hall was 'the director of my dreams' and that he was consequently moving into the subsidised sector (qtd. in Billington 2007: 149). Hall soon established himself as the pre-eminent interpreter of Pinter's work, directing the lion's share of Pinter premieres between 1965 and the early 1980s, the association no doubt contributing to the increasing perception among peers and critics of the dramatist as an establishment figure. John Bull, for instance, characterized Pinter as the 'Crown Prince' of a 'new mainstream' whose 'initial impetus came from the world of avant-garde Absurdism' but which increasingly reflected 'the conservatism of [...] commercial theatre' (Bull 1994: 56). Further to this, Hall integrated Pinter into, first, the wider work of the RSC as a director (see Chambers 2004: 133 and Billington 2007: 156–7) and, later, the management structure of the National Theatre as an associate director and formidable boardroom ally, as memorably detailed in fellow NT associate Michael Blakemore's memoir *Stage Blood* (2014). That both Hall and Pinter gained in authority and influence from the association confirms that nodal connections can be mutually, and highly, beneficial.

One project that demonstrates Pinter's professional links to the Theatre of the Absurd in a unique way is a projected film described by Michael Billington as 'a kind of Cinema of the Absurd' (Billington 2007: 191). This was a portmanteau feature proposed in 1963 by Barney Rosset of New York's Grove Press, the American publishers of Beckett, Ionesco and Pinter; each writer was to contribute a thirty-minute screenplay (see Knowlson 1996: 506 and Esslin 2000: 150). Years later Pinter was to recall a memorable pitch by Ionesco to the prospective producers: he saw sheep peacefully grazing on a Welsh hillside – suddenly they were all blown to pieces! The producers, agog, asked what came next, but Ionesco shrugged and replied, 'I don't know what happens afterwards.' As Pinter added, 'the film was never made'.[6] Beckett's contribution was later realized as *Film* (1965) starring Buster Keaton; Pinter's became the 1967 BBC television play *The Basement*; and Ionesco's piece *The Hard-Boiled Egg*, which did not include the sequence described above, materialized only as a published scenario.[7] In terms of theatre history, the unrealized project represents the tantalizing moment that the three playwrights most strongly associated with the Theatre of the Absurd almost-but-not-quite validated the term through artistic quasi-collaboration although not, admittedly, in the theatre.

Although the film foundered, Pinter and Beckett's joint involvement may have helped to strengthen the ties between them. Beckett's biographer James Knowlson describes their relationship: '[Beckett] met [Pinter] when in London or when Pinter came over to Paris. Pinter used to send him copies of his plays in typescript and Beckett had considerable respect for the English playwright's work' (1996: 654).[8] Beckett sometimes sent notes on Pinter's scripts, suggesting a degree of willingness to act as mentor – no small gift given Beckett's eminence. Though this resulted in few changes to the work itself,[9] Beckett's implied approval might be thought to have functioned like the royal crest on a jar of jam, an indicator of general approbation carrying great symbolic value. In this respect, Beckett may have been Pinter's most significant 'marquee' contact.

Describing the connections through which Pinter's early career was fostered confirms that there were strong and numerous professional links between Pinter and others associated with the Theatre of the Absurd either as practitioners or advocates. Arguably this group forms a distinct tribe within the UK's theatrical and cultural ecosystem of the late 1950s and early 1960s, open to the influence of the continental avant-garde and committed to drama as high art; as Irving Wardle observed, Donald McWhinnie's 'published statements suggest a fastidious distaste for mass entertainment' (Wardle 1968: 14). Alongside these values sat a wariness of the explicitly political, both in terms of the influence of Bertolt Brecht and the imperative towards social realism which followed the success of *Look Back in Anger* (1956). The exchange of views between Kenneth Tynan and Ionesco that took place in the pages of the *Observer* in June and July of 1958 gave explicit, impassioned expression both to these cultural positions and to their fiercely argued opposites, and elicited engagement, over three weeks' worth of comment pieces and expanded letters pages, from cultural luminaries including George Devine, John Berger, Orson Welles, Lindsay Anderson, Keith Johnstone, Ann Jellicoe and N. F. Simpson, not to mention a number of heavily invested members of the public.[10]

Considering the tribal aspects of support for or resistance to the Theatre of the Absurd raises the question of how far the proponents of the different modes of theatre vying for primacy in the late 1950s and early 1960s may also have felt common loyalties in terms of nationality, sexuality, gender or class. The potential influence of such factors is suggested by an exchange with Tynan that Pinter was to recall in 1997. Some years after the *Observer* critic had joined most of his colleagues in giving *The Birthday Party* a dismissive review (comparing the play unfavourably to the work of N. F. Simpson), the two found themselves sharing convivial drinks after a TV recording. The playwright remembered:

> He said to me, I assure you this is what he said, he said 'You know Harold, I didn't realise you were such a sort of pleasant fellow, I really had no idea', and I said 'Didn't you?' and he said 'If I'd known that I think

I would have taken a very different view of *The Birthday Party*. [...] I've been trying to unravel those words ever since.

(qtd. in Smith 2000: 73)

This suggests that there may indeed be more to unravel about Tynan's initial hostility to Pinter's work and also, potentially, his feud with Ionesco and mockery of Beckett (see Tynan 1958), but for the moment the exchange offers an intriguing glimpse of the social factors that exert a probably unquantifiable influence on the formation of the artistic networks that in turn shape theatrical history.

Pinter was not, of course, solely dependent on his connections to the Absurd. Even in his earliest days as a dramatist, he had a variety of other professional connections, most notably his relationships with the independent television companies which broadcast five Pinter teleplays between 1960 and 1963. As an ambitious writer with a family to support, the playwright took understandable advantage of whatever connections he could, whether from his expansive network of boyhood friends or from show-business contacts made as an actor. Even when this is taken into account, however, it remains clear that much of his early progress was facilitated by his engagement with a nodal network of influential professionals whose existing connections to other exponents of the Absurd, particularly Beckett, complemented their support of Pinter. As his success grew, he became less dependent on these connections and, for Zarhy-Levo, this is the significance of critics' adoption of the adjective 'Pinteresque' in 1964: 'its usage marks Pinter's acceptance, because it reflects the reviewers' assumption that hereafter Pinter's plays can be "sold" by a "Pinter" label, detached from the association with Beckett' (31). Although the new label connoted many of the same things as 'Theatre of the Absurd' (unsettling atmosphere, poetic dialogue, ambiguity), henceforth the association would become less significant – until suddenly it presented Pinter with a problem.

Leaving the Absurd Behind?

Harold Pinter's shift, in the 1980s, into political activism and overtly political playwriting has been much discussed.[11] It surprised many, because prior to this Pinter had repeatedly declined to engage in political debate: for instance, in December 1962, asked by *Encounter* for his thoughts on whether Britain should enter the European Common Market, he had responded, 'I have no interest in the matter and do not care what happens' (qtd. in Anon. 1962: 59). As Pinter was well aware, this now left him vulnerable to the damaging charge of inconsistency. His counter to this was to demonstrate that political concerns had been present in his work from the start, specifically in the early plays *The Dumb Waiter* (1959), *The Birthday Party* and the then-obscure *The Hothouse* (written in 1958); it may have been as a way of making this point that Pinter named his 1984 play about state oppression after a line spoken by Goldberg in Act III of *The Birthday Party*, 'One for the Road' (Pinter 1996: 73).

The assertion of a political purpose behind his early work became a consistent feature of Pinter's interviews from the 1980s on. 'I must repeat', he said in 1995, 'that *The Dumb Waiter*, *The Birthday Party* and *The Hothouse* are doing something which can only be described as political' (qtd. in Billington 2007: 286–7). Stage and television productions of all three pieces invited critics and audiences to see this for themselves: Pinter directed the stage premiere of *The Hothouse* in 1980 and high-profile television productions of *The Dumb Waiter* and *The Birthday Party* were broadcast in 1985 and 1986, respectively. In effect, Pinter was calling for a significant reassessment of plays which had thus far been considered examples of the largely apolitical Theatre of the Absurd. As discussed above, the playwright had not previously discouraged such interpretations in explicit terms but, to make his newly political focus tenable, this policy had to change. When, in 1985, Nick Hern put it to him that 'in 1958 your plays were seen as having no relation to the outside world at all', Pinter replied, 'Absolutely. They were dismissed as absurd rubbish' (qtd. in Pinter 1985: 10).

Although this is the only instance I've identified of Pinter taking direct issue with the term 'absurd', it forms part of a pattern nonetheless. When Michael Billington, then chief theatre critic of Britain's leading left-wing newspaper *The Guardian*, was chosen to write the authorized biography that would inevitably become the standard work on Pinter – replacing Martin Esslin's 1970 monograph, originally published as *The Peopled Wound* – it conveyed the implicit message that the playwright's work should be understood in relation to politics rather than existentialism. More specifically, because the book operated as a subject-sanctioned corrective to misrepresentations and misconceptions, we might see some significance in its assertion that *The Room* 'could not be further from the cul-de-sac of absurdism which presupposes that we live in an inexplicable universe' (Billington 2007: 92). Following the biography's publication in 1996, Billington became a long-standing advocate of Pinter, participating in and often chairing discussions of his work well into the twenty-first century, making him a very significant addition to the playwright's nodal network.

Pinter's efforts to update critical perceptions were successful, at least to an extent. It probably helped that the Theatre of the Absurd as a theatrical mode had quite quickly fallen out of fashion in the UK,[12] and it certainly helped that Pinter's claims for the political resonance of his early drama came gradually to be accepted.[13] Most important of all was the fact that the critical and commercial success of his work had over time allowed Pinter's reputation to float free from the construct with which he had initially been associated – in which respect, as in so many others, his career had followed the path taken by Beckett's. However, as Pinter had learned from the seeming immortality of an ill-judged phrase about 'the weasel under the cocktail cabinet' (Pinter qtd. in Taylor 1963: 285), once an idea is at large in cultural discourse it is very hard to eradicate it altogether.[14]

This has been made clear by the gradual revival of the fortunes of the Theatre of the Absurd in the twenty-first century. For one thing, a fresh wave of scholarship on the subject has included consideration of Pinter as part of the package.[15] For another, the recovery of the Absurd as a component of the theatrical repertoire, slowly building since Complicité's 1997 revival of Ionesco's *The Chairs* (1952) and continuing in such productions as the 2018 revival of the same playwright's *Exit the King* (1962) at the NT, has made Pinter's association with the genre both a selling point and a talking point once more. This is demonstrated by the fact that the promotional material for a 2018 production of *The Birthday Party* at the Harold Pinter Theatre referred to it as 'Pinter's landmark play about the absurd terrors of the everyday',[16] and by the headline of the review in the *Sunday Times*, which was 'Absurdly brilliant' (Hart 2018). As an emerging writer Pinter had acquiesced in the association between his work and the Theatre of the Absurd, an association which helped him gain the initial acceptance that was a precondition of his later eminence; the price appears to have been a seemingly ineradicable association with a theatrical mode that, as generally understood, only partially reflects his artistic aims.

Conclusion

The tenacity of Harold Pinter's association with the Theatre of the Absurd can partly be ascribed to the attractiveness of cultural shorthand, not least to journalists and marketing copywriters, but my argument in this chapter is that it also persists for a more fundamental reason. The dense network of nodal connections that links Pinter to numerous reviewers, producers, directors, actors, scholars, publishers and fellow playwrights, all in their different ways engaged in creating, producing and promoting an identifiable strand of post-war theatre, provides compelling reason to consider his early work as part of a larger cultural project that it makes sense to call the Theatre of the Absurd.

The powerful and extensive network whose efforts made such a decisive contribution to Pinter's early success worked to create space in British theatre and culture for a mode of avant-garde, formally experimental drama which was to prove surprisingly assimilable into the British theatrical mainstream. Granting the existence of the Theatre of the Absurd as a network opens the way to seeing the plays and performances for which it was responsible as a body of work available for consideration as a whole – while being mindful of the need to avoid reductive or totalizing interpretations of the kind that for so long veiled Pinter's political concerns – and to appreciating that its characteristics were determined as much by the cultural conditions in which it was brought into being as by the historical moment in which it appeared.

Notes

1 As Catherine Rees writes, the 'classification of Pinter as an Absurdist remains […] highly contentious', with some critics arguing that 'any such classification is an artificial and reductive way to discuss theatre' (Catherine Rees, 'Pinter the Absurdist' in Wyllie and Rees 2017: 25).
2 In the introduction to their recent book *Rethinking the Theatre of the Absurd*, Carl Lavery and Clare Finburgh list seven terms that have been suggested by critics as improvements on Esslin's – see Lavery and Finburgh (2015: 2).
3 For an alternative, but complementary account of Pinter's early career and its points of intersection with Beckett, see Jonathan Bignell's '"Random Dottiness": Samuel Beckett and the Reception of Harold Pinter's Early Dramas' (forthcoming).
4 Beckett also favoured McWhinnie as a director, insisting he direct *Eh Joe* for the BBC in 1966 (see Birkett 2015: 188).
5 Despite this impressive pedigree, the production received poor reviews and flopped. See Esslin (2000: 14), Billington (2007: 130) and http://www.haroldpinter.org/plays/frn_caretaker_fr61.shtml (accessed 11 May 2019).
6 Pinter told this story at the Barbican in London on 9 October 2002, where he was appearing in conversation with Michael Billington prior to a screening of *The Caretaker*.
7 'The Hard-Boiled Egg' appears in Ionesco (1976: 97–114).
8 For a detailed look at the relationship between Pinter and Beckett, see David Tucker's piece, '"That First Last Look in the Shadows": Beckett's Legacies for Harold Pinter' (Tucker 2016).
9 For one example of Beckett's comments on Pinter's work in typescript and their impact on the play as eventually performed, see Gussow (1994: 28–9).
10 For a summary, see Esslin (2001: 128–33). Letters on the topic were published in the *Observer* of 6 July 1958 ('Ionesco v. Tynan'), p. 19; 13

July 1958 ('The Ionesco-Tynan Controversy'), p. 14; and 20 July 1958 ('The Ionesco Controversy: Some Readers' Views'), p. 15.
11 For instance, in Basil Chiasson's 2017 book, *The Late Harold Pinter: Political Dramatist, Poet and Activist* (Chiasson 2017).
12 In the second edition of his book, published in 1968, Esslin asked if the Theatre of the Absurd had 'become no more than yesterday's fashion', concluding that 'in so far as it was a fashion, this is certainly so' (Esslin 2001: 430).
13 As acknowledged, for instance, by Chiasson, who writes of Pinter's 'earlier dramas which are taken to be political in the metaphorical sense, for example *The Birthday Party* and *The Dumb Waiter*' (Chiasson 2017: 41).
14 According to Taylor, Pinter used the phrase as part of an 'exchange at a new writers' brains trust' (Taylor 1963: 285). Pinter described the remark as a 'great mistake' in a speech given in 1970 (Pinter 1997).
15 For instance, *Reassessing the Theatre of the Absurd* includes the chapter 'The Pinteresque Oedipal Household: The Interrogation Scene(s) in *The Birthday Party*' (Bennett 2013: 53–69) and *Rethinking the Theatre of the Absurd* includes 'The Secluded Voice: The Impossible Call Home in Early Pinter' by Mark Taylor-Batty and Carl Lavery (Lavery and Finburgh 2015: 219–39).
16 As advertised at http://www.thebirthdayparty.london/ (accessed 6 March 2018).

Works Cited

Anon. (1962), '"Going into Europe": A Symposium', *Encounter*, December 1962, 56–65. Available online: https://www.unz.com/print/Encounter-1962dec-00056/ (accessed 7 January 2020).

Baker, W. (2018), *Pinter's World: Relationships, Obsessions and Artistic Endeavors*, Vancouver: Fairleigh Dickinson University Press.

Batty, M. (2005), *About Pinter: The Playwright and the Work*, London: Faber.

Bennett, M. (2013), *Reassessing the Theatre of the Absurd: Camus, Beckett, Ionesco, Genet, and Pinter*, Basingstoke: Palgrave Macmillan.

Bensky, L. (1977), 'Harold Pinter', in G. Plimpton (ed.), *Writers at Work: The Paris Review Interviews*, 347–68, Harmondsworth: Penguin.

Bibby, A. (2018), '5 Types of Professional Networks and How to Use Them', *Flexjobs*, 19 January. Available online: https://www.flexjobs.com/blog/post/types-professional-networks/ (accessed 3 April 2018).

Bignell, J. (forthcoming), '"Random Dottiness": Samuel Beckett and the Reception of Harold Pinter's Early Dramas', in N. Johnson, A. Rakoczy and M. Tanaka (eds), *Beckett Influencing/Influencing Beckett*, Budapest and Paris: Károli Gáspár University Press/L'Harmattan.

Billington, M. (2007), *Harold Pinter*, 2nd edn, London: Faber and Faber.

Birkett, J. (2015), *Undoing Time: The Life and Work of Samuel Beckett*, Sallins: Irish Academic Press.
Blakemore, M. (2014), *Stage Blood: Five Tempestuous Years in the Early Life of the National Theatre*, London: Faber and Faber.
Bull, J. (1994), *Stage Right: Crisis and Recovery in British Contemporary Mainstream Theatre*, Basingstoke: Macmillan.
Bull, J. (2000), 'Looking Back at *Godot*', in D. Shellard (ed.), *British Theatre in the 1950s*, 982–94, Sheffield: Sheffield Academic Press.
Calder, J. (2002), 'Martin Esslin', *Guardian*, 27 February. Available online: https://www.theguardian.com/news/2002/feb/27/guardianobituaries. booksobituaries (accessed 13 May 2019).
Chambers, C. (2004), *Inside the Royal Shakespeare Company: Creativity and the Institution*, London: Routledge.
Chiasson, B. (2017), *The Late Harold Pinter: Political Dramatist, Poet and Activist*, London: Palgrave.
'D.R.' (1959), 'Producing for Radio – from "Pop" Singers to Ionesco', *Manchester Guardian*, 6 April: 3.
Eltis, S. (2016), '"It's All Symbiosis": Peter Hall Directing Beckett', in D. Tucker and T. McTighe (eds), *Staging Beckett in Great Britain*, 87–104, London: Bloomsbury.
Esslin, M. (2000), *Pinter the Playwright*, 6th edn, London: Methuen.
Esslin, M. (2001), *The Theatre of the Absurd*, 3rd edn, London: Methuen.
Gussow, M. (1994), *Conversations with Pinter*, London: Nick Hern.
Hart, C. (2018), 'Absurdly Brilliant', *Sunday Times 'Culture'*, 21 January: 22.
Hinchcliffe, A. (1969), *The Absurd*, The Critical Idiom, London: Methuen.
Hinchcliffe, A. (1974), *British Theatre 1950–70*, Oxford: Blackwell.
Hobson, H. (1958), 'Larger than Life at the Festival', *Sunday Times*, 5 January: 19.
Hobson, H. (1984), *Theatre in Britain: A Personal View*, Oxford: Phaidon.
Ionesco, E. (1976), *Plays*, volume x, D. Watson (trans.), London: Calder.
Knowlson, J. (1996), *Damned to Fame: The Life of Samuel Beckett*, London: Bloomsbury.
Lavery, C., and C. Finburgh, eds (2015), *Rethinking the Theatre of the Absurd: Ecology, the Environment and the Greening of the Modern Stage*, London: Bloomsbury.
'Merlin' (1959), 'Mainly about People', *Sunday Times*, 27 December: 23.
Pinter, H. (1985), 'A Play and Its Politics: A Conversation between Harold Pinter and Nicholas Hern', in *One for the Road*, 5–23, London: Methuen.
Pinter, H. (1996), '*The Birthday Party*', in *Harold Pinter: Plays 1*, 1–81, London: Faber and Faber.
Pinter, H. (1997), 'Introduction', in *Harold Pinter: Plays 3*, London: Faber and Faber.
Prince, R. (2017), 'You Need Two Types of Professional Networks to Get Super-Rich', *Forbes*, 27 October. Available online: https://www.forbes.com/sites/russalanprince/2017/10/27/you-need-two-types-of-professional-networks-to-get-super-rich/#660cca0c4b3c (accessed 8 May 2019).

Rebellato, D. (1999), *1956 and All That: The Making of Modern British Drama*, London: Routledge.
Smith, I. (2000), 'Harold Pinter's Recollections of His Career in the 1950s: An Interview Conducted by Ian Smith at the British Library, 1997', in D. Shellard (ed.), *British Theatre in the 1950s*, 64–81, Sheffield: Sheffield Academic Press.
Taylor, J. (1963), *Anger and After: A Guide to the New British Drama*, rev. edn, Harmondsworth: Pelican.
Tucker, D. (2016), '"That First Last Look in the Shadows": Beckett's Legacies for Harold Pinter', in D. Tucker and T. McTighe (eds), *Staging Beckett in Great Britain*, 193–208, London: Bloomsbury.
Tynan, K. (1958), 'Slamm's Last Knock', *Observer*, 2 November: 19.
Wardle, I. (1968), 'Introduction', in *New English Dramatists 12: Radio Plays*, 7–21, Harmondsworth: Penguin.
Wyllie, A., and C. Rees (2017), *The Plays of Harold Pinter*, London: Palgrave.
Zarhy-Levo, Y. (2001), *The Theatrical Critic as Cultural Agent: Constructing Pinter, Orton and Stoppard as Absurdist Playwrights*, New York: Peter Lang.

3

The Elite Pinter and the Pinter Elite

James Hudson

On 27 October 2017, a copy of a letter Harold Pinter had written to Tom Stoppard in 2001 was posted to Twitter. In it, Pinter rebuffed Stoppard's invitation to a gala fundraiser, suggesting that he would 'rather die' than attend the dinner at a 'top London restaurant'. The tweet went viral, attracting over 18,000 'likes' (Tabard 2017). The text accompanying the photographed letter, by Twitter user @agnesfrim, added the punchline: 'My spirit animal is Harold Pinter' (2017). Many Twitter users identified with Pinter's posthumous statement, no doubt having used that idiom themselves in similar performances of social hygiene. Yet the spike of approval that greeted the remark was prompted, perhaps, not merely because so many recognized Pinter's characteristic frankness and expressive pugnacity, but because of the way these patented tropes were deployed to reject an evening of celebrity exclusivity and elite distinction. If the recent success of right-populist politics encapsulated by the election of Donald Trump and the 'leave' vote in the Brexit referendum of 2016 has made anything clear, it is that there is enormous political cachet to be gained from repudiating elites, whether one is a member of the elite or not. And yet it should be said that Pinter's refusal to associate himself with high-profile events and people was far from absolute. In Antonia Fraser's 2010 memoir *Must You Go?: My Life with Harold Pinter*, a book which *The New York Times* described as 'a lightly annotated social calendar, albeit one of the most enviable and kaleidoscopic of the 20th century' (Garner 2010), and *The Washington Post* called '*People* magazine for very smart people, an enchanting catalogue of celebrity names and sparkling events' (see 2010), Fraser conveys the impression of a life of stratospheric privilege quite in keeping with a playwright of Pinter's stature, although she crudely attempts to efface the realities of their participation in these echelons by remarking that she and Pinter 'belonged to the same class: […] the Bohemian class' (7). The reality is that Pinter's great success allowed him to breathe quite rarefied social air: it is unlikely that his description of having lunch at Buckingham Palace, as recounted to Mel Gussow, would have resonated as strongly on social media (qtd. in Gussow 1995: 154). A pre-eminent twentieth-century dramatist and permanent *habitué* of London theatreland with an artistic career garlanded with the highest literary honours, Pinter's artistic credentials were of the highest elite status, a status at odds with his lower-class origins.[1]

This chapter presents a dual perspective upon Pinter and the notion of the elite: one that considers the representation of elites in his writing for stage and one that examines his own elite status as an artist and public figure. The first section analyses the political, artistic and academic elites of Pinter's plays. It suggests that Pinter's conception and portrayal of elites can be understood as reflecting three paradigms of elite theory, each of which is contemporaneous with the period in which he is writing: C. W. Mills's notions of the operation of elites as defined in his seminal work *The Power Elite* (1956), the sociological work of Pierre Bourdieu, and theories of the way that elites function in neoliberal society. The second section of the chapter examines Pinter's elite status as an artist, specifically how this situated him within public discourse and codes of cultural appreciation. This approach builds on Yael Zarhy-Levo's work (2001) by demonstrating how Pinter's stock rose through his being associated with particular aesthetic movements thought to be elite, though the perception of him as an elite artist acquired unusual contours as his political activism increased and his artistic output changed in scope and form.

The Pinter Elite

Pinter's great abiding theme is arguably that of power (Gordon 2012), with every one of his plays staging a confrontation, or series of related confrontations, between characters exercising certain types of power over each other. Quite often the fault lines over which these contests are fought range over familiar categories of identity where power is unequally distributed: class, gender, race and nationality, occupation or the family. While, as Shamus Rahman Khan informs us, '[t]he study of elites is the study of power and inequality' (2012: 361), in reality what is at stake involves examining an ecosystem whereby economic, cultural and political power is dispersed through networks of educational, social and familial institutions as well as business and government, in such a way, as Rahman Khan defines it, that elites have 'vastly disproportionate control over or access to a resource' (362). At the beginning of Pinter's career, before he was considered an elite writer, elites went unrepresented in his theatre work; however, it could be argued that their influence pervades the suggestive and opaque contextual backdrops of both *The Birthday Party* (1958) and

The Dumb Waiter (1959). In this, Pinter's early career conception of elites corresponds at least partially to contemporaneous scholarship pioneered by the sociologist C. W. Mills, who defined the post-war power elite as 'those political, economic, and military circles which as an intricate set of overlapping cliques share decisions' (1999: 18). Central to Mills's critique is the view of an integrated set of groups operating anti-democratically outside the public sphere and issuing commands which must be obeyed by those outside the elite. As Mills's contemporaries Peter Bachrach and Morton Baratz maintained in 1962, power may be effectively exercised by 'confining the scope of decision-making to relatively "safe" issues' (938) – in other words, to limit the potential for the non-elite to influence the preferences of the elite. Certainly, characters in Pinter's early plays displaying a sterile antipathy to change and preferring stagnant occupancy of single locales can be seen as having inadequate scope to make decisions, while more empowered, assertive opponents circle them dextrously. Moreover, motifs identified by Martin Esslin that persuaded him to associate Pinter with the 'Theatre of the Absurd' were specifically linked to the notion that the fate of the individual in early Pinter plays was subject to vast, impersonal forces operating beyond their comprehension or capacity to influence. This is precisely the remove at which Mills's power elite exercised their collective will, having a 'jurisdiction over the public at large', as sociologist Will Davies puts it (2017: 229).

As Mills himself observed, 'All politics is a struggle for power; the ultimate kind of power is violence' (171). What Pinter's very first and very last plays share is a concern with the material effects of elite power as it manifests in certain types of violence. Pinter's first play, *The Room* (1957), ends with a vicious demonstration of brute violence perpetrated by the white delivery driver Bert Hudd upon the black visitor Riley, who visits Bert's wife Rose and implores her to 'come home'. Pinter's subsequent plays expanded beyond interpersonal rivalry to suggest a dimension whereby the violence enacted is performed at the behest of some higher authority. Indeed, in *The Birthday Party* and *The Dumb Waiter* Pinter appears equally exercised by the qualities and characteristics of those that implement elite power at its affective level as much as he is about those that encounter it. As Mark Taylor-Batty and Carl Lavery observe:

> McCann and Ben and Gus adopt positions within a system of authority that is more concerned with self-perpetuation than with the protection of those who serve to perpetuate it. Tellingly the status it affords them begins to erode once they begin to gain consciousness of this fact.
>
> (2015: 235)

That there is no more precise term than 'system of authority' to capture the type of social organism from which these characters emanate and whose policies they enact to exert its disciplinary effects accords neatly with the consciously nebulous perimeters of Mills's power elite. Pinter captured the sort of forces that Goldberg and McCann were intended to represent very clearly in a communication to Peter Wood, the director of the 1958 production of *The Birthday Party*, defining them as 'the hierarchy, the Establishment, the arbiters' (qtd. in Batty 2005: 21). Goldberg and McCann in particular can be understood as purveyors of a type of elite discursive technology, their idiolect a demonstration of interrogative dominance that operates above and beyond the grasp of the uninducted laity in the boarding house. In *The Dumb Waiter*, Gus and Ben are at once hitmen working for some clandestine criminal or governmental agency and also subject to a similar articulation of psychological manipulation by their superiors that transcends their capacity, as low-level operatives, to interpret it: they are metaphorically in the subterranean level of their organization, receiving orders from 'above'. The catatonic state of inarticulacy that is a consequence of the linguistic terrorization that Stanley is subjected to in *The Birthday Party* is a totemic paradigm of the potential of elite power to subjugate, neuter or achieve conformity in those who are subject to it. A feature common to these early plays is that those being victimized are exposed to the workings of power which may or may not be arbitrary but which is by definition punitive and extrajudicial: Goldberg and McCann operate on Stanley not to elicit information but to erode his faculties and achieve his compliance. While in Pinter's earlier plays the source of this authority is never investigated or disclosed, he was to resume this concern with elite power and its implementation in the tranche of work which has become known as his 'more precisely political' plays (Pinter 1998), where he was exercised primarily by specific atrocities mainly attributable to US adventurism and imperialism.

What was taken up in the interim frequently emerged as a preoccupation with problematic and unconventional aspects of bourgeois domesticity as Pinter began to situate his plays in middle-class milieus; indeed, the depiction of a dwelling inhabited by the working class in Pinter tends to evaporate in tandem with the UK's slum clearance programme of the 1950s and 1960s. Threats to relationships and an established status quo materialize in plays such as *The Lover* (1963), *Old Times* (1971) and *Betrayal* (1978), but little punctures the bourgeois assumptions of the *dramatis personae* or suggests a class strata existing beyond the social world they inhabit. This, of course, contrasts markedly with all three of Pinter's screenplays for Joseph Losey, with *The Servant* (1963) and *The Go-Between* (1971) particularly dramatizing the dynamics of a reckoning between a declining upper class and an emergent lower class. In *The Servant*, the relationship between Barrett, the manservant, and the wealthy pseudo-aristocratic Tony involves the enaction of a fairly straightforward Pinteresque power reversal: as Rebecca Dyer notes, 'Pinter and Losey transformed Maugham's "oily"-lidded, "repellent" servant into a powerful figure of class resistance and political change' (2015: 149). More sensitive than this perhaps is *The Go-Between*, in which the young, lower-class Leo is inducted into the wealthy Maudsley family only to be tainted by the hypocrisies of the upper classes and scarred by Marian's instrumental use of him to facilitate her love affair with the neighbouring gentleman farmer, Ted. Losey captures the sense of Leo as a mere object of curiosity for the Maudsleys in a shot where the boy stands on a seat in the middle of the sitting room while various members of the family scrutinize their class hostage. Leo's exploitation extends into adulthood, whereupon, at the end of the film, he is little more than an emotionally cauterized shell performing a final errand for Marian. In *The Servant*, a louche and anaemic upper class is poisoned by an unscrupulous emergent lower order: *The Go-Between* inverts this so that a benign and worthy lower class are toxified by their interactions with a callous upper class.

Like in Pinter's scripts for Losey, class boundaries in Pinter's mid-career plays are frequently antagonistic. Pinter's treatment of the issue in plays which feature the middle class once again corresponds to a contemporaneous turn in elite scholarship, namely Bourdieu's idea of cultural capital, where cultural dispositions serve as markers of elite status. *The Homecoming* (1965) and *No Man's Land* (1975) can each be seen to frame the conflict between characters as a series of aggressive negotiations oriented around socially acquired dispositions and preferences over-laced by patterns of domination and relative privilege. This resonates with what Bourdieu developed in *Outline of a Theory of Practice* (1972) and called *habitus*: 'this kind of practical sense for which is to be done in a given situation – what is called in sport a "feel" for the game, which is inscribed in the present state of play' (1998: 25). *Habitus*, for Bourdieu, is the crucial element in analysing the relationship between the given field of power and the agents competing within the field, a concept straightforwardly analogous to the way Pinter's characters pursue various trajectories through overlapping regions of social space. While there is frequently no guarantee that the logic that governs the actions of those within Pinter's plays corresponds to the same assumptions as those spectating them, Pinter's fictive world continually articulates a Bourdieuian conception of the social world as comprising a rule structure with an inbuilt capacity for improvisation and transgression: 'an infinity of practices adapted to endlessly changing situations, without those schemes ever being constituted as explicit principles' (Bourdieu 1977: 16). The protean capabilities of Pinter's characters and their often-inscrutable compulsions are prompts that remind us, as Bourdieu insists, that social reality is in a continuous state of flux, reproduction and renegotiation.

What is noticeable in this tranche of Pinter's plays is how inexpedient the strategic maximizing of cultural capital is shown to be: those considered elite often tend to lose out. In *The Homecoming*, Teddy's occupation as an academic is recognized, albeit without unalloyed endorsement, as constituting elite status that contrasts with their rather more modest home life, as Max says: 'How many other houses in the district have got a Doctor of Philosophy sitting down drinking a cup of coffee?' (Pinter 1997: 57). Though Teddy claims his powers of critical thinking allow him to remain above the fray and 'operate on things and not in things' (69), his status is progressively diminished sufficient that Lenny is able to suggest that he exploits his professional ties – in Bourdieu's terms, his social capital – to provide high-profile contacts to facilitate the proposed entry of Ruth into a life of sex work: '[Y]ou must know lots of professors, heads of department, men like that. They pop over here for a week at the Savoy, they need somewhere they can go to have a nice quiet poke' (82). The devaluation of Teddy's academic credentials and elite pretensions is at that point complete. While *The Homecoming* is best known as a play that exploits fissures and instabilities surrounding normative and reductive conceptions of gender roles, it is also a play where the standard trappings of class and professional status are junked alongside every other conventional propriety, with Teddy's aloofness not translating effectively in the expected hierarchical way.

In *No Man's Land*, class boundaries emerge once more, as D. Keith Peacock has already observed:

> Whereas in *The Caretaker* Aston and Davies met in a lower-class greasy-spoon café, Hirst met Spooner on middle-class Hampstead Heath. [...] The other two characters, Briggs and Foster, who are Hirst's butler and secretary, are lower-class and aggressive, but in consequence of their position of service to Hirst they are upwardly mobile.
>
> (1997: 113)

Hirst, like Pinter himself, is an elite man of letters, and the hedge-poet Spooner bases his supplication in the second act on their apparently improvised concoction of a shared upper-class Oxford education and high society background. Spooner seizes on this in a fraudulent attempt to conjoin his parlous state of social capital with Hirst's rather more considerable prestige, before being forced to switch to a plea for employment couched in terms of their mutual affinity for high culture. In doing so Spooner's final gambit becomes almost a tribunal for the power of cultural capital, which is the one category of Bourdieuian capital that both he and Hirst are rich in but one that ultimately fails to displace Briggs and Foster or secure him the position he seeks. Whereas the social accent in *The Homecoming* cleaves most closely to the constant and conflictual grating of each individual's *habitus* against the fluid structures of the environment in which they find themselves, where familial, legal and moral givens are thrown into disarray, in *No Man's Land* it is Spooner's appeal to discernment and taste which is most prevalent. As Bourdieu explains in *Distinction* (1984):

> Taste classifies and it classifies the classifier. Social subjects, classified by their classifications, distinguish themselves by the distinctions they make, between the beautiful and ugly, the distinguished and the vulgar, in which their position in the objective classifications is expressed or betrayed.
>
> (2010: xxix)

Spooner's appeal is once again fruitless, where, as in *The Homecoming*, the more earthly advances espoused by the lower-class characters work to edge out the more cerebral and refined pretentions of their competitors, successfully claiming the attentions of those either able to dispense patronage, as in Hirst, or willing to perform as a going concern, as in Ruth. Cultural capital in Pinter's plays tends to be susceptible to being undermined, as much as it is something that divides rather than unites, a key note struck in *Betrayal*, when Robert's rancour about Jerry and Emma's affair is mediated in terms of their shared attitude towards literature:

> You know what you and Emma have in common? You love literature. I mean you love modern prose literature, I mean you love the new novel by the new Casey or Spinks. It gives you both a thrill. (Pinter 2011a: 97)

It is in Pinter's late plays that the aestheticization of elites culminates. On Pinter's assumption of a more activist sensibility, Mark-Taylor Batty speculates:

> The ascent of a neoliberal discourse of consumption and traditionalism heralded by the election of Margaret Thatcher could well have focussed Pinter's mind back onto the machinations of a powerful elite.
>
> (2014: 163–4)

Taylor-Batty links Pinter's rediscovery of the text of *The Hothouse* (written in 1958 before premiering in 1980) around 1977–9 to the recalibration of his political calculus, at which point Pinter is concerned – arguably primarily – with the operation of elite power under societies guided by neoliberal ideas, a notion which Basil Chiasson has explored in depth (2014). In Pinter's final stage of theatre work, we are presented with what Taylor-Batty calls the 'establishment figures [of] the morally corrupt [...] Western political community' (2014: 164). Here Pinter once again shows an affinity with contemporaneous sociological interpretations of elite power distinct from its earlier Millsian or Bourdieuian articulations. Works such as *One for the Road* (1984), *Party Time* (1991), *The New World Order* (1991) and *Celebration* (2000) portray the ownership class of neoliberal society along with intellectual assistants and enforcing adjutants. It is an approach which finally delivers on the promise of Pinter's famous declaration in 1966 about flame-throwing politicians advocating for the Vietnam War (qtd. in Bensky 1967: 104), which is at its heart about holding political elites accountable for their actions.

Pinter appears most interested in neoliberalism as an anti-democratic project that is less about economic calculation and more as a style of technocracy that suppresses dissent and tends towards authoritarianism. The unlocalized nature of his later political dramas makes them quite distinct from their precursors and presents a composite picture of a repressive political elite both at work and at leisure, though noticeably the spirit of enjoyment is seldom far away from the dirty work of politics. It is not simply that the elites of *One for the Road*, *Party Time* and *The New World Order* exhibit an ironclad certainty in the rightness of the beliefs they espouse – a certainty that echoes Margaret Thatcher's pronunciamento 'There is no alternative' – but that the interrogations, torture and crackdowns undertaken to implement those beliefs clearly exert a powerful libidinal charge upon them which thrills and excites as much as it functions to constrain resistance.

Speaking about *Party Time* specifically, Pinter admitted that his objective was to achieve a faithful depiction of a category of people with the means to influence political events by whatever means they considered necessary:

> I believe that there *are* extremely powerful people in apartments in capital cities in all countries who are actually controlling events that are happening on the street in a number of very subtle and sometimes not so subtle ways. [...] It's a question of how power operates.
> (qtd. in Smith 2006: 92; emphasis in original)

The notion of power residing with a wealthy yet non-denominational elite dispersed all over the globe with an interest in preserving the status quo is perhaps the closest that Pinter comes to articulating a structural political critique aside from his specific aspersions to the imposition of US imperialism under neoliberalism. What Pinter augments in his elucidation of power here is that elites are not merely passive beneficiaries of the social relations empowering them. Rather, they actively mobilize to defend and further their interests, and these plays detail the processes by which this is achieved. As Chiasson points out, this is why the focus of Pinter's late plays tends to be constrained towards the language used by this privileged elite, because it is this that incarnates particular social realities:

> [H]owever, this does not constitute an attack upon class, privilege, social capital and money power so much as an exploration of language used in privileged, insulated, and atomized milieus […] Still, these later dramas […] make sensible for readers and audiences the extents to which modes of speech and orders of language are integral to circumscribing power and producing life practices and subjectivities […] which ratify the existing order of things.
>
> (2017: 112–13)

The stated political philosophy espoused in these plays rarely moves beyond single words extolled by characters who wield power that are simultaneously tokenistic and totemic: 'Democracy' in *The New World Order*, 'Peace' in *Party Time*, 'God' in *One for the Road*. While ideas, knowledge and ideology are plainly central to the maintenance of elite power, Pinter's notion of this appears less the Gramscian hegemony whereby the many are ruled by the few through acceptance of their ideas than the enforcement of ideological homogeneity unleashed by US support of dictators in key nations around the globe in the post-war period. It is an approach that recalls political theorist Ernesto Laclau's argument that the character of an ideology is determined less by its specific contents than by its process of 'articulation' (Laclau and Mouffe 1998: 105), which gathers together discrete elements that nevertheless possess a common nuclei of meaning. 'Democracy', 'peace' and 'God' are distinct words which suggest very different things, but following Laclau's designation they can plausibly be grouped by an 'articulating principle' that quilts them together to indicate a nebulously positive aspirant state to which the individual must subsume themselves. Indeed, 'God', 'peace' and 'democracy' work well as a specifically neo-conservative trifecta of abstract values propagated during the Bush-doctrine era of US foreign policy. Similarly, in a now-familiar global political context replete with transformative gains for far-right populists that have found considerable traction in pitting a conception of 'people' against 'elites', the disparagement of intellectuals and educators in *One for the Road* and *The New World Order* appears prescient. However, while this constitutes, as Pinter pointed out in his Nobel lecture, a critique of '[p]olitical language, as used by politicians' (2009: 288), the comparatively empty signifiers enunciated by these elites are demonstrably less important than the techniques of suppression and proscription employed to stifle dissent that successive late-career dramatic works reiterate. Charles Grimes has observed that Pinter's late plays 'depict a power structure seemingly impervious to critique and opposition' (2005: 31), just as Chiasson too has noted that 'the absence of voices in opposition to the official political line is a running theme in Pinter's political oeuvre' (2017: 35). As Pinter brings elites into the foreground, so does he emphasize their inevitable by-product, the figure of the oppressed that is incarcerated, tortured or murdered. Nowhere else in Pinter's *oeuvre* are power relations presented so asymmetrically as in these 'more precisely political' plays.

The Elite Pinter

Although at its heart an incontrovertible point, the notion that Pinter's work belongs to a class of elite cultural material, and that he himself was a member of an artistic elite, has some unusual contours which reward further exploration. The impetus for this can be traced to Pinter's education and early affinity for culture, particularly literature. It is well known that the encouragement of 'eccentric individualism' (Billington 1996: 11) under the tutelage of English teacher Joe Brearley at Hackney Downs Grammar School was formative in firing Pinter's imagination. Penelope Prentice writes evocatively about the transformation in Pinter's social circumstances engendered by his educational background, and particularly Brearley's influence:

> Harold seemed to have made himself into a Cinderella without a fairy godmother, to a man of the theatre in London. But what made such passage possible for all six boys [Pinter's adolescent friends] was a great teacher – of English, their beloved drama coach Joseph Bererely [sic] who singlehandedly provided a Pygmalian-type [sic] finishing school for those six well-brought-up boys, turning them from aggressively smart students into young gentlemen, actors who like Harold could don a passable BBC/Oxbridge accent.
>
> (2011: 26)

Prentice's description is intriguing because it interprets the effect of education less in terms of the cultivation of knowledge and the assumption of tastes for their own sake and more in terms of how such things are necessary acquisitions in the pursuit of social advancement. This emphasis on presentation over substance might perhaps be realigned in the light of an appraisal of Pinter's appreciation of high culture; as a motor for his success, it is less the assumption of the accoutrements of middle-class sensibility that were important and more an early affinity for elite art. The proof of this is that Pinter's early pursuit of acting as a career was marked by the inability of the young nonconformist to integrate smoothly with those of the class above him, his disenchantment stemming specifically from the 'class-consciousness [and] insular luvviedom […] of post-war RADA' (Billington 1996: 20). This was a good few years before a new generation of actors headed by the likes of Albert Finney and Tom Courtney were able to make a virtue of their working-class identity in a way that was simply not possible for Pinter in 1948–9. While Pinter may very well have been repelled by the hidebound practices of RADA and unwilling to ingratiate with his peers there, it is the profound engagement of a young working-class adolescent with a diverse range of elite artists and their work which nourished his imagination. The prodigious cultural spadework of Pinter's teenage years is a tale of relentless highbrow consumption: the modernist prose of Joyce, the enigmatic novels of Dostoyevsky and Kafka, the brooding menace of the poetry that pulsed in Webster's plays, and in film the surrealism of Luis Buñuel's *Un Chien Andalou* (1919) and the poetic realism of Marcel Carné's *Le jour se lève* (1939).

There is therefore a strong argument that Pinter's openness to elite art provided an invaluable store of cultural capital that helped pave his relatively idiosyncratic path towards an early career as a playwright. Even at this germinal stage, Pinter stood apart from his contemporaries as somewhat out of step with what was being considered significant developments in the theatre ecology of the period. He was associated with neither the Royal Court nor Stratford East, both hotbeds of theatrical innovation and enterprise that aimed to connect playgoing with younger and more nascently politicized audiences. Whereas the generic objectives of the generation inaugurated during this period of seismic change to the theatrical landscape were legible under discrete but overlapping epithets such as 'New Wave', 'Angry Young Men', 'Kitchen Sink' and 'Vital Theatre', in practical terms the exponents of these trends were fairly homogeneous in their shared commitment to authenticity of representation, specifically that of a recognizably lower-class idiom. All of Pinter's early staged works exhibited similar characteristics in their portrayal of a contemporary lower class both in language use and mise en scène, but most commentators were too caught up by the strategies of defamiliarization and the apparently elusive significance of the plays to pursue this line too far.[2] However, as Zarhy-Levo has shown, the very early negative critical reception of Pinter's plays as unfamiliar and 'puzzling' was rapidly reinterpreted as an attractive feature of his drama when the work was increasingly compared to Beckett and Ionesco, and what were initially taken as stylistic flaws became readily reconsecrated as attributes of an emerging variation on an existing theatrical model, the critical contours of which were becoming more and more finely limned in the early 1960s. As Zarhy-Levo notes, speaking of a consensus emerging between critics in the years 1959–64 who concurred that Pinter was both an original voice working within the perimeters of an identifiable tradition,

> reviewers repeatedly compare Pinter to Beckett and Ionesco, which seems to create the notion that Pinter can be regarded as a British representative of the European avant-garde. This notion might have had an impact on Esslin's decision to update his third edition [of *The Theatre of the Absurd*], which in turn contributed to Pinter's establishment as a British Absurdist.
>
> (25)

Zarhy-Levo further rightly argues that the ability of critics to identify Pinter with the Theatre of the Absurd was a crucial stage in formalizing a complete acceptance by the critical establishment, by which time the epithet 'Pinteresque' was coined and in free usage.

Varun Begley's (2005) characterization of Pinter as a modernist writer comes from a sense that his plays are somehow aesthetically autonomous in their formalism and an appreciation of how they derive inspiration from both high and low cultural influences, with popular forms including but not limited to music hall, vaudeville, detective fiction and gangster films all crucial elements woven particularly into his early stage work. While Begley insists that Pinter's appropriation of these forms was less parodic and satirical than academic critics might like to suppose, the fact is that Pinter became far more economical in his deployment of such 'low' cultural influences following the early 1960s, after he had found a different kind of elite employment as a screenwriter in his emerging collaboration with Losey. Thereafter, the late 1960s and early 1970s saw a period of work occupied with plays that were increasingly uncompromising, such as *Landscape* (1968) and *Silence* (1969), and the entirety of 1972 taken up with writing the impeccably high-art *Proust Screenplay*. Even before Pinter's work gradually stopped traversing class lines and settled into a more steady canalization of upper middle-class experience, it was progressively divested of 'low' cultural influences, as Susan Hollis Merritt says: 'After *The Caretaker* Pinter became more upscale, appealing to upper-middle class audiences' (2001: 144).

The culmination of this tendency in Pinter's stage work broached a synchronicity and reciprocity of tastes expressed within the plays and those that consumed them such that *Betrayal*, Pinter's play about marital embranglements of what would today be called the 'metropolitan elite', represented characters that were precisely the kind of people that came to watch the play. A letter from Peter Hall to Pinter in 1978 concerning potential royalties from *Betrayal* in the event of a US production seems to indicate that Pinter enjoyed the status of first among equals in the eyes of the artistic director of the National Theatre, even in comparison with other luminaries:

> You know my overriding worry: if you are seen to be treated differently to other major writers – Stoppard, Ayckbourn, Bolt – I am putting myself in an impossible position both as director of the play and as director of the theatre.
>
> (Hall 1978)[3]

Pinter's relationship with Hall gave him a platform that meant he could refuse any other accommodations that came his way, even from institutions of comparable prestige, which perhaps accounts for the tone of restrained pessimism that characterizes Stuart Burge's supplication on behalf of the Royal Court:

> In the hope that the entire contents of the Pinter cornucopia will not necessarily be the property of the National, I thought it would be good to assure you that we would be delighted if you felt enough confidence in us, to entrust one of your next works to our care and love.
>
> (Burge 1977)

Michael Billington famously deplored *Betrayal*'s display of class politics on the occasion of its National Theatre *première*, criticizing 'the pitifully thin strip of human experience it explores and its obsession with the tiny ripples on the stagnant pond of bourgeois-affluent life' (1996: 258). However, the play's chosen strata of representation may be less of a consideration in production today. In an interview for BBC Radio 4's *Front Row*, Samira Ahmed quizzed Zawe Ashton (who played Emma in Jamie Lloyd's 2019 production) about the characters' class context:

> Ahmed: It's certainly a very privileged world. One's an art gallery owner, one's a publisher, one's an agent. […] And that was an accusation that was made against it when it was first performed.

Ashton: I've never really thought of it like that. I was just really struck by how human, how universal it is.

(*Front Row*)

Billington's intervention, with its excoriation of *Betrayal* as a 'high-class soap-opera (laced with suitable brand-names like Venice, Torcello and Yeats)' (258) might have drawn attention to the extent to which the play, like much bourgeois culture more generally, tends to be promulgated as representing a universal experience free from the bounds of class which is often expressed in terms of it exploring the supposedly non-ideological sphere of the 'human'; but the reproach, perhaps more importantly, exhibits an awareness of Pinter as a type of brand, the integrity of which could be cheapened and debased if it traded too overtly in referencing its own elite hallmarks. To take one comparison, Peacock has pointed out the extent to which *No Man's Land* engages in literary allusion, expressing ideas which are comparable to T. S. Eliot's 'Burnt Norton' in the first of the *Four Quartets* (1936) (114). This style of indirect quotation of prior works is a quintessential element of elite literature; however, having characters directly reference Yeats and Ford Maddox Ford, as in *Betrayal*, was for Billington less a literary allusion and more a *faux pas*. The distinction between what is merely expensive and what is elite must be maintained.

In sum, what began as a popular form of theatre with certain elite pretensions became more of an elite form of theatre with popular pretensions, where, to use William Wordsworth's phrase, Pinter successfully 'creat[ed] the taste by which he [was] enjoyed' (2000: 657–8). Pinter's works attained the happy distinction of existing in a Goldilocks zone where they were simultaneously hailed as high art by the critical establishment but were also incredibly commercially lucrative for himself and the theatres they were staged in; where they found endless employment as fertile ground for academic enquiry but were equally enjoyable and satisfying, pleasure-giving commodities for West End, Broadway and provincial theatres alike. As Harry Derbyshire contends, these dualisms most likely existed in the form of productive antagonisms that characterized the way Pinter appeared in popular culture:

> Pinter is often invoked as a representative of a high, bourgeois and, sometimes, avant-garde culture, with which the implied reader or viewer is encouraged to establish a relationship. Sometimes a familiarity with this high culture is expected or encouraged; sometimes the reader or viewer is invited to join the commentator in rejecting it; but, most

commonly, there is an ambivalent mixture of the two, indicating a feeling of unease towards a perceived exclusivity.

(2001: 240)

As is well known, in his later years Pinter's celebrity existence became balanced against burgeoning human rights activism and increasingly strident support for political causes. As Derbyshire has observed, the former became a means to ventilate the latter, with Pinter 'capitalis[ing] on his fame as a means of promoting political causes' (231). However, the decision to use the mainstream media as a forum to circulate his political poems and screeds arguably damaged Pinter's reputation as an elite artist, since not only was open political activism and advocacy considered *déclassé*, but the blunt and unvarnished nature of the work and its arguments invited much opprobrium from critics and fellow artists (see Chiasson 2017: 139–40). With this decision, Pinter expended much of the cultural capital amassed over the years as a consequence of being considered a writer that did not deign to explain his work and became, as Hilary Wainwright put it, a 'left-wing dignitary' (2000: 49). Yet as a writer who possessed an acute conception of the political importance of the act of speech, Pinter's access to the press was a resource that as an elite he enjoyed and fully exploited.

Conclusion

In his retrospective appraisal of Mills's *The Power Elite* fifty years on, Stephen P. Dandaneau identified a telling cognate linking the Pinteresque and Millsian worldviews occasioned by Pinter's infamous Nobel speech, in which he chose to use his platform to excoriate US foreign policy:

> While Pinter never, of course, makes mention of C. Wright Mills, his characterization of the United States as every bit as undemocratic and menacing as the former Soviet Union is a bold statement perfectly consequent with both the spirit and the letter of Mills' now fifty year-old political sociology.
>
> (2006: 147)

As this chapter has shown, the nature of Pinter's chosen engagement with social systems, both their structures and the location of agency within them, is not only compatible with Millsian assumptions about the location of power and how it is exercised but also symmetrical with other contemporaneous articulations of elite theory. Ultimately Pinter's interest in the mechanisms and characteristics of power means that his work could hardly not engage with the notion of elites in some form. This chapter advocates for a way to appreciate Pinter's preoccupation with power that is linked to the status and functioning of elites: whether representing the manufacturers of Kafkaesque oppression of his early plays, transposing Bourdieuian notions of legitimation and authority bound up with class, professional merit and social prestige in the dramas of his mid-career, or offering searing portrayals of the officer class of neoliberal elite society in his final stage work. Yet within all this there remains the notion of Pinter as an elite himself, manufactured through immersion in elite cultural work, an uncompromising process of authorial self-curation and a serendipitous collision with the way theatre critics were interpreting work and forming cultural trends in his early career. Ultimately, both the Millsian conception of elites as individuals holding public status and possessing institutional authority and Bourdieu's analysis of human agents engaged in struggles whereby they maximize their control over specific social resources apply to Pinter himself, becoming a fixture in the commanding heights of Britain's prestige national theatre institutions, primarily the Royal Shakespeare Company and the National Theatre. There is far more to an appreciation of Pinter's social ascendancy than accounting for how the assumption of comfortable affluence was enabled by his professional success. It is noteworthy that *Celebration*, a play set in what one character calls the 'most expensive fucking restaurant in town' (Pinter 2011b: 454) and which situates vulgar and unscrupulous bankers and technocrats of the neoliberal corporate elite in their natural habitat, was also, according to Antonia Fraser, written to exorcise the experience of a genuine dining encounter that she and Pinter had shared 'when we had been very unlucky in our very, very loud neighbours at the next-door table in a famous West End restaurant' (279).

Notes

1. The 1990 Grove Press edition of the first part of Harold Pinter's Complete Works as I write features a large orange circle on the front, with the words 'Winner of the NOBEL PRIZE for literature' emblazoned on it.
2. Though by no means all. See Lacey (1995: 141) for a description of the way that Kenneth Tynan and John Arden detected the social realist relevance of the early Pinter.
3. Quoted here with kind permission from United Agents on behalf of the Estate of Peter Hall.

Works Cited

@agnesfrim (2017), 27 October. Available online: https://twitter.com/agnesfrim/status/923817584365047809?lang=en (accessed 3 April 2018).

Barach, P., and M. S. Baratz (1962), 'Two Faces of Power', *The American Political Science Review*, 56 (4): 947–52.

Batty, M. (2005), *About Pinter: The Playwright and the Work*, London: Faber and Faber.

Burge, S. (1977) Letter to Harold Pinter. 17 August. The British Library, Modern Manuscripts Collection, The Harold Pinter Archive, Add MS 88880/6/2.

Begley, V. (2005), *Harold Pinter and the Twilight of Modernism*, London: University of Toronto Press.

Bensky, L. M. (1967), 'Harold Pinter', in C. Marowitz and S. Trussler (eds), *Theatre at Work*, 96–109, London: Methuen.

Billington, M. (1996), *The Life and Work of Harold Pinter*, London: Faber and Faber.

Bourdieu, P. (1977), *Outline of a Theory of Practice*, Cambridge: Cambridge University Press.

Bourdieu, P. (1998), *Practical Reason: On the Theory of Action*, Stanford: Stanford University Press.

Bourdieu, P. (2010), *Distinction*, Routledge: Abingdon.

Chiasson, B. (2014), 'Pinter's Political Dramas: Staging Neoliberal Discourse and Authoritarianism', in M. Taylor-Batty (ed.), *The Theatre of Harold Pinter*, 249–66, London: Bloomsbury Methuen.

Chiasson, B. (2017), *The Late Harold Pinter: Political Dramatist, Poet and Activist*, London: Palgrave Macmillan.

Dandaneau, S. P. (2006), 'The Power Elite at 50: C. Wright Mills' Political Sociology in Midlife Crisis', *Fast Capitalism*, 2 (1): 147–59.

Davies, W. (2017), 'Elite Power under Advanced Neoliberalism', *Theory, Culture and Society*, 34 (5–6): 227–50.

Derbyshire, H. (2001), 'Pinter as Celebrity', in P. Raby (ed.), *The Cambridge Companion to Harold Pinter*, 230–46, Cambridge: Cambridge University Press.

Dyer, R. (2015), 'Class and Anticolonial Politics in Harold Pinter and Joseph Losey's *The Servant*', *Journal of Modern Literature*, 38 (4): 147–67.

Fraser, A. (2011), *Must You Go? My Life with Harold Pinter*, London: Phoenix.

Front Row (2019), BBC Radio 4, 20 March.

Garner, D. (2010), 'A Literary Romance, Rich in A-List Names', *The New York Times*, 28 October. Available online: http://www.washingtonpost.com/wp-dyn/content/article/2010/11/04/AR2010110407176.html (accessed 30 March 2018).

Gordon, R. (2012), *Harold Pinter: The Theater of Power*, Ann Arbor: University of Michigan Press.

Grimes, C. (2005), *Harold Pinter's Politics: A Silence beyond Echo*, Madison: Fairleigh Dickinson University Press.

Gussow, M. (1995), *Conversations with Pinter*, London: Nick Hern.
Hall, P. (1978), Letter to Harold Pinter. 17 May. The British Library, Modern Manuscripts Collection, The Harold Pinter Archive. Add MS 88880/6/33.
Khan, S. R. (2012), 'The Sociology of Elites', *Annual Review of Sociology*, 38: 361–77.
Lacey, S. (1995), *British Realist Theatre: The New Wave in Its Context 1956–65*, London: Routledge.
Laclau, E., and C. Mouffe (1998), *Hegemony and Socialist Strategy: Towards a Radical Democratic Politics*, London: Verso.
Merritt, S. H. (2001), 'Pinter and Politics', in Lois Gordon (ed.), *Pinter at 70: A Casebook*, 129–61, London: Routledge.
Mills, C. W. (1999), *The Power Elite*, New York: Oxford University Press.
Peacock, D. K. (1997), *Harold Pinter and the New British Theatre*: Westport: Greenwood Press.
Pinter, H. (1997), '*The Homecoming*', in *Harold Pinter: Plays 3*, 13–90, London: Faber and Faber.
Pinter, H. (1998), 'Interview on *The South Bank Show*', ITV, 29 November.
Pinter, H. (2009), 'Art, Truth and Politics', in *Various Voices: Sixty Years of Prose, Poetry, Politics, 1948–2008*, 3rd edn, 285–300, London: Faber and Faber. © The Nobel Foundation.
Pinter, H. (2011a), '*Betrayal*', in *Harold Pinter: Plays 4*, 1–117, London: Faber and Faber.
Pinter, H. (2011b), '*Celebration*', in *Harold Pinter: Plays 4*, 435–508, London: Faber and Faber.
Prentice, P. (2011), 'The Harold Pinter I Knew: Transcendence in Drama and the Man', *Cithara*, 50 (2): 23–38.
See, C. (2010), *Washington Post*, 5 November. Available online: http://www.washingtonpost.com/wp-dyn/content/article/2010/11/04/AR2010110407176.html (accessed 30 March 2018).
Smith, I. (2006), *Pinter in the Theatre*, London: Nick Hern.
Tabard. (2017), 'Diary: No Pause from Pinter on Stoppard Rejection', *The Stage*, 1 November. Available online: https://www.thestage.co.uk/opinion/tabard/2017/diary-no-pause-pinter-stoppard-rejection (accessed 4 November 2017).
Taylor-Batty, M. (2014), *The Theatre of Harold Pinter*, London: Bloomsbury Methuen.
Taylor-Batty, M., and C. Lavery (2015), 'The Secluded Voice: The Impossible Call Home in Early Pinter', in C. Lavery and C. Finburgh (eds), *Rethinking the Theatre of the Absurd: Ecology, the Environment and the Greening of the Modern Stage*, 219–39, London: Bloomsbury Methuen.
Wainwright, H. (2000), *Harold Pinter: A Celebration*, London: Faber and Faber.
Wordsworth, W. ([1815] 2000), 'Essay, Supplementary to the Preface of *Poems*', S. Gill (ed.), *The Major Works*, 640–62, Oxford: Oxford University Press.
Zarhy-Levo, Y. (2001), *The Theatrical Critic as Cultural Agent: Constructing Pinter, Orton and Stoppard as Absurdist Playwrights*, New York: Peter Lang.

4

'Too Much of a Modern?': Pinter's Jew*ish*ness

Eckart Voigts

Introduction: Universalizing Jewishness

Harold Pinter was very much a British-Jewish writer. In this chapter, I argue that the alarming inability of his characters to establish a rooted identity is located to a great extent in Pinter's experience of being raised as a Jewish boy in the East End – an identity to which many of his Jewish interpreters, from Martin Esslin onwards, have been acutely aware. I will make the case biographically, with reference to archival material, his second wife Lady Antonia Fraser's memoirs, the recently rediscovered record of their 1978 travel to Israel, *Our Israeli Diary* (2017), and Michael Billington's biography, with brief considerations of key early works such as *The Birthday Party* (1958) and *The Homecoming* (1965), as well as a short reading of *Ashes to Ashes* (1996). I will, however, make no 'identitarian' or essentialist claims about Pinter's Jewishness. Instead, I seek to outline how the precariously marginalized and insecure Pinter characters emerge from a Modernist Jew-*ish*-ness, which derives as much from Jewish writers such as Franz Kafka as from non-Jewish Modernist influences Pinter has acknowledged such as 'Joyce, Lawrence, Dostoevsky, Virginia Woolf, Rimbaud, Yeats' (Pinter 1998: 47) and, of course, Beckett. Pinter's Jew-*ish*-ness, therefore, represents the twentieth-century European experience in a much wider sense that clearly transcends the Jewish East End community from which Pinter emerged.

Is it possible that the academic, literary and theatrical communities in Britain have such a keen focus on the English Pinter that they have neglected the Jewish Pinter? A formalist interest in the absurdist and (post)modern theatre innovator, and particularly in his use of language, has long been documented. In the wake of Billington's biography and a further set of monographs (such as Baker 2008, Taylor-Batty 2014a, Wyllie and Rees 2016), attention has also focused on celebrating the English Nobel Prize winner as a man of letters and (as) political activist. In addition, recent biographical considerations were determined by issues of class, sketching his move from modest roots in Hackney and touring theatre, to become the cause célèbre of the London literary establishment, and marrying into the Kensington aristocracy via his second marriage to the eminent biographer Lady Antonia Fraser.

While the issue of Pinter's Jewishness is not new and has been championed as well as dismissed by various commentators, it can be argued that the network of his Jewish-European ancestry and his Jewish friendships and influences have not been given their due space in Pinter studies as well as his key cultural influences, many of which are rooted in the Jewish-European diaspora, with Kafka taking pride of place. Andrew Wyllie and Catherine Rees (2016: 51–4), for example, too readily in my view, dismiss specific Jewish dimensions in Pinter's work. They argue that biographical criticism that focuses on Pinter's Hackney background misses the point. They berate William Baker and Stephen Ely Tabachnik's *Harold Pinter* (1973) for displaying 'a repeated anxiety to establish Pinter's writing as essentially Jewish' (Wyllie and Rees 2016: 51). Wyllie and Rees are resolutely opposed to Billington's biographical reading and, naming conservative critic Harold Bloom, attack 'more explicitly political and more tenuous' attempts to 'recruit' Pinter's 'plays to the body of Holocaust literature' (51). Speaking for myself, I strongly dispute that there is an explicit political agenda in pointing out the not-so-tenuous Jewish dimensions in Pinter's work. In the words of Bryan Cheyette, Pinter 'universalized his Jewishness so as to make it unrepresentable' (1996: 36).

The Jewish East End and Pinter's Early Plays

The recent biographical turn in Pinter studies since the publication of Michael Billington's biography in 1996 (later revised in 2007) has brought his Jewish background into focus. Pinter was born on 10 October 1930 in Hackney, close to the traditional East End shaped by Jewish immigration. His family background is Ashkenazi (from Poland and Odessa) rather than Sephardic (from a Portuguese name such as Pinto or Da Pinta), as is sometimes suggested (Billington 2007: 3; see also Pinter 1998: 46). His father, the tailor Jack Pinter, was rather Orthodox, and his mother Frances, born Moskowitz, more secular and sceptical (Billington 2007: 2). Pinter's upbringing was different from the stoicist decorum of the 'stiff upper lip' or the tasteful temperance that have signified an enlightened gentlemanliness among the English elites since John Locke, Lord Shaftesbury or Lord

Chesterfield to the extent that it has crystallized to a prevalent stereotype. Pinter recalled: 'Many Jews lived in the district, noisy but candid' (qtd. in Billington 2007: 3). Billington suggests that up to 40,000 Jews lived in North London at the time (Billington 2007: 3).[1] It is true, of course, that Hackney Downs Grammar School was 'for young working-class scholars', as Taylor-Batty writes in *The Theatre of Harold Pinter* (2014: 2), but more than 50 per cent of the pupils and the great majority of Pinter's friends were not only working class but Jewish. For example, Pinter shared Hackney Downs Grammar School with fellow Jew Steven Berkoff and a group of Jewish friends, Morris 'Moishe' Wernick, Henry Woolf and Michael Goldstein. In archive material on Pinter, there is plenty of evidence how important these friendships were to him; in 1948 he planned a joint theatre company with this 'gang'.[2] Decades later he wrote to Wernick that their friendship was unique and that his love would even outlast his own death.[3]

To steal the title from Nathan Abrams's recent book, Pinter's Jewishness is 'hidden in plain sight' (2016) and English Pinter criticism, as David Jays has noted, '[touches] on many subjects – Pinter's place in the European intellectual tradition, his fervent political conviction, his passion for cricket – but never his Jewishness' (2000). A large number of key British theatre-makers are and have been of Jewish ethnicity, but many, such as Tom Stoppard or Mike Leigh, have only recently begun to articulate a Jewishness that was palpably but only implicitly present.[4] If it were not for predominantly American critics or Jewish critics, such as Martin Esslin in *The Peopled Wound* (1970), one can only wonder how much Pinter's ethnic background from Hungarian Jewry would have been remarked upon. Stoppard, who apparently only learned in 1993, at the age of 56, just how Jewish he was, is a case in point.[5] Ira Nadel as well as theatre critics John Nathan (2015), Jays (2000) and Billington (2012) have argued that Jewish identities bring an outsider's identity and outside (often European) perspective to British theatre. Billington, in a journalistic essay, has wondered 'how much an inherited sense of exile, loss and isolation offers a key to [British-Jewish dramatists'] work. Is there, in fact, such a thing as a Jewish theatrical identity?' (2012).

Pinter's (secular) Jewishness is thus a point of controversial debate. From the perspective of conservative Judaism, Pinter could be understood as a self-hating, self-abrogating Jew: Historian Geoffrey Alderman attacked Pinter for his lack of Judaism (2009), and Pinter significantly considered himself a Jew that writes rather than a Jewish writer (Pinter in Billington 2007: 189). Eli Rozik's survey of Jewish theatre and drama dismisses Pinter as a Jewish dramatist, adopting a kind of 'No Hebrew/Yiddish it ain't Jewish' essentialism and enlisting Pinter himself:[6]

> Playwrights of Jewish origin such as Arnold Wesker, Peter Shaffer, Arthur Miller and Harold Pinter made substantial contributions to the English-speaking theatre, and even to the English language. Although they occasionally used Jewish motifs, the main cultural tradition that underlies their writing was and is English. I was told once by Harold Pinter that for him English literature is his Bible.
>
> (2013: 189)

Indeed, writer Joshua Cohen has argued that Pinter deliberately downplayed his Judaism and that he is 'far too much of a Modern to identify as a Jew' (2005). This seems to set up a flawed dichotomy and Cohen is correct in his subsequent judgment that though he 'has downplayed his Judaism many times in conversation, and has consciously ignored it in his characterizations, [Pinter's] heritage infuses his work with a style that sets it apart from most English-language contemporaries' (ibid.).

Pinter's Modernism and Absurdism are in fact not opposed but linked to his Jewish upbringing, networking and collaborating, as well as to an undercurrent of Jewish-inflected themes and motifs in his work and particularly in his language. There are indications that in spite of his own disavowals Jewishness was at least an issue for Pinter, brought back to him for instance when he visited Israel for the first time in 1978. Fraser's *Our Israeli Diary* records how he remembers his Bar Mitzvah and learning Hebrew.[7] On this visit, the director of Jerusalem's National Theatre told Pinter in 1978: 'I am so *delighted* to see you here. I never thought you would come. You see, Jonathan Miller explained you were frightened to come to Jerusalem. [...] For the effect it would have on your work' (Fraser 2017: 28; emphasis in original). Later, Fraser notes, Pinter 'says he is very happy to be in Israel. [...] He feared to dislike the place, the people. Now, he doesn't' (55). In view of Pinter's political views since the 1990s, it is quite astounding to learn from Fraser's account that there is plenty of understanding for the Israeli position against a two-state solution: 'so close to the burgeoning Jerusalem: how can anyone expect the Israelis to welcome a *state* set up by Arafat and his murderous boys here?' (66). Finally, Pinter says in Jerusalem: 'I definitely *am* Jewish. I know that now. But of course that makes it more complicated. I am also English. And this is an Arab town' (83). Pinter's identity is essentially hybrid but, without a shadow of a doubt, being Jewish feeds into his aesthetic and cultural awareness of outsiders and liminal characters. This comes via his engagement with Jewish modernism. After encountering *The Trial* (1925) at the age of 17, Pinter read Kafka's works voraciously at the Hackney Public Library. When Pinter went to the Jewish quarters of Prague and Kolin during the filming of *The Trial* many years later (BBC 1993, dir. David Jones), he was, according to producer Louis Marks, extremely emotionally affected, although he deliberately universalized the Jewish elements one might have used in filming (see Baker 2008: 106).

Pinter, I argue, cannot be understood without taking into account his Jewishness, but it is a Jew*ish*ness in the sense suggested by Devorah Baum (2017). In her intriguing book on *Feeling Jewish* (2017) Baum explains that a sense of humour, self-hatred, paranoia or guilt are both Jewish and universal, so that '"just about anyone", regardless of his or her biology, belief, or background, might […] feel Jewish' (2017: 250). She quotes one of Kafka's diary entries on the impossibility for an individual to identify simply as a member of a specific group: 'What have I in common with Jews? I have hardly anything in common with myself' (7). What we can find in these statements are echoes of Sigmund Freud and Jacques Derrida, linking an imaginative diaspora to the discourse of constructed, unstable identities. For Baum, the Jewish experience is one of 'a diasporic people who are unsure of their place in the world – people who are persistently mobile, looking all the time over their shoulder, and jostling for position' (6). She never mentions Pinter, but Baum here gives an accurate description of many Pinter characters, particularly in his 1950s and 1960s plays that strongly resonate with his East End background. The equation of being Jewish with structures of feeling that are self-interrogating, European and modern, thus not Jewish but Jew-*ish*, is at the core of Pinter's aesthetics and it is also, in fact, what we detected in many of the interviews we conducted with contemporary British-Jewish playwrights in the context of a research project on British-Jewish theatre.[8]

There is, of course, no shortage of writers who have identified Pinter's Jewishness. Martin Esslin, who famously identified and coined the term the 'Theatre of the Absurd', argued in 1970 that Pinter's 'existential fear […] is […] based on the experience of a Jewish boy on the streets of the East End of London, of a Jew in the Europe of Hitler' (1970: 28). The Pinter of the 1950s had an acute awareness of being a precarious, marginalized, liminal figure – and so he generates characters with an alarmingly sketchy identity and a fractured past that is so characteristic of twentieth-century European Jewry, exemplified by the journeys of Gyula Márton Pereszlenyi, aka Martin Esslin. This attitude, pinpointed by Esslin, is echoed in Efraim Sicher's point that we find in Pinter 'the anxiety of the Jew on alien territory, cut off from roots but uncertain where he does belong' (1985: 97). Literary critic Harold Bloom claimed that Pinter's Jewish background does in fact bring his work closer to Philip Roth's American Jewishness than to 'Beckett's barren existentialism' (qtd. in Krasner 2016: 51),[9] which Bloom views as austerely Protestant. Daniel Salem's largely biographical approach, rich with interviews and information from sources close to Pinter, found two approaches to a Jewish Pinter: (1) the

Kabbalah and (2) humour. Salem argues that Pinter's hermetic and indirect writing resembles the style of Jewish mysticism, as expressed in the image of an 'obscure flame' (1986: 72–3), and that 'Pinter's comedy corresponds to Jewish humour, a desperate humour that often helps make bearable the unbearable' (75). We can recognize, with Baker and Tabachnik's 1973 monograph and Peter S. Golick's thesis on 'Jewish influences in the plays of Harold Pinter' from 1981, plenty of facetious references to archetypal *schlehmils*, *schlimazls* and *schnorrers* as quintessential Pinter characters (Golick 1981: 2). In *A Slight Ache* (1959), Golick suggests the wasp could be seen as an ironic comment on the WASP, the White Anglo-Saxon Protestant (53). We can, however, with Marc Silverstein, dismiss the identification of Jewishness in Pinter, arguing that in doing so one would construct a homogeneous ethnic identity that does not exist (154).

In addition, we frequently find generalizations on themes such as guilt and fear. Both Austin Quigley and Billington quote from an interview with Lawrence Bensky in 1966, observing how awareness of his Jewish identity influenced Pinter's fear of walking East London streets:

> If you looked remotely like a Jew you might be in trouble. Also, I went to a Jewish club by an old railway arch, and there were quite a lot of people often waiting with broken milk bottles in a particular alley we used to walk through. There were one or two ways of getting out of it – one was purely physical, of course, but you couldn't do anything about the milk bottles – we didn't have any milk bottles. The best way was to talk to them, you know, sort of 'Are you all right?' 'Yes, I'm all right.' 'Well, that's all right then, isn't it?' and all the time keep walking toward the lights of the main road.
>
> (Quigley 1975: 47–8; see also Billington 2007: 31)

Pinter also recalled the injustice that Oswald Mosley's Fascist gangs were allowed to thrive just after the world war and under a Labour government (Billington 2007: 29–30). Around the time of *The Birthday Party*, Pinter hit a man in a pub who addressed him as a 'filthy Yid' (139–40) – if there is still low-level anti-Semitism in Britain, in the 1950s it sometimes reached rather high levels (and I suppose it does again today).

Key plays that have been identified as carrying Pinter's Jewishness are frequent in his early work, for instance, *The Room* (1957), and *The Dwarfs*, written in the 1950s, adapted for radio in 1960 and the stage in 1963 and published as a novel in 1992. On several occasions in Pinter's early plays, the unstable identity of his characters is linked to their Jewishness. This is not so far-fetched, as many Jewish people from non-practising families that have shared in a history of forced migration – hardly an uncommon fate of European Jews in the twentieth century – did not know for sure about their Jewish identity (the example of Tom Stoppard mentioned above is a case in point). In *The Room*, the landlord Mr Kidd is not quite sure of his own Jewish identity: 'I think my mum was a Jewess. Yes, I wouldn't be surprised to learn that she was a Jewess. She didn't have many babies' (Pinter 1996a: 93). He mentions this to the character Rose, who is sceptical about Kidd's claims, while her own name also resonates with Jewish East End identity (see Baker 2008: 41). *The Dwarfs* is Pinter's semi-autobiographical novel informed by his circle of Jewish friends and which invokes the uncertain Portuguese-Jewish family background. The play version features the aggressive, almost surreal repartee and cross-talk of a youthful gang of East End Jews, including characteristic Yiddishisms such as *schmutta*, meaning 'rags' (Pinter 1996b). While Pinter does not create sketchy and precarious identities only for his Jewish characters, we can conclude that the awareness of being a latently insecure outsider in 1950s England that he transmitted to many of his characters can be attributed in part to his composite Jew*ish*ness: a sense of instability, a self-interrogating European modernity and, as two new essays argue, his indefinability and un-English language (Lawson, forthcoming), as well as his engagement with themes of belonging and authoritarianism (Taylor-Batty, forthcoming).

It is hardly surprising that discussions of Pinter's Jewishness focus very much on his major early plays, *The Birthday Party* and *The Homecoming*. What is fascinating in *The Birthday Party* is maybe less that *schlemihl* and *schnorrer* Stanley Webber, whose pyjamas and name may suggest not only Ashkenazi origin but also the Holocaust, is obviously a persecuted Jew in an insecure, threatened position – and for instance, Billington's reading quoted above seems to forget that not only the authority figure Goldberg, but also the victim Webber are Jewish. More intriguingly, both agents of persecution – Goldberg and McCann – represent colonized Ireland and also Jewishness. For Silverstein, Goldberg (above all in his invocation of Uncle Barney) represents the dangers of assimilation so that Jewishness becomes a cipher for integration and cultural powerlessness (42). I am far from reading *The Birthday Party* allegorically – for instance with Baker and Tabachnik, who make Goldberg a concentration camp kapo (60) – but it is not too far-fetched to associate Monty, the 'organization' that realigns Stanley, with the Hebrew God who meets Moses on Mount Sinai, an altogether observant, threatening and revengeful entity in the Torah. Taylor-Batty is right that Pinter universalized his authoritarianism as, to quote Pinter himself, he had 'no desire to write a whole play about Jews or the Jewish situation' (in Taylor-Batty 2014a: 29). This is not to say that his railing against 'Our mentors. Our ancestry' (ibid.) does not focus to a large extent on Judeo-Christian patriarchal monotheism. What makes the play fascinating is that Pinter dramatizes the debilitating effect the authoritarianism deriving from monotheistic surveillance has on his authority figures too, from Goldberg and McCann to the 'devilish' Nicolas in *One for the Road* (1984) and Devlin[10] in *Ashes to Ashes*. Billington concludes that the character of Goldberg, whose reminiscences of Jewish life recall Pinter's own 'while satirising the Jewish tradition', is also a 'terrified, even beleaguered figure', exposing 'Pinter's own ambivalence' (2007: 82, 138). Pinter himself of course played Goldberg several times, and in the Pinter Archive at the British Library, I even found a letter signed, ironically, 'Monty Pinter' (Pinter 2002). It is striking that Pinter as an actor tended to represent totalitarian persecution rather than victimization, for instance when he played the tyrannical Director (D) in David Mamet's film version of Beckett's 1982 play *Catastrophe* (2000), Lenny and then Max in *The Homecoming*, and Nicolas in *One for the Road*.[11]

The Homecoming recalls the perils of Jewish and non-Jewish intermarriage. Billington's biography suggests that Pinter did not intermarry with his girlfriend Pauline Flanagan because she was a Roman Catholic, Irish *shiksa*, and the issue returned with Vivien Merchant, whom he married on Yom Kippur in the absence of his parents (2007: 92–3). *The Homecoming* is set in a quintessentially Jewish place, North London Hampstead. The play seems to dramatize, among other things, the generational conflicts between a Jewish butcher's family and the son who has escaped to academia in American-Jewish circles. Pinter was anxious to protest that *The Homecoming* was no 'localised Jewish family drama' (Billington 2007: 280). However, Joey is a boxer, just like the miraculously disappeared Judah, Pinter's uncle, and the first version of the absent character MacGregor was Berkowitz (286). Pinter finally admitted that Max was based on the father of his boyhood friend, Moishe Wernick (281–2). Wernick's secret marriage and departure to Canada and his return in 1964 provide the rough plot framework. 'None of this makes the play a specifically Jewish drama,' Billington (282) argues but later concludes that 'it is a socially accurate study of […] a group of […] Hackney predators' (289). It is certainly also more than that, but the strategy, to use a Jewish family to make universal points about families as *Tribes* (2010), to invoke Nina Raine's play, can be observed in almost all British-Jewish playwrights, from Arnold Wesker and Mike Leigh to Raine, Julia Pascal and Ryan Craig. With Craig's *The Holy Rosenbergs* (2011) and *Filthy Business* (2017), the family is specifically Jewish. But I admit that in Pinter it is not *just* Jewish, which accounts for the fact mentioned by Bryan Cheyette (1998: xxxiii) that Pinter's abstracted Jewishness enabled him, unlike Wesker for instance, to inhabit a central position within the English literary scene.

Pinter and the Holocaust

As an actor, then, Pinter appeared in 'Jewish' roles like Goldberg. As discussed above, his role as D in Beckett's *Catastrophe* might be seen as reprising Goldberg's nasty aggression. For the Beckett biographer Jim Knowlson, however, it is another of the play's characters, the Protagonist (P), who 'recalls images of the concentration camp or holocaust victim' (1997: 679). Further evidence of a Jewish perspective can therefore be found in Pinter's engagement with the Holocaust, both in his directing (Robert Shaw's *The Man in the Glass Booth* in 1967; see Grimes 2005: 234) and his screenwriting. His film adaptation of *Reunion* (1989) from the 1971 novel by Jewish writer Fred Uhlman is a good example of Pinter's renewed interest in this crucial moment of modern Jewish history. In a DVD featurette (*Reunion* 1989/2014), director Jerry Schatzberg recalls how Pinter became involved in his adaptation, which tells the story of the youthful friendship between a German Jew, the doctor's son Hans Strauss (Christien Anholt), and the aristocratic Konradin von Lohenburg (Samuel West), an emerging Nazi in Stuttgart in the early 1930s. When two screenwriters Schatzberg and his producer had approached about the screenplay were not available, they were surprised to learn that Pinter had not only read the novel on recommendation of his mother, but that he loved Uhlman's book and was keen to get involved in the project. Schatzberg and Pinter even went to Stuttgart to hunt for locations and Pinter has said that he never undertook as much historical research in any of his projects (Grimes 167). Crucially, Pinter introduced the 'contemporary' level to the story, the Jewish Hans (Jason Robards) returning to Stuttgart at an old age to investigate his own memories and the inadequate ways contemporary Germany is dealing with its Holocaust guilt (see Grimes 167 who sees *Reunion* as romanticizing the German resistance, in which Konradin is finally discovered to have been involved with).

Finally, in *Ashes to Ashes* even the title might be seen to reference the Holocaust. As Billington's biography of Pinter notes, his writing of the play was triggered by Gitta Sereny's biography of Albert Speer (1995). He had read Sereny's biography when he directed fellow Jewish writer Ronald Harwood's *Taking Sides* in 1995. Pinter says, 'Reading the book also triggered lots of other associations. I've always been haunted by the image of the Nazis picking up babies on bayonet-spikes and throwing them out of windows' (qtd. in Billington 2007: 375).

While this powerful and influential play was highly praised and frequently discussed by critics (Reitz 1998; Merritt 2000; Neumeier 2003; Scolnicov 2008; Angel-Perez 2009), it resonated particularly with continental and

Jewish commentators. In my archival research, I was able to look at a letter Sarah Kane sent to Pinter, documenting how deeply impressed she was by *Ashes to Ashes* (Kane 1996). Indeed, the play's premise – to cast atrocities reminiscent of the Holocaust in middle England – recalls Kane's *Blasted* (1995), which premiered a year earlier, also at the Royal Court.[12] The play focuses on a woman (Rebecca) being interrogated by a man (Devlin) who might or might not be her doctor, therapist, partner, interrogator or torturer. It is set in an English country home (maybe in Dorset, as Rebecca claims, in any case very Southern) while at the same time invoking the horrors of the European Nazi past, something English critics quickly leapt on in disbelief, criticizing Pinter for suggesting that even democracies might allow or even foster atrocities (Billington 2007: 385). This key aspect of the play is deliberate, as Pinter pointed out: 'I'm talking about us and our conception of the past and our history and what it does to us in the present' (qtd. in ibid.).[13]

The play opens on Rebecca recounting a sadomasochistic encounter with an unnamed man (possibly Speer). Described as a kind of torture he makes her kiss his fist, puts his hand around her throat, 'gently but truly' (Pinter 2011a: 397), she claims, and she responds, her 'legs [...] opening' (397). The encounter suggests sadomasochistic undertones, according to Billington, 'a mixture of sexual enforcement and willing submission' (2007: 652). Rebecca recalls that her lover once took her to a damp factory without bathrooms, Speer's factories about which Pinter had read in Sereny's book. Later, she recalls that he worked in a travel agency, and as a guide, tearing 'all the babies from the arms of their screaming mothers' (Pinter 2011a: 407) – and the term 'guide' clearly invokes the German *Führer*. In the unnamed Speer figure, Pinter mixes the mundanely private and the Jewish Holocaust experience as part of European history.

Rebecca could have been partly inspired by a German woman with English ties, who came to be infatuated with Speer when he was an old man (Billington 2007: 384). According to Fraser, however, Pinter sees her as a version of himself: '"She is the artist who cannot avoid the world's pain"' (2010: 257). In yet another reference to Jewish tradition, Elisabeth Angel-Perez (2009) suggests that Rebecca is possessed by a dybbuk, a spirit of the dead, in a metaphor of collective suffering that, according to Hanna Scolnicov (2008), is present in Jewish narrative.[14] Scolnicov argues against Katherine Burkman's (1999) point that both characters act out aspects of Speer's personality. Echoing the Jewish/Irish pairing of Goldberg and McCann from *The Birthday Party*, Rebecca is likely to be Jewish and Devlin Irish. According to Scolnicov, they represent a female/male dichotomy, but also the Jew/Gentile divide, rather than a quasi-monologue that represents aspects of Albert Speer's character. Scolnicov says Pinter 'found to deal with this difficult topic was to write not about the Shoah, but about the memories of the Shoah' (2008). In an interview with Mireia Aragay, Pinter stated that the play was not about Nazi Germany, but 'the images of Nazi Germany', for him the calculated bureaucratic nature of the Holocaust (Pinter 1998: 226–8). This statement gives further weight to Taylor-Batty's reading, who associates the play with contemporaneous images of Nazi Germany such as Spielberg's *Schindler's List* (1993) and Alan Pakula's *Sophie's Choice* (1982) (see Taylor-Batty 2014a: 183).

Turning the tables, eventually Rebecca attacks Devlin, arguing that he has brought on the genocide exemplified by the babies torn from their mothers' arms. Devlin misquotes the Jewish Shema Yisrael prayer 'Hear, O Israel: the LORD our God, the LORD is one' when he says, 'He's the only God we have' (Pinter 2011a: 412). Devlin's words may be seen as a reprise of Pinter's frequent attacks on authoritarian order derived from monotheism. The passage is reminiscent of the interrogator/torturer Nicolas in *One for the Road*, who also invokes a monotheistic foundation to his creed, while at the same time protesting that he is not Jewish: 'I run the place. God speaks through me. I'm referring to the Old Testament God, by the way, although I'm a long way from being Jewish' (Pinter 2011b: 225).

Conclusion

To conclude, I will sum up the results of this foray into the Jewish dimension of Pinter's writings in four brief theses:

(1) Harold Pinter is a British-Jewish writer and can hardly be fully understood if separated from his Jewishness, but he is more than just a British-Jewish writer as his plays easily transcend this kind of pigeonholing.
(2) Pinter's Jewishness must not be seen in opposition to his Modernism: on the contrary, his early readings are in Kafka, his school initiation to European Modernist writers in a circle of Jewish friends and his particular influence on and exchange with other Jewish modernist/postmodernist writers such as Arthur Miller, Patrick Marber or David Mamet. This suggests that his Jewish background prepared him to make the somewhat insular British theatre slightly more European. He found a universalizing form, however, that feeds into an existential rootlessness and diasporic insecurity that is, on the one hand, very Jewish, but on the other makes plays such as *The Homecoming* more universally valid to, say, the culturally very specific Jewish family plays

of Ryan Craig (*The Holy Rosenbergs* and *Filthy Business*), Julia Pascal (*Crossing Jerusalem*, 2003) or even Nina Raine (*Tribes*).[15]

(3) This is not to say in a circular, essentialist fashion that Pinter wrote the way he did because he was Jewish. Nor can we construct Jewishness as a stable reference area – it is rather a plural, fluid set of attitudes, memories and identity markers. Pinter may not write about Jewishness so much but about Jew*ish*ness, a precariousness and volatility of existence and identity that should not be construed as constrained by a distinct ethnic identity. Pinter's Jewishness is thus the result of his discursive engagement with Jewish culture, through literary sources such as Kafka or the language and other semiotic systems he encountered from his East End youth onwards. Pinter's Jewishness is thus produced, performed, transformed by friends such as Morris Wernick, Henry Woolf and others, as well as redefined, recovered and destructed by his own changing attitudes, disavowals, rediscoveries and so on.

(4) Themes of persecution, violence, trauma, memory, self-interrogation, Pinter's East End language patterns and family scenarios, the acute awareness of being an outsider who does not belong and whose position remains unstable emanate both from his Jewish biography and from the experience of European Jewry in twentieth-century Europe. His characters seem to live in a permanent state of diaspora, with an unclear past and a precarious future. Being Jewish thus inevitably links Pinter to being European and to being Modernist. I suggest that the emerging biographical details in recent years as well as thorough textual readings of his plays suggest that British Pinter criticism should not forget this particular network of Pinter as a British-Jewish writer.

Notes

1   According to sociologist Ernest Krausz, who puts the number at 30,000, there was a marked shift in the Jewish population from the poor post-war East End to North West London: 'It has been estimated that the East End, which at the beginning of the twentieth-century contained about 125,000 Jews and in 1929 still had some 85,000 Jews, was left with no more than 30,000 Jews within a few years after World War II. The northwest London area alone was said to have contained some 85,000 Jews by 1950' (Krausz 2019).

2   Morris Wernick was to be business and stage manager, B. J. Law director and Henry Woolf, Ron Percival and himself actors. See MS 89094: 1948–

2013 in the Harold Pinter Archive held in the British Library. Subsequent manuscript references are to this collection.
3   The letter is undated. MS 89094/5: 1965–2005.
4   David Herman has argued that European locations, biographical vagaries, disguises and unrest as themes in Stoppard's work can be related to his Jewishness (Herman 2015: 193). Arguably, until *Leopoldstadt* (2019), Tom Stoppard has rarely used directly autobiographical material. Similarly, Linda Grant has described Mike Leigh's *Two Thousand Years* (2006) as his first Jewish play but found that aspects in his work, such as the focus on families and sibling rivalry, thwarted idealism, diaspora and tragicomedy in the work of 'this most English of playwrights and film-makers' (Grant 2006) can be traced to his Jewishness.
5   Nadel argues that Stoppard was more assimilated than Pinter or Wesker: 'Other British dramatists of Stoppard's generation, notably Arnold Wesker and Harold Pinter, both Jewish, took a less adaptable view of British life: they maintained the rigid stance of an outsider in their work' (2002: 42).
6   Rozik only accepts theatre as Jewish that has (1) a Jewish or Judaized narrative, (2) a Jewish set of beliefs and/or values, (3) Jewish language and (4) an obvious Jewish author (playwright or director). A very problematic set of essentialist categories, especially with respect to narratives, beliefs, values and even personnel (what about devised work?) that does not seem to account for the mixing of ethnic identities, which is general practice in a globalized world.
7   'H. talks about his instruction for Bar Mitzvah, two nights a week learning Hebrew. "I haven't thought about it for years." How astounded his parents were by his gesture of revolt against the formal religion two years later. How they have mellowed' (Fraser 2017: 9). Fraser and Pinter pass the Wailing Wall without even noticing: 'H. definitely felt no atavistic twinge here' (Fraser 2017: 16).
8   For more information, see https://britishjewishtheatre.org/.
9   Pinter actually formed a friendship with Roth, as Pinter's wife Antonia Fraser stated in a letter to *The Times* after Roth's death (Fraser 2018). I am grateful to Basil Chiasson for directing my attention to this letter.
10 The etymology of the name 'Devlin' is not entirely clear. A web search yielded possibilities such as 'Old Nick' from 'Old Iniquity', the name of the devil in medieval plays, mentioned in the OED. Other theories of derivation point to the Dutch *Nikken*, the devil, which again comes from the Anglo-Saxon *nac-an*, to slay. The Irish name Devlin subtly invokes 'devil' but is derived from the Irish *Dobhuilen* or 'Raging Valour', an Irish nobleman.
11 Pinter as director in *Catastrophe* (1999, RTÉ, Blue Angel); Pinter as Lenny in *The Homecoming* (1969, Palace Theatre, Watford, dir. Stephen Hollis); Pinter as Max in *The Homecoming* (2007, BBC Radio 3, dir. Thea Sharrock);

Pinter as Nicolas in *One for the Road* (2001 ACT Productions & Gate Theatre, Dublin, dir. Robin Lefevre).

12 The possible influence of *Blasted* on *Ashes to Ashes* is explored by Taylor-Batty (2014b) who argues that there are direct links between both plays.

13 In a private letter Ian McEwan sent to Pinter on 23 September 1996, McEwan seems to agree that the play imagines the Holocaust in Dorset or Surrey. Pinter Archive 88880/6/15.

14 'If we understand her as being Jewish, then the Shoah is an integral part of her heritage. The Jewish conception of national history is perhaps best exemplified by the injunction of the prayer from the Haggada, read on the eve of Passover, that, in every generation, every Jew must see himself as if he himself came out of Egypt. … This attitude is so deeply ingrained, that the Shoah too is grasped as a national tragedy, personally affecting also those Jews that did not live in Europe, or were born only after the Holocaust' (Scolnicov 2008: n.p.).

15 Pinter supported Raine's work, and they communicated about a private performance of *Ashes to Ashes*. See Pinter Archive. Production correspondence; 1997–9. Add MS 88880/6/17 '"Ashes to Ashes". Correspondence with Nina Raine relating to staging a private performance; 29 July 1999–20 Sept. 1999.'

Works Cited

Abrams, N., ed (2016), *Hidden in Plain Sight. Jews and Jewishness in British Film, Television, and Popular Culture*, Evanston: Northwestern University Press.

Alderman, G. (2009), 'Harold Pinter – A Jewish View', *Current Viewpoint*, 6 May. Available online: http://www.currentviewpoint.com/cgibin/news.cgi?id=11&command=shownews&newsid=1075 (accessed 30 June 2020).

Angel-Perez, E. (2009), 'Ashes to Ashes: Pinter's Dibbuks', in B. Gauthier (ed.), *Viva Pinter: Harold Pinter's Spirit of Resistance*, 139–60, New York: Peter Lang.

Baker, W. (2008), *Harold Pinter*, London: Continuum.

Baker, W., and S. E. Tabachnick (1973), *Harold Pinter*, Edinburgh: Oliver and Boyd.

Baum, D. (2017), *Feeling Jewish (A Book for Just about Anyone)*, New Haven: Yale University Press.

Billington, M. (2007), *Harold Pinter*, London: Faber and Faber.

Billington, M. (2012), 'J Is for Jewish Dramatists', *The Guardian*, 14 February. Available online: https://www.theguardian.com/stage/2012/feb/14/jewish-dramatists-modern-drama (accessed 30 June 2020).

Burkman, K. H. (1999), 'Harold Pinter's *Ashes to Ashes*: Rebecca and Devlin as Albert Speer', in F. Gillen and S. H. Gale (eds), *The Pinter Review Annual Essays 1997–1998*, 86–96, Tampa, FL: University of Tampa Press.

Cheyette, B. (1996), 'Englishness and Extraterritoriality: British-Jewish Writing and Diaspora Culture', in E. Mendelsohn (ed.), *Literary Strategies: Jewish Texts and Contexts*, 21–39, Oxford: Oxford University Press.

Cheyette, B. (1998), *Contemporary Jewish Writing in Britain and Ireland: An Anthology*, Lincoln: University of Nebraska Press.

Cohen, J. (2005), 'Harold Pinter, Son of a Tailor and Weaver of the Absurd, Awarded a Nobel', *Forward*, 21 October. Available online: https://forward.com/news/2095/harold-pinter-son-of-a-tailor-and-weaver-of-the-a/ (accessed 30 June 2020).

Esslin, M. (1970), *The Peopled Wound: The Plays of Harold Pinter*, London: Methuen.

Fraser, A. (2011), *Must You Go? My Life with Harold Pinter*, London: Phoenix.

Fraser, A. (2017), *Our Israeli Diary, 1978: Of That Time, of That Place*, London: Oneworld.

Fraser, A. (2018), 'Philip Roth, Harold Pinter, Claire Bloom and Me — What a Foursome We Made', *The Times*, 27 May. Available online: https://www.thetimes.co.uk/article/antonia-fraser-philip-roth-harold-pinter-claire-bloom-and-me-what-a-foursome-we-made-r3zptbf30 (accessed 30 June 2020).

Golick, P. S. (1981), 'Jewish Influences in the Plays of Harold Pinter'. MA diss., Concordia University, Montréal.

Grant, L. (2006), 'Mike Leigh Comes Out', *The Guardian*, 18 April. Available online: https://www.theguardian.com/film/2006/apr/18/theatre.religion (accessed 30 June 2020).

Grimes, C. (2005), *Harold Pinter's Politics: A Silence beyond Echo*, Madison: Fairleigh Dickinson University Press.

Herman, D. (2015), 'Jewish Émigré and Refugee Writers in Britain', in D. Brauner and A. Stähler (eds), *The Edinburgh Companion to Modern Jewish Fiction*, 188–98, Edinburgh: Edinburgh University Press.

Jays, D. (2000), 'Missing', *New Statesman*, 30 October. Available online: https://www.newstatesman.com/node/152277 (accessed 30 June 2020).

Kane, S. (1996), The British Library, Modern Manuscripts Collection, The Harold Pinter Archive, Add MS 88880/6/15.

Knowlson, J. (1997), *Damned to Fame: The Life of Samuel Beckett*, London: Bloomsbury.

Krasner, D. (2016), *A History of Modern Drama II: 1960–2000*, Oxford: Wiley-Blackwell.

Krausz, E. (2019), 'London: Postwar Period'. Available online: https://www.jewishvirtuallibrary.org/london (accessed 28 August 2019).

Lawson, P. (forthcoming), 'The Theatre of Harold Pinter: Staging Indefinable and Divided "Jewishness"', in S. J. Ablett, J. Malkin and E. Voigts (eds), *A Companion to British-Jewish Theatre since 1956*, London: Bloomsbury.

McEwan, I. (1996), Letter to Harold Pinter, The British Library, Modern Manuscripts Collection, The Harold Pinter Archive, Add MS 88880/6/15.

Merritt, S. H. (2000), 'Harold Pinter's *Ashes to Ashes*: Political/Personal Echoes of the Holocaust', in F. Gillen and S. H. Gale (eds), *The Pinter Review: Collected Essays 1999 and 2000*, 73–84, Tampa, FL: University of Tampa Press.

Nadel, I. (2002), *Double Act: A Life of Tom Stoppard*, London: Methuen.

Nathan, J. (2015), 'Visionary behind the Shock of the Young Vic', *The Jewish Chronicle*, 20 April. Available online: https://www.thejc.com/culture/theatre/visionary-behind-the-shock-of-the-young-vic-1.66131 (accessed 30 June 2020).

Neumeier, B. (2003), 'Identität und Gedächtnis in der britisch-jüdischen Literatur der Gegenwart: Harold Pinter's *Ashes to Ashes*', in D. Lamping (ed.), *Identität und Gedächtnis in der jüdischen Literatur nach 1945*, 156–71, Berlin: Erich Schmidt Verlag.

Pinter, H. (1996a), 'The Room', in *Harold Pinter: Plays 1*, 85–110, London: Faber and Faber.

Pinter, H. (1996b), 'The Dwarfs', in *Harold Pinter: Plays 2*, 77–105, London: Faber and Faber.

Pinter, H. (1998), 'A Speech of Thanks', in *Various Voices: Prose, Poetry, Politics 1948–1989*, 46–9, London: Faber and Faber.

Pinter H. (2002), Letter to Henry Woolf, The British Library, Modern Manuscripts Collection, The Harold Pinter Archive, Add MS 89094: 1948–2013.

Pinter, H. (2011a), '*Ashes to Ashes*', in *Harold Pinter: Plays 4*, 389–433, London: Faber and Faber.

Pinter, H. (2011b), '*One for the Road*', in *Harold Pinter: Plays 4*, 221–247, London: Faber and Faber.

Pinter, H. (n.d.), Letter to Moishe Wernick, The British Library, Modern Manuscripts Collection, The Harold Pinter Archive, Add MS 89094/5: 1965–2005.

Quigley, A. E. (1975), *The Pinter Problem*, Princeton, NJ: Princeton University Press.

Reitz, B. (1998), '"Forget Things and You'll Go to Pieces": Jüdische Identität zwischen Erinnerung und Annäherung, Utopie und Holocaust im englischen Drama der Gegenwart', in B. Neumeier (ed.), *Jüdische Literatur und Kultur in Großbritannien und den USA nach 1945*, 25–42, Wiesbaden: Harrassowitz Verlag.

Reunion/L'ami Retrouvé (1989), [Film] Dir. Jerry Schatzberg. Paris: Les Films Ariane et al.

Rozik, E. (2013), *Jewish Drama and Theatre: From Rabbinical Intolerance to Secular Liberalism*, Chicago: Sussex Academic Press.

Salem, D. (1986), 'The Impact of Pinter's Work', *Ariel*, 17 (1): 71–83.

Scolnicov, H. (2008), '*Ashes to Ashes*: Pinter's Holocaust Play', *Cycnos* 18 (1). Available online: http://revel.unice.fr/cycnos/index.html?id=1665 (accessed 30 June 2020).

Sicher, E. (1985), *Beyond Marginality: Anglo-Jewish Literature after the Holocaust*, Albany: State University of New York Press.

Silverstein, M. S. (1993), *Harold Pinter and the Language of Cultural Power*, Cranbury, NJ: Associated University Press.

Taylor-Batty, M. (2014a), *The Theatre of Harold Pinter*, London: Bloomsbury Methuen.

Taylor-Batty, M. (2014b), 'How to Mourn – Kane, Pinter and Theatre as Monument to Loss in the 1990s', in M. Aragay and E. Monforte (eds), *Ethical Speculations in Contemporary British Theatre*, 59–75, Basingstoke and New York: Palgrave Macmillan.

Taylor-Batty, M. (forthcoming), 'A Jew Who Writes: The Shadow of the Holocaust in Harold Pinter's Work', in S. J. Ablett, J. Malkin and E. Voigts (eds), *A Companion to British-Jewish Theatre since the 1950s*, London: Bloomsbury.

Wyllie, A., and C. Rees (2016), *The Plays of Harold Pinter*, London: Palgrave Macmillan.

5

Pinter's Connections with the Middle East

Ibrahim Yerebakan

The contemporary history of the Middle East has been dominated by tumultuous events: Muslim-Muslim conflicts, terrorism, ethnic purifications, occupations by powerful nations and, most recently, cannibalism in Syria's inter-ethnic violence where warring factions commit atrocities and display them online – the latter a phenomenon one expert refers to as 'YouTube war' (Baker 2013: 15). Before the internet carried images of these disturbing realities to Westerners and before conflict in the Middle East inspired analysts to speak of the inhumane acts of violence and the causal factors perpetuating them, Harold Pinter was voicing his concern that the Middle East was one of the most unstable regions in the world.

Pinter's concern with the Middle East goes back to his first two overtly political plays, *One for the Road* (1984) and *Mountain Language* (1988), and persists with his sketch *The New World Order* (1991) and several political poems, including 'American Football: A reflection upon the Gulf War' (1991) and 'Democracy' (2003). That concern, however, is most evident in a number of speeches he made and/or published in opposition to the exercise of Western foreign policy and can be found by looking to histories which have yet to be introduced into the study of Pinter's activism. Pinter's critique of the Middle East was in fact a critique of Western nations whose foreign policies played a key role in the instabilities there, and it stemmed from his compassion for civilians and interest in their plight. This component of Pinter's activism was significant in the sense that his first-hand experiences and persistent engagement with the region provided much of the impetus to bring public attention to this corner of the world, and can thus be appreciated for how it initiated intense political debate, specifically in the aftermath of the 1990–1 Gulf War. For example, when Turkey was under military rule in the 1980s, Pinter vigorously condemned the state's human rights record. His political critique also accounted for Israel's suppression of the Palestinian people and the first and second invasions of Iraq and their attendant war crimes, such as the Abu Ghraib prison abuse scandals and the burning and burying of 'an untold number of Iraqis alive' (Pinter 2009b: 223).

Although scholars have examined Pinter's political speeches, their discussions and analyses have not focused upon Pinter's profound connection and association with the Middle East specifically during his time as an activist. One of the least explored moments in Pinter's activism is his views on the interminable Israeli-Palestinian conflict, including his criticism of Israel – directed at the state and not its people – and his empathy for Palestinians expressed in interviews and public speeches. By contrast, Pinter's trip to Turkey with Arthur Miller in 1985, the only Middle Eastern country he ever visited while on duty as an activist, has been much discussed, particularly his direct contact with those affected by the military dictatorship, and focuses on how the worst examples of human rights infringements sharpened his new-found commitment as an activist in defence of oppressed Others. It is nevertheless important to revisit this history in more detail and, in doing so, to offer a non-Western appraisal of Pinter's time in Turkey and in the Middle East more generally, one that engages with Pinter's reports about his first-hand experiences in this region, moments in his published speeches, Western news sources and with first-hand accounts of Turkish critics.

The Centrality of the Middle East

In 2002, prior to the emergence of a culture of suicide bombing, Pinter warned that the West's interest in the Middle East as a means of expanding America's status as a superpower, along with its allies, would only lead to an escalation of violence, with profound global consequences. Pinter straightforwardly declared, 'If they bomb Iraq, it can only inflame a whole world of terrorism. The reaction would be severe, quite apart from the fact that it could be a humanitarian catastrophe' (qtd. in *Newsnight* 2002). In pointing his finger at the West, particularly America, for sociopolitical turmoil in the Middle East, Pinter focused on the consequences brought about by Western foreign policy. Western democracy has indeed not prevailed in Iraq nor managed to stabilize the region in the wake of destruction and reconstruction in the name of freedom. On the contrary, all attempts to counter terrorism with what arguably constitutes Western state terrorism have only served to ignite ultra-nationalism and religious radicalism and, more ominously, have provoked anger and anti-Western sentiment in the region.

Pinter's critiques of such policies were, in effect, a way of questioning the West's integrity, calling attention to its avoidance of accountability. However, it was also a way for him to depict the West as participating in the spread of terrorism. In his Nobel lecture, he branded America's invasion of Iraq 'a bandit act, an act of blatant state terrorism, demonstrating absolute contempt for the concept of international law' (Pinter 2009a: 295). Elsewhere in the lecture he observed,

> Early in the [West's] invasion [of Iraq] there was a photograph published on the front page of British newspapers of Tony Blair kissing the cheek of a little Iraqi boy. 'A grateful child', said the caption. A few days later there was a story and photograph, on an inside page, of another four-year-old boy with no arms. His family had been blown up by a missile. He was the only survivor. 'When I do get my arms back?', he asked. The story was dropped. Well, Tony Blair wasn't holding him in his arms, nor the body of any other mutilated child, nor the body of any bloody corpse. Blood is dirty. It dirties your shirt and tie when you're making a sincere speech on television.
>
> (296)

At once, this scene indicts Blair and brings the victims of political violence into the frame, placing the former British prime minister in the role of terrorist and demonstrating a profound sympathy for children and civilians who are caught up in conflict zones.

Pinter's interpretation of 9/11 at the time was that it was predictable, to be expected even, given the way successive American governments have steered their military in the Middle East. For Pinter, the attack on New York City was 'an act of retaliation against the constant and systematic manifestations of state terrorism on the part of the United States over many years' (262). He also focused on the way actions prompt reactions: 'People do not forget', he once insisted, '[t]hey do not forget the death of their fellows, they do not forget torture and mutilation, they do not forget injustice, they do not forget oppression, they do not forget the terrorism of mighty powers. They not only don't forget. They strike back' (262). In depicting 9/11 as a retaliation invited by the American state, Pinter was not gloating, nor was he sympathizing with anti-West terrorists. His emphasis of action and reaction, of cause and effect, was an appeal for America to be responsible in its use of political power.

Pinter also repeatedly articulated his concern over another sensitive issue in the region, the protracted conflict between the state of Israel and Palestinians. The subject of Zionism as a state ideology and Israel's use of disproportionate force against Palestinians, however, has received comparatively little attention in Pinter scholarship, despite Pinter's outspoken claims. During a visit to Jerusalem with Lady Antonia Fraser in 1978 Pinter declared, 'this is an Arab town,' suggesting that Israel was not only for Israelis (qtd. in Fraser 2017: 83). In one of his last exclusively political interviews with Ramona Koval, Pinter denounced crucial support the American government was giving to

Israel, which he described as an apartheid state still lording over land it had captured (Gaza). It was not Israelis that Pinter condemned but the Israeli state's regional policies: '[T]he injustice to the Palestinians now has become an absolute outrage. Now that's something worth talking about. We don't even know whether Saddam Hussein has any weapons or not. But we do know that Israel has, and they've used them too' (Pinter qtd. in *Newsnight* 2002).

He also argued that anti-Islamic discourses in the West, Israeli aggressions in the region and the interventionism of the West would only exacerbate terrorism and racism and reinforce neocolonialism in the whole region:

> I would particularly like to remark upon Israel's position in this now. Until Israel takes a totally different attitude to the Palestinian state of affairs, we're going to get nowhere. Because it reverberates, rebounds, and is never-ending. And Israel has a great responsibility, as, of course, the United States, which arms Israel to the hilt, also has. [...] And until we see that military force gets nobody anywhere – I'm talking about that, the iron fist – it doesn't work.
>
> (Pinter qtd. in Koval 2006)

At base, Pinter was calling for a more sober approach both to the performance of Israel's role given its disproportionate power and to the West's performance of its role as a superpower mediating Israel's relation to Palestine. The only way to deal with the 'terrorism', Pinter claimed, was to 'try to understand it and to try to take other means towards it. As I say, to use your common-or-garden intelligence, [and] not become hysterical' (qtd. in *Newsnight* 2002). The hysteria and arrogance to which Pinter referred have arguably increased since the early 2000s, as prejudices and bigotries in the West against Islam shape social relations and sit at the forefront of Western politics, particularly in America and Britain. These prejudices manifest, for example, in the immigration policies of far-right and conservative politicians calling for a complete or restrictive ban on Muslim immigrants from entering their countries. Far-right parties such as the British National Party (BNP) and United Kingdom Independence Party (UKIP) in the UK have a history of making anti-Muslim comments, demonizing Islam as being in permanent conflict with the West. Former UKIP leader Gerard Batten described Islam as a 'death cult' (Walker 2018). Elsewhere, French politician Marine Le Pen compared Islamic prayers in the streets to Nazi occupation (*Telegraph* 2010). American President Donald Trump has on occasion made anti-Islamic statements such as 'Islam hates us', and therefore the 'United States can't allow people into the country who have such hatred for the U.S. and people who are not Muslim' (Sherfinski 2016).

At the same time, Pinter's avoidance of Palestinian terrorism and violence in his political discourse is contentious. One example – albeit still largely unremarked upon – occurred during a visit to Israel in 1978. Lady Antonia's diary entry relates that Pinter had expressed relief that 'four Palestinian terrorists have been shot dead at Orly Airport in Paris [...] without managing to spray the innocent tourists of EL AL with their machine guns' (Fraser 2017: 131–2). His criticism of Israel and its Zionist state ideology might be seen as informed by a distinction between Palestinian violence, which is characterized by a tit-for-tat pattern, and the state violence of Israel, which is defined by systematic and routine brutality, dispossession, humiliation, collective punishment and detention without charge. In this way, Pinter's recurring fascination with bullies and the seizure of power in his plays inspires him to see the state of Israel as enjoying and exercising a disproportionate amount of political power. It might also be informed by the fact that he identified, more than anything else, with the humanism underpinning his politics: 'I deplore what is happening in Israel,' he asserted in conversation with Mireia Aragay in 1996 and clarified that 'I've made my position very clear. Not as a Jew, but as a citizen, as a man' (Pinter 2009b: 253).

Although he never explicitly offered a picture of what another, better world might look like, Pinter's critique of Western foreign policy and its effect upon the Middle East implicitly called for the establishment of a more inhabitable world through more peaceful relations between political adversaries in the Middle East. Believing that one day '[w]e will celebrate when Arab and Jew live as equals in a peaceful Middle East' (Pinter qtd. in *The Guardian* 2008), Pinter maintained his hopes that a peaceful coexistence between two communities on the same land would become possible only through mutual respect and understanding. His emphasis on Arab and Jew, rather than the states of Israel and Palestine, again underscores that Pinter had more faith in citizens than regimes.

The Centrality of Turkey

Encountering Turkey First-Hand

Although Pinter was born into a Jewish family, he only came into first-hand contact with the Middle East in 1978, when he and his wife visited Jerusalem and Gaza, and then in 1985 when he and Arthur Miller visited Turkey from 17 to 22 March. The latter trip was an eventful visit on behalf of PEN International in the company of Miller to investigate reports of human rights violations and, specific to PEN's agenda, the status of writers and intellectuals whom the Turkish state saw as dissidents. The visit was neither a holiday, nor part of a literary event but focused rather on promoting civil liberties, a kind of 'peace mission' to draw widespread attention to those suffering in Turkey's prisons under military rule. During the visit Pinter and Miller met with prominent Turkish politicians, the intelligentsia, the Turkish Peace Association and some family members of those imprisoned. At a press conference at the conclusion of their visit Pinter stated, 'From the information we have received since we have been in Turkey, which we regard as authentic, we believe that gross violations of the human spirit through physical torture is a present fact in Turkey' (Gursel 1985). Pinter subsequently confirmed in an interview that while in Turkey he saw first-hand the consequences of state violence used upon a people:

> It was a very vivid and highly illuminating trip in a number of ways. […] Well, the first time that I'd ever been in a place where I actually met people who had been tortured. But, as you know, torture and this kind of treatment not only tend to destroy the person suffering it, but the whole of his family. For example, one trade union leader I met in Istanbul – a very distinguished man, by the way – had been very badly tortured. He was out of prison, and very shaky indeed, but his wife was actually mute; she's lost her power of speech altogether. I think she saw him in prison and hasn't spoken a word since.
>
> (qtd. in Ford 1989: 4)

Pinter focused upon how torture harms not only the individual subjected to it but also the local community they inhabit; his articulation of his experiences goes beyond the confines of interview rooms, public platforms and newspapers, and speaks of the human pain, suffering and torment caused by brutal regimes while inviting the wider world to be attentive to the bitter realities of both this country under dictatorship and beyond.

Pinter's analysis and critique of what was happening in Turkey drew attention to less obvious causes at work from beyond the Middle East. Assessing the political situation in Turkey after returning home, Miller stressed that the country was not democratic 'but [more accurately] a military dictatorship', the situation purely 'a consequence of the new, tremendous United States contribution to the military – about $900 million per year – and a not very dramatic American emphasis on human rights' (Kamm 1985). At the time of Pinter and Miller's visit, Turkey was, despite being under military rule, fully endorsed by the West – and America in particular – which 'seemed happy to overlook its suppression of democracy, so long as it also staved off (or was seen to stave off) the communist threat' (Freely 2010: 31).

Discovering Another Turkey

In addition to accounting for Pinter's concern with the plight of citizens from regions affected by political upheaval, local war and Western interventionism, it is also important to consider Pinter's activism from the standpoint of what inhabitants of the Middle East have reported about him. One fascinating aspect of Pinter's visit to Turkey was how he and Miller were chaperoned by a then young Orhan Pamuk and a professor of psychology, Gunduz Vassaf. Years later, Pamuk recounted vividly:

> Together we visited small and struggling publishing houses, cluttered newsrooms, and the dark and dusty headquarters of small magazines that were on the verge of shutting down; we went from house to house, and restaurant to restaurant, to meet with writers in trouble and their families. [...] I remember how we discussed the street vendors, the horse carts, the cinema posters, and the scarfless and scarf-wearing women.
> (2006)

Pamuk explains how he had been offered the job of serving as Pinter and Miller's guide because he was fluent in English and how he saw an opportunity to spend a few days in the company of two famous writers. Pamuk confesses that until his experience with the men, he had remained indifferent to the phenomenon of Turkish intellectuals running into trouble with the regime. He also stresses how he 'felt drawn to this world through guilt' and 'shared shame' in every meeting he attended, 'room after room of troubled and chain-smoking men' (ibid.). Even in inhospitable conditions, Pinter's friendship and solidarity appear to have had an important impact on intellectuals like Pamuk, who would become a Nobel laureate in 2006, directly following Pinter's own win in 2005.

During their visit, Pinter and Miller met with political figures, including two former Turkish prime ministers, and even Necmettin Erbakan, the leader of the anti-Western, pro-Islamic National Salvation Party. These were all legitimately elected politicians, all deposed and dispossessed of their language by the 1980 coup. When Pinter asked whether the National Salvation Party was banned, Erbakan reportedly said, 'Yes, like all other political parties, my party was banned just after the military takeover with a unanimous decision taken by the members of the governing military council' (*Cumhuriyet* 1985: 8). Miller intervened, 'When do you think this ban will come to an end?' Erbakan replied, 'Our party will forever remain banned, like other political parties.' Pinter asked, 'Could the party be re-established in a new format?' Erbakan only smiled, 'No, certainly not' (8).

Pinter's first-hand encounters with beleaguered political figures, intimidated by the military and dispossessed of their right to exist, and his desire to hear their stories are echoed in many of his political dramas that typically feature authoritarian figures silencing and denying a voice to political dissenters or political outliers. In Pinter's dramatic sketch *Precisely* (1983), for example, Roger and Stephen ponder what they might do with those who contest their estimation of the death toll of a bomb strike; in *One for the Road* we discover that Nicolas has subjugated Victor and Gila for challenging the status quo, and the disappearance of their boy, Nicky, may well have to do with the fact that the child spat at his soldiers; in *Party Time* (1991) Dusty's outspokenness about her brother Jimmy's sudden absence is met with Terry's threats, and Jimmy's appearance as a broken and disoriented figure in the final scene gives a clear sense of the consequences for speaking out against the club and its regime. *The New World Order* marks a kind of climax of this thematic concern, where a blindfolded and seated man is unable to speak at all; the fact that he has affronted the state in some way goes without saying at this stage of Pinter's journey writing political drama.

It is significant that during Pinter and Miller's informal yet direct inquiry into the state of human rights they encountered a range of political viewpoints but made no distinctions among those they met: between those on the political right and left, or between scarfed or scarfless women. Because of their plight as ordinary people who had endured appalling deprivations and assaults, systematic or otherwise, Pinter saw them as 'exactly the same as you and I' (Ford 1989: 4), no matter how far away they were from Western eyes and how much they seemed to be 'others'. Pinter's art and activism have been characterized as 'motivated by the passionate empathy that he felt for the outsider' (Heawood 2008), and here in the specific context of his encounter with locals on that PEN mission in Turkey one finds a formative empirical example which simultaneously offers a specific point of reference for what might have inspired features of his political dramas and his frequent focus on the plight of victims in his activism.

The State and the Media: Censorship, Silence, Historical Revisionism

Although Pinter and Miller expressed their desire to meet Turkey's cabinet members, apart from the leaders of the outlawed parties, to discuss human rights issues, their request was reportedly declined (Genc 2016). The PEN ambassadors also encountered other kinds of silence. The Turkish media at that time, including right-wing publications, were subject to martial law and so were fully controlled by the military; as with imprisoned and tortured writers, any dissenting voices in the mainstream could be shut down by the authorities without warning. Miller's testimony is revealing: 'We couldn't find an editor who wouldn't say that he cannot tell the whole truth' (Kamm 1985). One finds here a point of origin that informed Pinter's predilection – in the context of his public statements, dramatic work and interviews – to interrogate the close relationship between the state and the media, often highlighting the ways in which the media is typically an arm of the state in both authoritarian and democratic nations.

Pinter's experience of media censorship in Turkey emerged quite early in his activism in the form of his abhorrence at the state's control of the media and critical depiction of it as a tool 'used politically all over the world. There is such a relationship between the media and the people in political power' and 'a very corrupt state of affairs' (Pinter 2009b: 253–4). His criticism of mainstream media censorship in his own Western context is all the more interesting with the knowledge of what he witnessed first-hand in Turkey. In 1990 he commented, 'England is the only country, as far as I know, in which a legitimately elected MP of a certain party is not allowed to speak on TV' (qtd. in *BBC Third Programme* 1990). Some fifteen years later when commenting on the reception of his Nobel lecture in the British media, Pinter stated, 'It wasn't passed over. It was totally ignored by the BBC. It never happened' (qtd. in Billington 2006). While Pinter's dramas depict the subjugation and silencing of political dissent, it is notable that his concern with media censorship materialized in his last political drama, the sketch *Press Conference* (2002), the only work that features the media explicitly and portrays it as failing to respond critically to an obviously fascistic government. The central character, a former chief of the secret police now turned minister of culture, offers a detailed account of the fate of political dissenters such that the journalists gathered before him are loath to respond critically.

The culture of censorship in Turkey took on a curious form as public interest about the writers' visit was aroused, resulting in substantial coverage on the front pages of both right-wing and the left-wing Turkish newspapers. Liberal *Hurriyet* commented upon the participation of the writers in the court hearings of members of the Turkish Peace Association:

> World-famous writers Arthur Miller and Harold Pinter have attended the case of the Members of the Turkish Peace Association, put on trial by court martial. While Arthur Miller took constant notes on the process, Pinter kept quiet and was content with watching the case. However, upon the completion of the trial in a space of ten minutes, both writers got surprised and bewildered at the duration of the trial process, and then asked their associates whether it was all over.
>
> (1985: 13)

Innocuously enough, media representations of the court attendance relayed facts without editorializing. However, surveying the coverage reveals that the media spoke about the event almost univocally, arguably as a manifestation of self-censorship imposed out of fear of not provoking the authoritarian state. There was a deliberate avoidance of statements that might be construed as critical of the state's treatment of political prisoners and also a refusal to look beyond the horrors of the courtrooms. Instead, the papers took up rather rudimentary subjects and were content with selectively reporting the 'brighter' sides which emphasized the presence of two elegantly dressed, world-famous dramatists and 'foreign guests', with Pinter's and Miller's celebrity receiving more attention than the court case report itself. The front pages bore leaders such as: 'Miller and Pinter at the Peace Court Case' (1) and 'Two celebrated writers deeply impressed by the Bosporus: They attended the court case during the day and toasted Turkish raki during the night' (*Milliyet* 1985: 1).

Those same newspapers changed their tone and content once the writers returned to America to give a press conference tied to the publication of their report for International PEN Club and the submission of the document to Amnesty International, to be subsequently presented by the organization to the British Foreign Office and to the State Department. In *The Washington Post* the Turkish press claimed that as soon as Miller and Pinter returned home, they spoke of Turkey in their own media with great disrespect and, moreover, observed that the writers' press conference about their visit and the report was rather political in its content. The front page of daily *Milliyet* declared: 'They came over to Turkey, banqueted and vomited poison back home' (1985: 1). Turkish friends in the US Congress were quoted by *Milliyet* as saying that the publication of these embarrassing, anti-Turkey statements made by Pinter and Miller in *The Washington Post* would impede official talks and negotiations and would only 'enable [the] Greek lobby, in particular, and those who conspire a propaganda campaign against Turkey to gain an upper hand just before the Premier Ozal's visit to Washington' (7). The stark difference between Pinter and Miller's account and that of the Turkish press underscores the disjuncture between the playwrights' investment in human rights and the media's status as an arm of the state and thereby its implication in the maintenance of the status quo and of power.

It also highlights the media's carefully crafted framing of events, something which also concerned Pinter as an activist. The sharp contrast was that while the Turkish media saw the press conference back in America as an insult and offence to the Turkish Republic and its people, Pinter himself 'praised the Turkish people for their dignity' and he and Miller were 'deeply moved and impressed by the intelligence, the grace and the dignity of so many of the people we have met in Turkey' (*Washington Post* 1985). Similar to the example of Pinter's representation of Israel, his collaborative work with Miller to bring widespread attention to the appalling state of affairs in a country under military dictatorship consisted of both a vigorous criticism of the Turkish state's systematic human rights violations and an affirmation of its citizens. In those troubled years in Turkey, the Turkish media would have worked in fear of legal censure, with dozens of journalists already living out hundreds of years of prison sentences for presenting divergent narratives themselves informed by pacifism and non-violent opinions.

One significant visual aspect of the Turkish media coverage was the tendency for accompanying courtroom pictures to show, deliberately or otherwise and without exception, only the PEN ambassadors and their interpreters, thus avoiding displaying the photographs of the prisoners on trial. It was common practice during the days of military rule to bring prisoners to the site of the courtroom in military truck convoys. During such transfers, the routes to the site would be closed to local traffic until the convoys reached the final destination safely. Most often, sports complexes would serve as the sites for courts handling large quantities of trials. Pictures related to the handling of the trials' processes and pictures of the prisoners hardly appeared in the media. Prisoners would sit in a courtroom in white prison uniforms – a grim reminder of a burial garment – with shaven heads while often 'protected' by two soldiers. By absenting the lived reality of prisoners from the media frame, the press atomized Miller and Pinter, detaching them from the political reality and human beings to which they were actively connected and instead portraying them as individuals, outsiders or even human rights tourists.

Despite the scale of public attention in Turkey and, as this chapter has shown, the well-publicized reception of Pinter and Miller's visit by the Turkish media, some Western newspapers minimized the Turkish media's involvement, thus presenting a strikingly different picture of reality. According to *The New York Times*, 'Arthur Miller and Harold Pinter, the playwrights, held a well-attended news conference on human rights in Istanbul recently, but not a word about it appeared in the Turkish Press' (Kamm 1985). Assessing the event, Mustafa Gursel in *The Washington Post* similarly commented: 'Playwrights Arthur Miller and Harold Pinter were censored from the pages of the Turkish press today after having given a press conference here in which they were strongly critical of the human rights record of this NATO ally' (Gursel 1985). Censorship evidently takes many forms, and these Western media dailies appear to have been engaged in the representation or suggestion of a kind of censorship that did not, in fact, exist.

While the Turkish media's representation of Pinter and Miller's presence in the courtroom and visit more broadly is easily understood, one wonders: did Western news outlets simply ignore or misread or did they actively censor the Turkish media's involvement? Were *The Washington Post* and *The New York Times* led to misrepresent the situation because of presumptions they made about the freedom of Middle Eastern, and more specifically Turkish, journalists? If this was the case, then the fact that a presumption of a certain kind of authoritarianism prevented the Western media from seeing the actual form of authoritarianism that was at work draws our attention back to Pinter's own critique of Western media in his activism, suggesting just how complicated the exercise of media bias and the enactment of censorship can be. Pinter never spoke of (and was thus perhaps unaware of) these two completely inconsistent interpretations of the same event; meanwhile, they have concurrently gone unremarked upon in Pinter scholarship. This 'new' history in Pinter's activism contributes to a still quite latent discussion of the ways Pinter was subject to media censorship: from the many times his contributions to British newspapers had their titles changed to the effect of altering his meaning, to the refusal of publication of his political poems, to the way in which the publication of his notorious appeal for a fair trial for Slobodan Milošević divested it of context and nuance.

Trying to Tell 'the Real Tale': The Turkish Embassy Anecdote Revisited

One of the most salient moments in the writers' visit – and arguably the most widely discussed example of Pinter's time in the Middle East thanks in part to his own piece, 'Arthur Miller's Socks' (1985), written in tribute to Miller on the occasion of his eightieth birthday – was a dinner party given at the American Embassy in Ankara on 21 March 1985 in honour of the playwrights. The reception got off to a bad start as one of the invited local guests, who was reportedly politically left-leaning, was praising the authors' stance against the military rule in Turkey before a politically conservative guest joined the fray. She reprimanded Miller and Pinter, insisting that they should leave Turkey's internal problems to the Turks. Pinter was reported to have reacted ferociously, shouting from the other end of the table: 'I throw these offensive words back to your face' (Genc 2016). This version of events comes from Yalcin Dogan, a liberal Turkish journalist and party guest who witnessed the fracas unfold. Dogan's vantage provides an added dimension to a well-known anecdote which routinely depicts the drama as transpiring between Pinter and the American ambassador to Turkey. The conflict subsequently came to be identified as a symbol of the dramatist's protest, under any circumstances, against human rights violations.

A decade later, in the *Hurriyet*, Dogan gave this exclusive first-hand account of what exactly happened there:

> Almost everyone on the dinner table has got into an explosive debate on the existence of systematic torture in Turkish prisons, and America's support of the military dictatorship in Turkey. There is only one person who is terribly embarrassed by this debate; it is American Ambassador Robert Strausz-Hupé, the host, posturing himself as if he were a shadowy figure of the Turkish state. The Ambassador takes the floor. He is defending to the death the 1980 military coup in Turkey. Considering the Ambassador's manner of speech, there is no need to look for the address of the 1980 coup in Turkey elsewhere. No sooner has the Ambassador finished his final words than Pinter jumps up from his chair: 'These words are insults to all of us, sitting here, on this very table. Defending a military regime is an insult to humanity'. Pinter's words and his manner of utterance were very tough indeed; pounding his fist on the table, he stood straight up. Fruits and desserts were left uneaten. Just then the dinner abruptly came to an end.
>
> (2005: 8)

Pinter admitted sometime later that being thrown out of the ambassador's dinner was 'one of the proudest moments in my life' (1990: 5). More importantly, this alternative historical report of the notorious confrontation offers a characterization of Pinter that does not come directly from the man himself but instead from a Turkish observer. Moreover, it offers a characterization of Pinter's activism which defines, more clearly than most accounts of that activity, how unswerving and vociferous Pinter's belief in the value of human life was, his lobby for human rights and his critique of political rationality, and it enhances the narrative of how Pinter was variously defamed and even censored for his politics.

In his proudest moment, Pinter, enquiring into the realities behind the 1980 coup while at the ambassador's dinner table, once again brought public attention to bear not only on the bloodiest military regime in the history of modern Turkey but also more significantly on the United States' endorsement of this 'friendly' dictatorship under the pretext of protecting a NATO country against Communism. Interestingly enough, the same Western media that were so critical of insufficient Turkish media coverage of the PEN ambassadors' visit had earlier on shown little interest in the 1980 military intervention into Turkey and its deplorable consequences. Only a few critical statements emerged on the matter of the green lights, active backing by Western governments and the West's contentious support for NATO's military intervention. The seventh president of Turkey, Kenan Evren, a self-appointed general-turned-politician, was welcomed enthusiastically by Western states and their leaders during official state visits until his ten-year term came to an end in 1989.

Pinter and Turkey: Visible Influence, Sustained Engagement

Pinter's fact-finding mission to Turkey and his staunch criticism of Potemkin democracies such as Turkey through the 1980s was impactful. The story of drawing attention to and critiquing another country's human rights problems and exhibiting his solidarity with the persecuted and prosecuted received much international attention, from Human Rights Watch and Amnesty International in particular. As a result, visible pressure upon the Turkish state, robustly undergirded by the spirit of international solidarity, saw the court cases dropped one by one; even life imprisonments and death penalties were commuted to less severe punishments. Shortly after the PEN visit, the defendants of the Turkish Peace Association who had initially faced hundreds of years of prison sentences were acquitted. Former president of English PEN, Maureen Freely, disclosed the significant impact of the 'ruckus at the US Embassy in Ankara, and the gloriously quotable lecture Pinter gave on torture. The story got a lot of coverage, causing the leaders of the so-called Free World a great deal of embarrassment, and it was not long afterwards that the writers and artists they had come to help began to see their cases dropped' (Freely 2014). Still, unhealthy prison conditions, harassments, intimidations, torture, pronouncements of death and life sentences left an indelible mark on each prisoner.

   It is understood that after a certain period of time the decisions to arrest, punish, imprison and inflict all manner of sufferings upon the regime's political opponents were arbitrarily and, suddenly, revoked by the very same authorities. This of course calls to mind the final scene of *Mountain Language* when the authoritarian state figures suddenly declare to the trembling prisoner and his prostrate mother that they have changed the rules, and they can speak their mountain language. Although the arbitrarily imposed ban on communicating in one's mother tongue has been lifted just as arbitrarily, 'Until further notice. New rules' (Pinter 2011: 265), the swiftly changing rules and the physical and mental abuse are what shock and incapacitate the mountain people, rendering them unable and perhaps now unwilling to utter a word, let alone communicate or converse. For example, when the Prisoner says to his mother, 'We can speak. You can speak to me in our own language'

(265–6), the old woman remains mute and does not respond to the 'new rules'. Another concrete outcome of the international pressure Pinter and Miller mobilized was that the official ban on speaking the Kurdish language was lifted in 1991, 'after three years of debates, studies and broken promises of reform' (Pope 1991: 11).

Pinter maintained his commitment to human rights issues in Turkey, fixing a critical eye on the nation until the end of his life. In 2004, he and friends including Miller and Noam Chomsky joined a campaign against the Ilisu Dam Project in southern Turkey on the River Tigris aimed at protecting the rich archaeological heritage site and the medieval town of Hasankeyf. As for the plight of Turkish writers, Pinter never ceased speaking passionately and in detail about that political reality. He championed the poetry of the long-imprisoned Turkish writer Nâzim Hikmet, sending a congratulatory message to the celebration held in 2002 on the centennial anniversary of the poet's birthday at Queen Elizabeth Hall in London. In January 2007, in poor health, Pinter participated in a vigil outside the Turkish Embassy in London to protest the murder of Hrant Dink, an Armenian-Turkish newspaper editor and human rights activist. Pinter's presence and his concern for the murder of Dink bolstered ongoing pressure applied to the Turkish authorities to bring the activist's assassins to justice.

Dictatorships, state violence and the imprisonment, torture and murder of civilians as well as Western interventions into foreign nations entailing significant violence and high numbers of civilian casualties continue today. Pinter made it his business to resist, acknowledge and inquire into these realities. While it is easy to regard him as a political commentator speaking from the safe haven of his own nation, the story of his journey from one corner of the world to a country ruled by martial law and his first-hand experiences turns out to entail not just personal contact with the victims of state oppression and violence but also the administration of support and solidarity, the provision of a forum to speak and gather as a community of dissenters and an influence upon others and their attitude towards and knowledge of what transpires in their own communities and country. As this chapter has shown, an explicit focus on and more thorough excavation of the history of that first-hand experience enrich our appreciation of the complicated nature of the media's representation – both in Turkey and internationally – of Pinter's activism.

The case of Turkey reveals that Pinter's scathing critique of the effects of state violence is a double-sided coin whose other, less-visible side consists of an open mind and heart in the face of realities which can easily harden and embitter anyone directly affected and, moreover, overwhelm those of us who dare to look. While the story of Pinter in Turkey highlights the extent of the divide between two worlds, East and West, it also suggests the extent to which one person can participate in changing political circumstances and, at the same time, the extent to which Pinter was never really acting alone as an activist. While Pinter's engagement with the Middle East was wide-ranging – from Iraq, to Israel, to Palestine and beyond – his relationship to and physical presence in Turkey is a standout moment in his career that continues to offer much in the way of thinking further about his activism and his art.

Works Cited

Baker, A. (2013), 'The Youtube War', *Time*, 27 May: 15–19.

BBC Third Programme (1990), [radio] 'Pinter at Sixty: An Interview with Harold Pinter', BBC 3, 7 October.

Billington, M. (2006), 'An Interview with Harold Pinter', *The Guardian*, 14 March. Available online: https://www.theguardian.com/stage/2006/mar/14/theatre.stage (accessed 11 December 2008).

Chrisafis, A., and I. Tilden (2003), 'Pinter Blasts "Nazi America" and "Deluded Idiot" Blair', *The Guardian*, 11 June. Available online: https://www.theguardian.com/uk/2003/jun/11/books.arts (accessed 24 December 2011).

Cumhuriyet (1985), 22 March: 8.

Dogan, Y. (2005), 'A Dinner with Pinter', *Hurriyet*, 19 October: 8.

Ford, A. (1989), 'Radical Departures: An Interview with Harold Pinter', *The Listener*, 27 October: 4–6.

Fraser, A. (2017), *Our Israeli Diary, 1978: Of That Time, of That Place*, London: Oneworld.

Freely, M. (2010), 'Two for the Road: Harold Pinter and Arthur Miller in Turkey', in J. Glanville (ed.), *Beyond Bars: 50 Years of the Pen Writers in Prison Committee*, 39 (4), 27–40, Newbury Park, CA: Sage.

Freely, M. (2014), 'Friendship Is the Essence of PEN', *The Guardian*, 13 March. Available online: https://www.theguardian.com/books/2014/mar/13/maureen-freely-pen-friendship (accessed 24 July 2016).

Genc, I. (2016), 'Harold Pinter: The Nobel Laureate, Friend of the Oppressed', *Kurdi Bianet*, 24 December. Available online: http://bianet.org/kurdi/yasam/182041-harold-pinter-ezilen-halklarin-nobelli-dostu (accessed 18 October 2017).

Gursel, M. (1985), 'Turkey Censors Blast on Rights by 2 Authors', *The Washington Post*, 24 March. Available online: https://www.washingtonpost.com/archive/politics/1985/03/24/turkey-censors-blast-on-rights-by-2-authors/ab907085-0726-4ed9-b6b1-b3ba2a02b55b/?utm_term=.b05dec18c8be (accessed 20 April 2018).

Heawood, J. (2008), 'For Pinter, the Outsider Came First', *The Independent*, 27 December. Available online: https://www.independent.co.uk/voices/commentators/jonathan-heawood-for-pinter-the-outsider-came-first-1212426.html (accessed 22 October 2018).

Hurriyet (1985), 18 March: 1, 13.
Kamm, H. (1985), 'Two Playwrights Deplore Turkish Rights Record', *The New York Times*, 28 March. Available online: https://www.nytimes.com/1985/03/28/world/2-playwrights-deplore-turkish-rights-record.html (accessed 29 June 2017).
Koval, R. (2006), 'An Interview with Harold Pinter', *The Edinburgh International Book Festival*, 1 October. Available online: https://www.abc.net.au/radionational/programs/archived/bookshow/harold-pinter-nobel-prize-winning-playwright-and/3348870#transcript (accessed 25 October 2020).
'Marine Le Pen: Muslims in France "like Nazi occupation"' (2010), *The Telegraph*, 12 December. Available online: https://www.telegraph.co.uk/news/worldnews/europe/france/8197895/Marine-Le-Pen-Muslims-in-France-like-Nazi-occupation.html (accessed 23 April 2020).
Milliyet (1985), 20 March: 1.
Milliyet (1985), 27 March: 1, 7.
Newsnight (2002), [TV programme] 'An Interview with Harold Pinter', BBC2, 24 October.
Pamuk, O. (2006), 'Freedom to Write', *The New York Review of Books*, 25 May. Available online: http://www.nybooks.com/articles/2006/05/25/freedom-to-write/ (accessed 18 April 2018).
Pinter, H. (1990), 'Arthur Miller's Socks', in C. Bigsby (ed.), *Arthur Miller and Company*, 4–5, London: Methuen.
Pinter, H. (2009a), 'Art, Truth and Politics', in *Various Voices: Sixty Years of Prose, Poetry, Politics 1948–2008*, 3rd edn, 285–300, London: Faber and Faber. © The Nobel Foundation.
Pinter, H. (2009b), 'Writing, Politics and *Ashes to Ashes*: An Interview with Harold Pinter', in *Various Voices: Sixty Years of Prose, Poetry, Politics 1948–2008*, 3rd edn, 238–54, London: Faber and Faber.
Pinter, H. (2011), '*Mountain Language*', in *Harold Pinter: Plays 4*, 249–267, London: Faber and Faber.
Pope, H. (1991), 'Turkey Lifts Ban on Speaking of Kurdish', *The Independent*, 13 April: 11.
Sherfinski, D. (2016), 'Donald Trump: "I Think Islam Hates Us"', *The Washington Times*, 10 March. Available online: https://www.washingtontimes.com/news/2016/mar/10/donald-trump-i-think-islam-hates-us/ (accessed 23 April 2020).
Walker, P. (2018), 'Ukip's Gerard Batten Reiterates His Belief That Islam Is a "Death Cult"', *The Guardian*, 18 February. Available online: https://www.theguardian.com/politics/2018/feb/18/ukip-gerard-batten-islam-muslims-quran (accessed 23 April 2020).
'We're Not Celebrating Israel's Anniversary' (2008), *The Guardian*, 30 April. Available online: https://www.theguardian.com/world/2008/apr/30/israelandthepalestinians (accessed 23 June 2018).

Part Two

Pinter as Playwright, Playwrights and Pinter

6

'An insistence in my mind': Pinter's Writing Ethic

Steve Waters

This chapter is a playwright's attempt to identify the specific power and singularity of Harold Pinter's achievement, by means of looking closely at the scattered yet telling accounts of his writing process he offers. In so doing, I challenge Michael Billington's endeavour in his seminal *The Life and Work of Harold Pinter* (1996) to unify Pinter's plays under a legible, humanist rubric. Instead, in order to account for the extraordinary power of his work up until *A Kind of Alaska* (1982), I take him at his word, acknowledging his refusal to explain the mysteries behind his work and his wider repudiation of ideologies beyond it. To that end I track how his aesthetic runs counter to the main currents of British new writing from the 1950s to the 1970s and treat *Old Times* (1971) and *No Man's Land* (1975) as emblematic of this writing ethic, as allegories of his writerly predicament.

On First Looking into Pinter

For many of my generation, coming of age in the 1980s, Pinter provided our first encounter with a living playwright, indeed with the very notion that playwrights might be still alive and at work. I was 16 when I first came across him, his name promising a terrain, a genre even as much as a writer, with a cache of excitement and risk. *The Caretaker* (1960) was recommended to me by my English teacher. I hadn't read any plays other than those by Shakespeare and Webster and was all set to sneer in a punky resistance to what I imagined would be its pretension. The play's effect on me was startling – I was blind-sided by it, shaken by its mysteries. I had no way of *reading* it. It wasn't like the television and films I had consumed. I felt affronted at what I imagined to be the play's emptiness; my petit bourgeois soul felt there to be an absence of available meaning and effect. Very little contemporary theatre made it into that lightless enclave of the Midlands where I grew up; this play seemed to be a message from another star altogether.

The next encounter was when I was an undergraduate at Oxford. There was a much-feted student production of *The Homecoming* (1965). As so often in my life I missed it and, resenting the chatter and the excitement, I got hold of a copy to puncture the hype. I still remember how I felt putting that text down after reading it in one electrified sitting. I was more alive and alert, as if an adrenaline surge had been triggered by the tough, cold laughter the play offers. The implacable logic that takes Ruth into the heart of a wounded male household felt so unarguable that I emerged from the play as if from a dark dream. Pinter noted elsewhere a similar effect on his friend and teacher Joe Brearley who slammed down the manuscript and walked wordlessly to the sea (Batty 2001: 155–6).

It was over a decade before I finally saw the play in Roger Michell's astonishing production for the National Theatre in 1997, performed by Michael Sheen, Keith Allen, David Bradley, Eddie Marsan, Sam Kelly and Lindsay Duncan. We all have our definitive productions of the key Pinter plays, but simply to list those actors is to feel the necessity of this one, the way it effortlessly situated Pinter in the BritPop era. It is one of the greatest experiences of my life. I can still hear Christopher Shutt's sound design calmly marking the sound of Teddy and Ruth's late-night arrival and still see the yawning vastness of William Dudley's design. The material is laden with misogynist tropes, staging potentially hackneyed conflicts – fathers versus sons, brothers sparring over trophy wives – but, as is so often the case with Pinter, he takes an available formal template only to empty it of its usual concerns. *The Homecoming* exhibits all the hallmarks of the default 1960s drama, a boiler-plate Grammar school boy *heimkehr* play full of class niggling and dialectal crackle. Yet set it against analogous contemporary dramas by Dennis Potter, David Storey or David Mercer, wherein socially mobile young men return to excoriate their insular families, *The Homecoming* steps out of such ideologically limited contexts into a space beyond context itself. Peter Hall's sense of the 'piss-take' as the fundamental Pinter gesture is apparent everywhere in the snarling comic jumps and swerves the action takes, with never any attempt made to securely locate us with either brother, father, uncle or wife (Hall 1993: 190). We move from moment to moment locked in immaculate confrontation and a kind of shocking refusal of elucidation, of alibis, confronted and confounded by Pinter's ineluctable voice, his ethic of writing without apology. *The Homecoming*'s very refusal to explain or account for itself epitomizes Pinter's indefatigable defence of the centrality of the playwright in theatre and the autonomy of their task; in the astute words of the critic George E. Wellwarth, it 'represents the quintessence of Pinter's dramaturgy' (Wellwarth 2001: 107).

There are few playwrights who offer such frank reports from a masculine unconscious. Yet puzzlingly Billington's essential and canonical critical biography, *The Life and Work of Harold Pinter*, seems determined to unify of Pinter's work into a politically humanist project, with terrifying works such as *The Homecoming* 'redeemed' as a proto-feminist work (Batty 2001: 65). Surely the sublimity of Pinter's early plays lies precisely in how they sidestep and refute contemporary politics? This very singularity defines Pinter's ethic of playwriting, a dark undiluted regressive intensity that makes his work so rich and strange and quite distinct from the daylight practice of so much contemporary playwriting. And it seems to emerge from the suggestive end state described in *No Man's Land*, 'which never moves, which never changes, but which remains forever, icy and silent' (Pinter 1997a: 399). Too often we have been encouraged not to take Pinter at his word; Billington's attempt to unify his career backwards from the insistent public figure of the 1980s and 1990s belies Pinter's earlier reluctance to explain his own work, his clear horror at the accumulation of commentary induced by his writing and his distaste for what he calls 'ideology'.

'Too much of an individual': Pinter against the Post-War Grain

Perhaps Pinter's enduring power derives from this twenty-year refusal to include the audience. From *The Room* (1957) to *Betrayal* (1978), his plays turn their back on us and remain counter to the spirit of their times, a deep structure of optimism governing what Eric Hobsbawm characterized as the 'Golden Age' between 1950 and 1975: amelioratory, egalitarian, social democratic (Hobsbawm 1996: 225). It is a shock to think of *The Caretaker* or *The Homecoming* as being contemporary with the Beatles or Harold Wilson. Yet now that that era seems behind us, Pinter's dramas have become even more pertinent, not simply as anatomies of power but as expressions of masculine closure. This surely ultimately derives from his biographical trajectory. As an only child Pinter's first imaginative acts were the forging of 'a small body of imaginary friends in the back garden when I was about 8 or 9 […] definitely all boys' (Batty 2001: 5). Later this closed group was re-fashioned with his cadre of mates from Hackney Downs Grammar School, united by their refusals of authority. If the *locus classicus* of much of the work of post-war writers such as David Hare was the so-called 'People's War' (after Angus Calder), for Pinter the trauma of evacuation seems to have offered him the first image of power as an impersonal imposition. Likewise, the warm glow projected back onto the post-war reforming Government of Attlee of 1945–51 is belied by Pinter's experience of anti-Semitic East End fascists shielded by the police. Yet his plays offer little evidence that his Jewish heritage per se presented a counter-weight to such experiences; latterly of course he found himself at odds with his father's Zionism (Billington 1996: 345). It is notable that, until *Ashes to Ashes* (1996), the Holocaust is barely mentioned directly in Pinter's plays (even if it informs the dread underlying *The Birthday Party* (1958)) and how, unlike Arthur Miller or David Mamet, Pinter resisted recasting a play such as *The Homecoming* to speak to a specific Jewish familial context, a decision both Arnold Wesker and Steven Berkoff have challenged (Batty 2001: 109).

Indeed, Pinter's central political act as a young man, his refusal of conscription in 1948 at age 18, was another gesture that put him at odds with the 'benign' socialism of his time or imperatives of community, party, ethnicity. These forces may be seen as displaced into the psychic imperatives embodied by the intrusive Goldberg and McCann in *The Birthday Party*, retaining trace elements of the toxic racism which generated them, but serving only to further define an ethic of apartness. This ethos is confirmed in an article tellingly entitled 'Writing for Myself' in 1961 which, in the age of existentialism, roll-neck sweaters and Jean-Paul Sartre's injunction to be *engage*, fearlessly proclaims, 'I'm not committed as a writer [...] not conscious of any particular social function' (Pinter 1996a: x). Of all the long litany of fates outlined by Goldberg and McCann, the former's threat of 'you'll be integrated' (Pinter 1996b: 78) is perhaps the most chilling and apposite, redolent of the normative psychological behaviourism of the age. Equally the gurgling gibberish that then issues from Stanley is prompted by a demand for his 'opinion', something neither he nor his author were prepared to offer (78). Was that coyness, non-conformity or a refusal to show forth a self? It certainly defined the fate of Pinter's early work as an outlier of the English stage. A stand-off with the Oxbridge director of that first production, Peter Wood confirms the gap between Pinter and his peers. Wood, like Goldberg, wanted Stanley to articulate his position; Pinter rejoined, 'Stanley *cannot* perceive his only valid justification – which is he is what he is – therefore he certainly can never be articulate about it' (Pinter 2009a: 22; emphasis in original). Note here that riposte barely amounts to a justification, more a visceral refusal to justify. As he later comments to Mel Gussow in 1988: 'Between you and me, the play showed how the bastards [...] how religious forces ruin our lives. But who's going to say that in the play? That would be impossible' (qtd. in Gussow 1994: 71).

No Room at the Court: Pinter and the English Stage Company

Understanding Pinter's divergence from the heroic days of post-war English theatre further pins down his singularity. The flowering of the British stage as a home for new writing is evident in the efforts of directors such as George Devine crafting a benign theatrical environment in which to 'develop' it. Pinter's dissent or exclusion from such collaborative consensual processes is apparent from the outset. As an actor he was rejected after auditioning for Michel Saint-Denis and Devine's Group Company at the Old Vic; as his girlfriend of the time Dilys Hamlett tellingly notes, '[T]he school was run on group principles and Harold was felt to be too much of an individual' (Batty 2001: 36). He was similarly ill at ease in RADA because of its middle-class nature but equally because of his resistance to the workshop ethos. No ensembles, no sacrificing of the self for the unity of the theatrical moment for Pinter, who famously learned his craft with stubbornly maverick actor-managers like Anew McMaster and Donald Wolfit, themselves the tail end of a tradition of an English stage which disavowed 'process' and overt technique.

And it is not as if Pinter wasn't aware of this new context for playwriting; after all, he played Cliff in a regional revival of *Look Back in Anger* (1956) and under-studied for N. F. Simpson and John Osborne plays at the Royal Court. Yet there's little evidence Pinter ever sent his plays there and less likelihood. Certainly, despite the initiating experience of his friend Henry Woolf's prompt to write *The Room* or his experiences at the BBC, the idea of being *commissioned* to write, of the genesis of his work arising extrinsically, was an anathema to him. Yet the commission was intrinsic to the Court and has become the given institutional practice of British new writing ever since. It embodies a kind of Welfare State approach to theatre, interventionist, redistributing opportunity, the theatre acting in lieu of the state, distributing gifts and engineering outcomes. The English Stage Company's point of origin speaks to this problem or this lack; famously, the first call from the Court drew a great deal of blanks, with Devine taking it upon himself to create as much as discover his new writers. Witness, for example, the cultivation of novelists such as Angus Wilson or Nigel Dennis as the forgers of this new aesthetic, side by side with Devine's sustenance of a quite different new writing of a European lineage: Eugène Ionesco, Samuel Beckett, Jean Anouilh. The happy discovery of *Look Back in Anger* seemed to trigger a new momentum and a new desire. In fact, as Dan Rebellato (1999: 1–9) notes, this was a piece of persistent myth-making; the displaced and defeated residuum of Terence Rattigan and Noël Coward, or even T. S. Eliot infected the dramaturgy of Osborne and the Court as much as it transcended it with new social contents. Yet it is hard to imagine Pinter coming out of that stable: 'script without decor', the workshop ethos of Keith Johnstone or across town, the different Brechtian inflections of Joan Littlewood. The notion of the pet writer at the centre of a culture of development (the Court) or as a jester in the midst of an ensemble (Littlewood) makes Pinter's achievement entirely incomprehensible.

It is surely significant that until *Ashes to Ashes* had its British premiere during Stephen Daldry's tenure in 1996, no Pinter play received its debut at the Court, yet his work reveals the archetypes of that scene. I would not be the first person to recognize that Stanley in *The Birthday Party* is a sort of anti-Jimmy Porter, marooned in digs, yet incapable of Porter's glib tirades. Stanley is hardly an angry young man, even if he fits the demographic. When Goldberg and McCann appear, it is as if Archie Rice and a renegade from a Brendan Behan play rock-up. Is it in some ways, then, an unwitting satire on the dreams of duffle-coated CND marchers of the New Left as much as anything? It is also striking how little sympathy the denizens of the Court felt for Pinter's work. In a generally positive account of *The Caretaker*, its poster boy, John Arden, felt obliged to take Aston's speech about electroconvulsive therapy to task: 'If it's true why isn't Mr Pinter writing that serious social play to denounce the cruelty prevalent in mental hospitals?' (Arden 1960: 30). Precisely because Pinter refused the very premises of 'the serious social play' that has been the mainstay of the Court ever since, his work set against its implicit social instrumentality.

West End Boy: Pinter and the Repertoire

Thanks to the producer Michael Codron, Pinter begins his career in the blank spaces of the West End where failure is remorseless and there is no supporting context to offer protection – no 'right to fail' here! The harrowing experience of the premiere of *The Birthday Party* in 1958 places Pinter at the centre of a theatre culture which, from thereon in, had little idea of what he or his work was about. That a major period in his career occurred in collaboration with the late Peter Hall, then, seems highly significant but equally odd. After all, Pinter's gnomic modernity sits uneasily alongside the values of Hall's Royal Shakespeare Company (RSC) with its Brechtian urgencies and company ethos. Billington notes the hostility of the RSC's artistic team, Peter Brook and John Barton in particular, to Hall's wish to stage *The Homecoming*

(Billington 1996: 175). They understandably protest that any contemporary work in that repertoire should offer a latter-day version of the Shakespearian tradition, a response to Brecht, not 'a very tight East End domestic drama', a world away from the centrality of the history plays as a core statement of Hall's epic vision (Batty 2001: 175).

The transition then with Hall into the National Theatre paradoxically continues Pinter's immaculate isolation marooned on his own theatrical 'no man's land' apart from the currents of new work elsewhere on the British stage. Given the present volume's concerns with networks and collaboration, this may seem a perverse formulation; clearly there are passionate and sustained working relationships in Pinter's career, but largely intimate ones with specific directors: Hall, Joseph Losey, David Leveaux. Nevertheless, it is impossible to imagine him sitting with Max Stafford-Clark in the merry mêlée of the Joint Stock rehearsal room, just as it is inconceivable that he might turn out a modernized version of a Brecht play. For example, he was notably, if Hall's diaries are to be believed, hostile to Howard Brenton's work (Hall 1983: 412). Indeed, the defining impact of Brecht on British post-war theatre, however unevenly manifested, seems to have entirely passed Pinter by. In an interview with Billington in 2006 at the point of his reception of the Nobel Prize, Pinter commented: 'Yes, Brecht was very important to me to read and I greatly admire his poetry' (Pinter 2006). Yet that influence is impossible to discern in his major works which offer a sustained refusal to contemplate history in its immediate forms, let alone solidarity or economism. More importantly even Pinter's political works eschew anything resembling Brecht's aesthetic. Instead, his dramaturgy resembles the crumbling West End piles within which so much of his work began, retaining the supporting structures of Aristotelian form only to dismantle them to reveal what Larkin called 'the solving emptiness / That lies just under all we do' (Larkin 1964: 33).

Pinter's aesthetic affiliations in writing for the stage are to a pre-modernist English stage of mid-century stagecraft; his plays breathe the trapped air of the West End with its oddly anachronistic spirit. His forays into directing are equally telling in this respect – Jean Giraudoux, a comradely attachment to the boulevard work of Simon Gray, ventures into James Joyce and David Mamet and, wonderfully, Noël Coward and his production of *Blithe Spirit* (1941) (Pinter to the cast: 'Coward calls this an improbable farce [...] I do regard it as improbable and I do not regard it as a farce' (Batty 2001: 72)). With the exception of Giraudoux, it is an entirely Anglo-Saxon repertoire, in contrast with Pinter's passionate engagement with European modernism in his reading.

Leaving Clues for Yourself: Pinter's Process

What's striking through all this is the sheer consistency of Pinter's creative process which begins with the genesis of *The Room*, 'written in 4 days':

> I started at the top and at a certain point there was a knock at the door and someone came in and I had absolutely no idea who he was, who he might be or what he might say. I let it run, let it happen and found he did have a voice and that he was the landlord.
>
> (Pinter qtd. in Batty 2001: 72)

What's notable here is the disavowal of any planning or plotting and the sheer refusal to know more than the characters know, to conceive of back stories or concepts. Pinter resists processes most contemporary dramatists undertake as a matter of course. His methodology yields a headlong process of invention mirroring the very tale it tells. This naked playwriting, deriving its impetus from the foundational image, is pregnant with possibility. It is also inherently scenic, as if no moment or event can be imagined in advance, forcing the imagination into the grain of the moment. As Leveaux noted:

> I think when he's writing a play there's almost an unchecked open channel between his unconscious and the page. When he finishes that process, the door closes in some way and he is something of a stranger to the work itself.
>
> (qtd. in ibid. 108)

Note those open and shut doors; the imaginative act is spatially conceived. Pinter may rewrite within that interval of time but never dares to go back and tamper, to 'wring the play's neck' once more, as he puts it (qtd. in Gussow 1994: 59-60). It is worth comparing this with a natural reviser like Brecht whose filing cabinet bulged with drafts of his work. Pinter's protectiveness of that initial moment of invention extends to his resistance to subsequent interpretation and elucidation. He is the least *intellectual* writer for the stage; his work is of course fiercely intelligent, but to be intellectual is to reflect, and reflection seems an anathema to him.

This writing ethic is movingly expressed in his speech on the acceptance of the German Shakespeare Prize in Hamburg in 1970; it is rare to find Pinter as confessional as he appears to be here. He notes that the 'dangers of speaking in public' derive from the constant risk of adding to the creation of the public 'Harold Pinter': 'I don't know the man they're talking about. I know the plays, but in a totally different way, in a quite private way' (Pinter 2009b: 48–9). Here he reveals his plays' essentially private, even inviolable nature. Later in the speech Pinter alludes to the theatre-making process, but he disavows any theoretical vantage point, describing rehearsal wonderfully as 'a kind of stumbling, erratic shorthand, through which facts are lost, collided with, fumbled, found again' (49), a private realm of painfully achieved public meaning. The reaching for theatrical facts, 'legitimate and compulsory facts', leads him to outline his inner aesthetic: the search for a truth that must be 'scrupulously protected', to achieve a 'necessary shape' (49–50).

The evident affinity here with poetry is critical to understanding Pinter's process; his aesthetic might be compared with the imagist imperative of Ezra Pound or William Carlos Williams with the latter's injunction for 'no ideas but in things': 'I can sum up none of my plays. I can describe none of them, except to say: That is what happened' (52). The speech is full of pain and fear and difficulty: finding a bulwark against mendacity, secondary thinking, cliché, half-truth, evident in his sideswipe at 'group theatre' which presents 'sweat and assault and noise' but is underpinned by 'nothing but valueless generalizations' (52). This develops a credo outlined first in a piece for *Cambridge University Magazine* in 1958 and reiterated in a speech made in 1962 at the National Student Drama Festival in Bristol:

> The more acute the experience, the less articulate the expression ... To supply an explicit moral tag to an evolving and compulsive dramatic image seems to me facile, impertinent and dishonest [...] no conflict between audience and play, no participation, nothing has been exposed. We walk out as we went in.
>
> (Pinter qtd. in Billington 1996: 94)

Here again we see his resistance to glib craft, critical exegesis and his underlying commitment to an abrasive relationship between 'play and audience', with truth emerging through conflict. The idea of theatre as an act of exposure wherein the truth lies hidden is crucial again to the potency of his work. Channelling Wallace Stevens, he announces the aim of achieving 'an evolving and compulsive dramatic image' free of superimposed secondary meaning (Pinter 1996c: x). That phrase, for all Pinter's aversion to accounting for himself, is astute. Part of the force and mystery that keeps his work alive is inherent in its implied organicism, the growth of a play rooted in a primary image that is unstable and is in motion.

This surely accounts for the astonishing grip of *The Homecoming*, the play Pinter most often acknowledged to be closest to this idea of 'necessary shape'. Peter Stein accounts for its effect as that of 'a play-machine at work' (qtd. in Billington 1996: 178). That mechanical image – or in Wellwarth's designation its 'nuclear structure' (2001: 105) – goes some way to account for the play's irresistible force which seems beyond intentionality, both of writer and of character. Again and again in Pinter's best work, the hackneyed question 'who is the protagonist' proves impossible to answer. It is hard to imagine a Pinter play named after a character; in the main they take the name of a space or a process before giving way to abstract nouns. *The Homecoming* is less a story, and more of an event, a collective transformation, which no one seems to govern and which could not be imagined in advance – if a single moment of the play felt willed or calculated in the way most plays invariably do, nothing within it would work. This is why critiquing it for its misogyny or recuperating it for its feminism is a category error.

There is a useful clue to his work's mysterious birth in the same talk to the National Student Drama Festival:

> You arrange *and* you listen following the clues you leave for yourself through the characters. And sometimes a balance is found, where image can freely engender image and at the same time you are able to keep your sights on the place where the characters are silent and in hiding. It is in the silence that they are most evident to me.
> (Pinter 1996c: xiii; emphasis in original)

This is an eloquent self-analysis which foregrounds interactions between conscious craft and unconscious discovery; perhaps Pinter's refusal to construct 'wilful' characters ready to unleash action derives from his own modest account of his creative process. While the discourse of character creation can be precious, it is also instructive. When pressed on his writing and drafting process, Pinter frequently talks of a play emerging in days and then being consolidated within a month. Billington offers us details of the differing drafts of, say, *The Homecoming* with a shift from lines unattached to a given character or context to the precise world of family belligerence that ultimately emerged. This process of consolidation is surely what the younger Pinter refers to in his notion of arranging and listening, of paradoxically 'leaving clues for yourself'. There seems to be a primary state of finding material, immortalized in those epiphanies he speaks of that span his career – the moment in the taxi that begot *No Man's Land*, running up three flights of his Regents Park house to begin *Old Times* – wherein first lines open up an image and an event, lines that are nearly always performative: an invitation to a drink, 'As it is?' as Hirst asks in the former (Pinter 1997a: 321), or the guided visualization in the latter:

Kate (*Reflectively*) Dark.

Deely Fat or thin? (Pinter 1997b: 245)

'In the desert': *Old Times* and *No Man's Land* as Allegories of Writing

Pinter's imaginative process is quite often enacted or allegorized in his plays. *Old Times* is a particularly clear case in point: the emergence of Anna resembles this notion of a creative seeking out, a reaching into 'the place where the characters are silent and in hiding' (Pinter 1996c: xiii). As if in an exorcism, Kate and Deely bring her into being from her stance with her back to the audience in their opening catechism. If the play is seen from Deeley's vantage, it enacts this troublesome process of images engendering themselves and indeed the very irrefragability of character, whether present in memory or through re-enactment. Deeley's insistent questions to Kate and Anna resemble the author gnawed away at by 'the insistence of [his] mind', Kate offering up clues to her own intractable past and self, Anna erupting into the action to bring the past gushing onto the stage, at which point we are, without comment, into the hoped-for scene. Image engenders image; the verbal gives way to the visual. If we can read Deeley as the playwright (after all he is the director, as he jokes, 'I wrote the film and directed it. My name is Orson Welles' (Pinter 1997b: 280)), the action enacts the usurpation of his function; the usurpation of the playwright's function is effected by *the play*.

Anna and Deeley then compete to control the ineffable Kate; they battle to, as it were, write her. Anna's accounts of her are contested or endorsed by Deeley who notes, 'I couldn't have put it better myself' (273). Kate then turns away, resists this naming, this writing: 'You talk of me as if I was dead' (272–3). Deeley's retreat into tears and impotence by the close only confirms his marginalization from the act of storytelling, superseded by Kate as she is finally goaded out of her own hiding place. In some ways the gradual shedding of naturalistic appurtenances preceding this play, the shift into abstraction marked by *Landscape* (1968) and *Silence* (1969), makes more excruciating the struggle to 'engender images' out of the ensuing spatial vacuum. Much of the battling of *Old Times* is over the gifts of imagination, disputed fragments of memory, little islets of concrete concern: the screening of *Odd Man Out* (1947), the Wayfarers Tavern, scenes that loom out of a vacuum. When there is so little present to play with, a dearth of action and immediate event, the products of the imagination take on an almost supernatural power.

Without overplaying this, I suspect a similar laying bare of the device accounts for the critical role *No Man's Land* plays in Pinter's oeuvre. It is worth acknowledging his angry dismissal of the characterization of the 1970s as a drought of 'writer's block'; in truth his output across several media kept him busy in all decades of his career. But as he notes in Hamburg at the beginning of that decade, being bereft of a play, of that insistence, which he describes as his current predicament, is a state of pain: 'When you can't write you feel you've been banished from yourself' (Pinter 2009b: 52). This de-territorialized image is apt when we think of *No Man's Land*, conjuring up Hirst's predicament trapped in his dark Hampstead fastness. Marooned in the airless task of adapting F. Scott Fitzgerald for the screen and in a taxi, for Pinter, the first line emerged:

> I had the image of two people standing up in a room and one offering the drink [...] I was thrust into a situation where they knew more about it than I did. So I had to find out, I had to pursue it [...] the *donnee*, the given fact. If I don't have that, I'm in the desert.
>
> (qtd. in Batty 2001: 417)

This play, then, is a confrontation with the primal scene of Pinter's imagination: the ruined house of mid-century English theatre within which he learned his craft. The casting of John Gielgud and Ralph Richardson for the first production is hardly accidental; the world and aesthetic of the play was a resurgence into the midst of the 1970s nationalized social democratic art, of the wreck of the theatre it displaced, stuck in dead conventions and settings, cast in a literary language of the 1930s. If *Old Times* is a confrontation with the personal sources of his gift, *No Man's Land* feeds off the inner theatrical form it takes, voided of urbane glitter. There are few plays as excitingly morbid as this.

The entire absence of women too, after their triumph in *Old Times*, seems significant: this sterile quartet of men embody the recurring homosociality that defines Pinter's work – as if, in Briggs and Foster, Lenny and Teddy gate-crashed into the genteel social withdrawal. Billington remarks that after he described the play to Pinter as a projection of his 'darkest fears', Pinter gnomically replied, 'there'd never been a Briggs and Foster in [his] life protecting him from the outside world' (245). Yet at least three of the four characters conceive of themselves as writers; where in their midst is Pinter to be found? The four men offer a kind of psychomachia, playing out the versions of self that Pinter has to draw on: Hirst, trapped, sodden in drink, facing the past; Spooner, a fragile, wheedling arriviste; Foster, a coat-hanging talent of a secondary order; and the necessary Briggs, that recurrent figure of violent philistinism that tends to generate the laughter and the fear in so much of Pinter's work. Hirst's paralysis is central, embodied in his role as gate-keeper and critic, stymied by his paralysing superego, failing to re-animate the sources of his art, the figures in his photograph albums that Briggs declares, 'They're blank, mate, blank. The blank dead' (Pinter 1997a: 383). Spooner, the interloper syndrome embodied, re-animates him at least, forming an image of bohemian indigence, blagging and ligging, name-dropping and embroidering. Spooner's spiel is snobbery and chauvinism, the dry well of English national identity and sentiment: 'All we have left is the English language. Can it be salvaged?' (324).

Again, Pinter's process is laid bare here: Hirst's silence generates Spooner's free associations; echoing Davies filling up the vacuum created by Aston, Spooner offers a talking cure that allows the detritus of the English imagination to be purged and called out, the endless recourse to emptied out nostalgic cliché, 'We share something. A memory of the bucolic life. We're both English' (335). Such allusions always have a grotesque freight and the deracinated and de-territorialized figures of Davies and Spooner seem totemic for Pinter, brutally evacuated to Cornwall and Norfolk. Spooner's audit of these tropes seems as much a kind of saturation therapy leading to Hirst's collapse; when he returns revivified he's in his more official mode, defended by his protectors, less vulnerable, more urbane: 'I came round to human beings in the end' (350). His second collapse as he seeks to assert a past and uncover the *donnée* of his dream of a man drowning leaves the stage for Briggs's and Foster's mercantilist view of art: 'It's the cloth bell-pull. It's organisation' (355). The direst fate for a writer is to be a world-facing commodity overseen by financial advisers.

This frank self-excavation is perhaps the endgame of Pinter's creative journey, the last gasp of that very singularity he worked out of and defined. Thereafter a more publically motivated, extrinsic project took place. That house of the play perhaps defines the end state of his true project and its terminal risks – the writer trapped in his very process, the world reduced to threat and charade. All of this is by way of saying Pinter's work is unique, his example is exemplary. His great plays, like chimeras, inviting you in and keeping you out at once; repetition does not exhaust them, they remain bottomless with mystery, yet neither are they prey to the fey or the whimsical. For me, the diminished artistic power of his work in his later career derives from his honourable submission to the idea of the citizen-playwright which he spent the first half of his career keeping rigorously at bay. As he became more agreeable, more readable, more 'clear', his works became legible and locked in to their moment. No matter. The power of his work still defines what theatre might be and what playwrights might still do.

Works Cited

Arden, J. (1960), 'The Caretaker', *New Theatre Magazine*, 4: 29–30.
Batty, M. (2001), *Harold Pinter*, Plymouth: Northcote House.
Billington, M. (1996), *The Life and Work of Harold Pinter*, London: Faber and Faber.
Gussow, M. (1994), *Conversations with Pinter*, New York: Grove.
Hall, P. (1983), *Peter Hall's Diaries*, J. Goodwin (ed.), London: Hamish Hamilton.
Hall, P. (1993), *Making an Exhibition of Myself*, London: Sinclair-Stevenson.
Hobsbawm, E. (1996), *The Age of Extremes: A History of the World, 1914–1991*, London: Vintage.
Larkin, P. (1964), *The Whitsun Weddings*, London: Faber and Faber.
Pinter, H. (1996a), 'Writing for Myself', in *Harold Pinter: Plays 2*, vii–xi, London: Faber and Faber.
Pinter, H. (1996b), 'The Birthday Party', in *Harold Pinter: Plays 1*, 1–81, London: Faber and Faber.
Pinter, H. (1996c), 'Introduction: Writing for the Theatre', in *Harold Pinter: Plays 1*, vii–xvi, London: Faber and Faber.
Pinter, H. (1997a), 'No Man's Land', in *Harold Pinter: Plays 3*, 315–399, London: Faber and Faber.
Pinter, H. (1997b), 'Old Times', in *Harold Pinter: Plays 3*, 243–313, London: Faber and Faber.
Pinter, H. (2006), 'I've Written 29 Damn Plays. Isn't That Enough?', *The Guardian*, 14 March. Available online: https://www.theguardian.com/stage/2006/mar/14/theatre.stage (accessed 25 June 2018).
Pinter, H. (2009a), 'On *The Birthday Party* I', in *Various Voices: Prose, Poetry, Politics 1948–2008*, 3rd edn, 20–4, London: Faber and Faber.
Pinter, H. (2009b), 'On Being Awarded the German Shakespeare Prize in Hamburg', in *Various Voices: Prose, Poetry, Politics 1948–2008*, 3rd edn, 48–52, London: Faber and Faber.
Rebellato, D. (1999), *1956 and All That: The Making of Modern British Drama*, London: Routledge.
Wellwarth, G. E. (2001), 'The Dumb Waiter, The Collection, The Lover, and The Homecoming: A Revisionist Approach', L. Gordon (ed.), *Pinter at 70: A Casebook*, 95–108, London: Routledge.

7

Beyond the Mainstage: Harold Pinter at the Royal Shakespeare Company

Catriona Fallow

In a letter to the Royal Shakespeare Company's (RSC) chairman, Sir Fordham Flower, dated 17 June 1966, Harold Pinter expressed both his gratitude and regret that he was unable to accept a position to serve on the company's board of governors (Pinter 1966). In restating his fondness for the RSC and admiration for the company's founding artistic director, Peter Hall, Pinter was careful to explain that to take up such a position, and to honour the role by giving it the time and commitment it would require, would be to risk both the time and scope to do what the world had come to know him for best: writing (ibid.). This articulation of what Pinter considered to be his chief occupation, tempered by an implicit grasp of the rigours of theatrical administration, speaks to the competing imperatives that drove Pinter, creatively and professionally, during his multifaceted, polymathic career as not only a writer for stage, screen and radio but also a director, actor and advocate. That Pinter was even offered the role of governor at this stage of his career is testament to his growing significance in Britain's theatrical landscape during the 1960s and, specifically, his work with the RSC during the company's first decade.

This letter, and the offer that precipitated it, came at a time when the RSC was still consolidating its identity, practices and structure as a company, and while Pinter's career and status were accelerating rapidly. By 1966, the RSC had already staged three major Pinter works in its London venue, the Aldwych: *The Collection* (1961) in 1962, co-directed by Pinter and Hall, *The Birthday Party* (1958) in 1964, directed by Pinter, and Hall's world premiere of *The Homecoming* in 1965 which would become a landmark production, going on to garner numerous accolades in the UK, on Broadway and, later, as a film in 1973. The company then went on to premiere three other Pinter plays on stage: *Landscape* and *Silence* in 1969 and *Old Times* in 1971.[1] While *Old Times* was in production at the Aldwych, Pinter directed his third RSC production, *Exiles* (1919) by James Joyce. Over nine years, the RSC was responsible for what are still considered to be some of the most significant examples of Pinter's work for the stage as both a writer and a director.

What is less documented and discussed are the small, fleeting instances of Pinter's work for the RSC that took place not on the company's main London stage but as part of their smaller, short-lived initiatives that sought to engage new audiences, particularly those beyond London and Stratford-upon-Avon. These lesser-known productions of Pinter's work at the RSC offer a new perspective on Pinter's collaboration with one of Britain's leading theatrical institutions and an opportunity to reflect on the versatility of Pinter's writing in contrasting contexts during this crucial decade for British theatre. They also serve to emphasize the plurality and significance of the different working practices employed by the RSC early in its history and to underscore the role of new work by contemporary writers like Pinter to the company's emerging identity and practice.

This chapter reappraises the current discourses on Pinter's relationship with the RSC, and Hall specifically, in order to situate the different imperatives that underpinned both mainstage and community-focused engagement initiatives where Pinter's work appeared. Reflecting on how Pinter's own formative experiences of regional touring as an actor shaped the dramaturgy and portability of his plays, this chapter goes on to consider two key examples of small-scale stagings of Pinter's work at the RSC: Actors Commando's *How to Stop Worrying and Love the Theatre* in 1966 (performed live and as part of a televised BBC broadcast) and Theatregoround's regional touring production of *The Dumb Waiter* (1959) in 1967. By focusing on Actors Commando and Theatregoround's shared imperative to engage audiences in ways that went beyond the RSC's primary repertoire in Stratford and London, this chapter concludes by considering the role these productions had in shaping public perceptions of the accessibility of Pinter's work, while simultaneously consolidating and validating the writer's canonical status.

Mainstage Success: Pinter and Hall

Pinter and Hall's professional collaboration and friendship is a key part of any account of either practitioner's career and forms the cornerstone of the majority of current studies of Pinter's work with the RSC. Despite his initial interest, Hall was unavailable to direct the first productions of *The Birthday Party* in 1958 and *The Caretaker* in 1960 before assuming his role at the RSC. He would, however, go on to direct every major stage premiere of Pinter's work for the next two decades.[2] Both men referred to the significance of one another's work numerous times throughout their careers, with

Pinter reportedly describing Hall as 'the director of my dreams' and Hall confirming that 'I've never worked with any dramatist in my life where I knew so instinctively what he was driving at and what it was he wanted. [...] I found a great deal from him as a writer and I think he found a great deal from me as a director' (Billington 1996: 149, 140). Critics and scholars have similarly continued to emphasize the centrality and symbiosis of this creative partnership to both men's work and careers.[3]

In terms of the impact the pair's working relationship had on the company, one thing that is repeatedly articulated in both Pinter and RSC scholarship is how Pinter's presence helped to realize one of Hall's key ambitions: if the company's remit was to interrogate anew Shakespeare's plays and ways of staging them, Hall believed that it must also pursue a rigorous engagement with the work of contemporary dramatists. This commitment to new work was also vital to attracting the best actors, both new and established, to work with the company long term, actors who, as Flower observed, 'will not these days accept long-term contracts for solely Shakespearean work' (1964). According to former RSC literary manager Colin Chambers, for Hall, securing actors long term was 'the prerequisite for creating a vibrant theatre of reanimated Shakespeare and vital new and modern plays presented in an invigorating symbiosis' (2004: 12–13). In his history of the company, Chambers goes on to suggest that Pinter 'defined the importance of the writer at the early RSC through his partnership with Hall and his own involvement with the company as a director as well as a playwright', describing his plays as 'iconic of RSC new writing' (133). The work of contemporary dramatists like Pinter was therefore fundamental to shaping the company's early identity. However, the decision of a self-declared Shakespearean company to also stage new plays was not without controversy.

The most ubiquitous and widely cited example of the contested position of new work at the RSC during the mid-1960s is the context surrounding the company's productions of *The Birthday Party* in 1964 and *The Homecoming* the following year. Now commonly known as the 'Dirty Plays' scandal, it followed a season of new works at the Aldwych that included Pinter's *The Birthday Party* and which theatre impresario and RSC Governor Emile Littler publicly denounced as a 'programme of dirt plays' (qtd. in Norman 1964).[4] Littler's disavowal of the company's London season sparked heated debate both internally within the RSC and from mainstream commentators and members of the public. Though Pinter and his play were no stranger to critical scrutiny thanks to the early negative responses to *The Birthday Party*'s brief run at the Lyric Hammersmith, London in 1958, the dirty plays controversy was different in that it centred less on the supposed intellectualism and inaccessibility of Pinter's, as well as other writers', work and instead critiqued the work on moral grounds. As one of a number of letters sent by concerned members of the public to Flower following Littler's statement to the press bemoaned, '[M]odern plays seem always to dwell on the sordid side of life and unpleasant people', concluding that 'dirt, for dirt's sake is neither clever nor avant garde' (Strauss 1964). The debate, then, had less to do with any single work and more with what the collective presence of such work represented in the context of a newly subsidised Shakespearean company with the Queen as its patron.

This shaped perceptions of the suitability of future new works, including Pinter's next play, *The Homecoming*. As Mark Taylor-Batty notes:

> When *The Homecoming* arrived in their mail, the [RSC] board members would have viewed it in the context of this history of subversive material and the reputation they sought for the still young company. They disapproved of the play and voiced their objection at seeing it enter the repertoire at the Aldwych. Hall listened to their concerns and went ahead regardless.
>
> (2005: 43)

However, it was not just the RSC Board who were ambivalent or resistant to Pinter's latest play. In his memoir, *Making an Exhibition of Myself*, Hall recalls his colleagues' initial responses: 'Peter Brook thought the play too small for the large spaces of the Aldwych. So did John Barton. Michel St Denis felt that it was not poetic enough. Clifford Williams and Trevor Nunn were less specific, but neither said anything to stop the strong tide of objection' (2000: 200). Pinter, too, had concerns about the suitability of his work for the Aldwych stage. In his discussion of directing Pinter, Hall recounts how the writer was 'worried initially by the largeness of the stage. Would it have sufficient claustrophobia, sufficient tension? The "open living area" came from responding to the strengths of the wide stage. So the Aldwych, in some sense, provided the image of *The Homecoming*' (2001: 151). The subsequent widespread success of this production, then, offers a clear example of how writing for the RSC's mainstage presented unique challenges and opportunities for Pinter and which, in turn, shaped the play.[5]

Brook's objection and Pinter's initial hesitation concerning the size of the Aldwych, however, also serve to underscore the suitability of Pinter's works for smaller-scale productions and, in the context of a newly established and still underfunded repertory company like the RSC, the attendant financial benefits. With a cast of just six in *The Homecoming*, four in *The Collection*, two in *Landscape*, three in *Silence* and three in *Old Times*, and all set in single-location interior spaces, Pinter's best-known works with the company presented both artistic and practical advantages. As Jamie Andrews observes,

> Not only did Pinter add to the lustre of Hall's ambitions for the RSC to stage challenging new work, but his small casts were also financially attractive to the company's management in comparison to major Shakespeare revivals. As Hall admitted in a letter […] 'Plays like *The Homecoming* are, in fact, a great help to us. They do not cost as much to do, they relieve our company on some nights, as they have small casts, and their modern interest is such that they boost our general Box Office take.'
>
> (2012: 171)

But the suitability of Pinter's work for RSC's stages, its role in shaping and realizing the company's core principles and ideologies and its potential audience appeal were not limited to the Aldwych stage during the 1960s. While widely publicized media battles about the validity of certain new works at the RSC raged in the mainstream press at the same time as *The Homecoming* continued to garner critical acclaim, a different strand of RSC programming was beginning to emerge away from the company's mainstages. In the following sections, I move away from the dominant narratives and examples of Pinter's affiliation with the RSC in order to offer a more complete picture of the range of contexts in which his work appeared – and to what purpose – during the 1960s.

Juxtaposing Pinter: *How to Stop Worrying and Love the Theatre* (1966)

Organized and implemented by director and writer Michael Kustow in 1965, Actors Commando – as it was provisionally named before being rebranded as Theatregoround – initially comprised a group of four Stratford-based RSC actors. Though short-lived, the very name suggests a force on the move with direct, perhaps even insurgent action – a 'commando' being a solider specially trained to carry out raids. In this case, however, rather than 'parachuting in' to conflict, these RSC company members sought to intervene directly in audiences' local milieux in order to 'overcome the socially divisive protocols of theatre-going' by touring 'a thirty-minute programme of excerpts from Shakespeare and other writing' to 'local halls and workers' canteens, followed by a talk with the audience afterwards' (Chambers 2004: 41-2).

As the initiative grew following these initial performances, its ideological ambitions became even more explicit. In the summer of 1965 an article for the RSC's members' magazine, *Flourish* (of which Kustow was the founding editor), insisted that in order to reach new audiences,

> [t]heatre publicity in the 'quality' Press is not enough; it does not reach the people we want to meet. In this situation the first move must come from the theatre-people themselves. This entire project is based on the wager that by going out and offering themselves and their work, theatre-people can help to cross the barriers that exist.
>
> (1965)

Based on his earlier experiences with Théâtre National Populaire in France, where the emphasis was on 'getting the best social mix in an audience, not necessarily the biggest crowd', for Kustow, mobility was key to offering audiences 'a taste' of theatre (qtd. in Lawson 1975: 80). The imperative, then, fell on the organization to be mobile – rather than its audiences – in order to provide access to those who perhaps would not normally encounter the company's work. However, in the case of Actors Commando, and later Theatregoround, the emphasis was initially not placed on a specific show but on the *idea* of theatregoing itself.

Later, in the autumn of 1965, Kustow developed the concept further by creating *Theatregoround*, a touring production in which six RSC actors – Michelle Dotrice, Gabrielle Hamilton, Paul Hardwick, Davyd Harries, Michael Jayston and Richard Moore – offered audiences what Kustow described as 'a misguided, lunatic and yet rather worthwhile attempt to tell the history of the theatre in an hour and half' (81). This pilot programme, dubbed *How to Stop Worrying and Love the Theatre*, consisted of a condensed selection of material from Sophocles, Aristophanes, Shakespeare, Molière, Victorian melodrama and Pinter. Initially performed in a number of London boroughs, John Wyver describes how at the time the initiative was 'sufficiently novel for the idea to be taken up by the BBC for a programme in its *Sunday Night* strand of arts features' (2019: 57).

Wyver offers an overview of the fifty-minute-long programme broadcast on 20 February 1966, noting that the footage was shot 'primarily with electronic cameras by a mobile outside broadcast unit at Rutherford School, Paddington' (57). Following an introduction from the host, René Cutforth, commentary from Hall and insights into a rehearsal session with Kustow and the actors, the programme presents a selection of performance extracts, including a scene from *The Birthday Party*. The scene is played on a small, hexagonal, slightly raised stage with a free-standing curtain rail behind with the curtains drawn open to reveal production paraphernalia, such as lighting equipment. Three actors enter the playing area from the back of the space, dressed in non-descript dark trousers and long-sleeved sweaters. These don't appear to be costumes per se but rather 'everyday clothes' (58). The only essential item of costuming is a pair of glasses, worn by actor Davyd Harries as Stanley who perches upon a small stool facing out towards an unseen audience, flanked by the other two performers, Richard Moore as Goldberg and Michael Jayston as McCann. The scene begins with Goldberg demanding: '[T]ake off his [Stanley's] glasses' (Pinter 1996: 43).

During the interrogation that ensues, the camera cuts sharply between the actors' faces, capturing the mocking disdain of Moore's Goldberg, the ominous sneering of Jayston's McCann and the darting eyes and sweaty brow of Harries's Stanley. These cuts both complement and intensify the pace of Pinter's already rapid-fire dialogue at this moment in the play. But for the interplay of emotion across the actors' faces and the occasional darting head movements of Stanley as he looks between his interrogators, all three remain almost entirely still for the majority of the scene. This interpretation contrasts with the stage directions in Pinter's original script. There is no '*turning, crouched*' from Stanley as he puzzles, 'What wife?' (ibid.). In the RSC's production he remains seated, facing out towards the audience (or to camera for the viewers at home). When Goldberg asks a second time, 'Why did you kill your wife?', Stanley is not '*sitting, his back to the audience*' (ibid.) but instead only slightly turning his head, eyes wide with surprise. The BBC's recording of the production, particularly the frequent close-ups of Harries's face, leaves no question as to Stanley's increasing distress or confusion and also little potential for ambiguity regarding the power dynamics between the three men. McCann's ensuing exclamation, 'There's your man!' (ibid.), provokes laughter from an audience which sounds live but remains unseen onscreen during this extract. The tension continues to be amplified by the rapidly changing camera angles and the breakneck pace of the dialogue.

When Goldberg, seeming to lose patience, demands, 'Speak up Webber. Why did the chicken cross the road?', Moore's face abruptly appears in shot, close to Harries's as the camera zooms in to a tight close-up on both, sweat visibly shining on Harries's contorted face as he struggles to utter: 'He wanted to – he wanted to – he wanted to...' (Pinter 1996: 45). McCann's interjections are heard off-screen while the camera remains tightly focused on Goldberg and Stanley until, at last, Stanley screams, the camera zooming out again to a wide shot of the trio. Shooting from stage left, next to McCann, the camera captures Goldberg standing up straight while Stanley buries his head in his hands. Goldberg looks across to McCann and intones the scene's final line, 'He doesn't know' (46).

While impossible to speculate about general audiences' responses to this work, in either its live or broadcast iterations, Kustow's own account of the piece goes some way towards describing how the framing and splicing together of these performance extracts was key to enabling audiences to engage with this material:

> [F]rom melodrama [specifically *Under the Gaslight* (1867) by Augustin Daly] we leapt into Pinter and *The Birthday Party*. The audience, all turned on by melodrama, could see, all of a sudden, the very wholesome base of melodrama in Pinter himself. They took *The Birthday Party* without thinking what a hifalutin, philosophical, complex statement it was, and instead saw these two guys working over this poor guy with his spectacles.
>
> (qtd. in Lawson 1975: 81)

The scene's minimalism coupled with the camera's framing of the scene and subtle changes to blocking and stage directions certainly support this reading. The close scrutiny of the actors' faces, the paucity of any traditional, naturalistic theatrical scenography or costuming to connote character or context and no apparent details on who the characters actually are serves to focus the attention on the 'working over' of one man by two others. For Kustow, it is the scene's juxtaposition with melodrama that enables audiences to better connect to the simplicity of the scene and thereby understand Pinter's writing as just one example or fragment of theatrical practice in dialogue with other, older theatrical forms.

This one-off broadcast, however, is unlikely to have been many British viewers' first encounter with *The Birthday Party*, or other examples of Pinter's work, on the small screen. On 22 March 1960, for example, *The Birthday Party* was broadcast in full by the commercial ITV company Associated-Rediffusion, directed by Joan Kemp-Welch, and, according to Andrews, reached 'an estimated 11 million people, and was enthusiastically received by the critics' (161). Moreover, as Jonathan Bignell and William Davies argue, television's role in shaping Pinter's career trajectory and cultivating 'widespread recognition of his distinctive "brand"' was essential and meant that 'his representation of ordinary people and everyday speech was, despite the artifice with which Pinter turned these domestic stories into "menace", an aspect of a cultural current that sought to connect with mass audiences and engage with contemporary experience' (2020: 486). While it may be tempting, then, to agree with Kustow's suggestion that juxtaposing Pinter with melodrama enabled the audience to better comprehend the play, British audiences' familiarity with Pinter – and *The Birthday Party* specifically – on the small screen must also be accounted for.

What Kustow's emphasis on the benefits of juxtaposing Pinter with earlier theatrical forms does usefully direct attention to are Pinter's earliest professional engagements in theatre as an actor appearing primarily in touring repertory companies. Performing as part of Anew McMaster's company in Ireland from September 1951 until early 1953, followed by three months under contract with Donald Wolfit's company at the King's Theatre Hammersmith in London, Pinter continued to appear in regional repertory theatres across the UK until 1957 (performing under the name David Baron).[6] During this time, he was exposed to a wide-ranging repertoire and a variety of theatrical genres from comedy and tragedy, to drawing room comedies and thrillers. As William Baker notes, 'All the while, Pinter was learning stage techniques which reappear in his subsequent work', offering the example of Mary Hayley Bell's *The Uninvited Guest* (1953), in which Pinter appeared in April 1955 and which 'contains a key interrogation scene [where] [a]n escaped mental patient performed by Pinter has his back to the audience. He is fiercely questioned by the other characters', thereby linking this to the scene in Pinter's *The Birthday Party* (2008: 35). Writing on the influence of these early experiences of repertory more broadly on Pinter's practice, Michael Billington has described how the 'grinding system [was] hardly conducive to psychological probing or intellectual agonising; which is why Pinter, however meticulous a director, has always been suspicious of too much theorising' (1996: 50). Kustow's pairing of Pinter with melodrama as an aesthetic experiment and his attention to the effect of such a juxtaposition offers another, richer way to understand how Pinter eschewed conceptual or 'hifalutin' theorizing in his own work and how his own acting experiences on the road informed his writing for the stage.

It is now widely agreed among Pinter scholars that there is a 'close connection between Pinter's writing and acting' (Gussow 2001: 257). To explore this connection further, I turn now to another example of Pinter's work 'on the move' for the RSC – a full-length production of *The Dumb Waiter* – that both echoes and evolves the ideas, aesthetics and ambitions initiated in *How to Stop Worrying and Love the Theatre*.

Portable Pinter: *The Dumb Waiter* (1967)

Kustow's initial vision for the RSC's mobile unit was officially 're-devised, re-staffed and re-titled' (Kemp 1968) as Theatregoround on 1 November 1966 following an anonymous donation of £10,000.[7] Now under the directorship of Terry Hands, who had joined the company in July that year, Theatregoround operated primarily out of a red double-decker bus, touring Britain with a portable stage, mobile exhibition and box office. Its work was similarly motivated by a desire to reach out to regional, non-theatregoing audiences and students. Rather than offering a 'taste' of live theatre via limited performances or one-off broadcasts like *How to Stop Worrying and Love the Theatre*, this incarnation of Theatregoround attempted to amplify and sustain any potential impact, both during and after the performances, by working more closely with schools and education centres, offering programmes based around core texts that were available in conjunction with packages of documentation for teachers to use in schools.

What remained constant through this work was the imperative to democratize and diversify the company's audience or, as Hands describes, 'to build the audience of tomorrow, not just to please the audience of today [Hall] wanted Theatregoround to reach out to that new audience, to go anywhere and everywhere' (qtd. in Rutter 2012: 205). This objective was explicit in Theatregoround's marketing, with early publicity flyers proclaiming:

> Theatres tend to cater for a very small section of society. But the theatre audience does not have to be a select few. Class barriers, high prices, inconvenience, a feeling that it is only for the educated these are some of the obstacles that keep people away from the theatre. But theatres could be opened to a wider audience, become much more a part of daily life. This is what Theatregoround is trying to achieve.
>
> ('Theatregoround' Publicity Flyer)

Clearly reasserting the sentiments of Actors Commando's early publicity (and perhaps downplaying any related commercial imperatives to swell audience numbers), statements such as this read almost as a call to arms and could be usefully understood in the context of the rhetoric of the New Left that had begun to proliferate in Britain from the mid-1950s onwards. For example, in the first issue of the *New Left Review*, published in February 1960, cultural theorist Stuart Hall claimed, 'We have to go into towns and cities, universities and technical colleges, youth clubs and Trade Union branches and – as [William] Morris said – make socialists there' (1960: 2). In the case of Theatregoround, rather than trying to overtly politicize their audiences by aligning with a particular position, the 'politics' at work here is arguably in the desire to simply create audiences, to assemble a group of people who hitherto had not experienced this kind of work and – at its most utopian – to erode the very class barriers that theatre perpetuates.

These ambitions resonated strongly with the aims and working practices of other Fringe organizations of the late 1960s and early 1970s. By taking performance out of conventional, purpose-built theatre spaces, groups such as Portable Theatre, Agitprop Street Players (later renamed Red Ladder in 1971), Brighton Combination, Joint Stock, Foco Novo and the Women's Street Theatre group sought to engage their audiences in the public sphere, thereby – it was hoped – democratizing access to theatre and amplifying any latent or overt political messages within their work. Though never discussed explicitly in relation to these other Fringe organizations, Theatregoround's operations can be understood as a precursor to these better-known, autonomous small-scale touring operations. From the perspective of recalibrating understandings of Pinter at the RSC, it is significant that his work appeared in this more overtly politicized strand of the company's practice, thereby connecting this early work to the broader historical narratives concerned with the politicization of theatre in the UK.

A politicized interpretation of Theatregoround's ambitions for their work, however, is complicated by its position within the wider structures of the RSC itself. Typically, the rise of alternative, Fringe theatre is thought to represent an overthrow of the largely naturalistic, building-based, capitalist theatre practices of major theatrical organizations like the RSC and the West End. Here, the 'alternative' Theatregoround posed was in opposition to its own progenitor, the wider company. Theatregoround audiences, therefore, were at once encouraged to perceive theatrical works and the practice of theatregoing in general as accessible to all, while the RSC itself concurrently continued to represent the theatrical establishment, catering primarily and consistently for audiences in London and Stratford-upon-Avon. In that sense, the RSC was at once responsible for the creation and consolidation of canonical mainstage productions while at the time stripping away the supposed barriers to audiences' access to such material. This disjuncture mirrors the tension Kustow invokes between high intellectualism and accessible storytelling, situations and conventions in Pinter's plays and is particularly striking in the context of the RSC, a company that is, as discussed above, regarded as instrumental in the establishment, acceleration and maintenance of Pinter's career. On the one hand, Pinter is placed within the pantheon of great writers who have shaped Western theatre – Sophocles, Aristophanes, Molière and Shakespeare – to the effect of valorizing his status and cultural capital. On the other hand, initiatives like Theatregoround work to destabilize this notion, to demystify Pinter's plays and make intelligible the supposed 'wholesomeness' of the work.

There are indications that, as with Kustow's perception of *How to Stop Worrying and Love the Theatre*, Theatregoround's framing and treatment of the texts they put on stage did have the capacity to subvert popular perceptions of both Shakespeare – still the company's primary focus – and the work of contemporary writers like Pinter. Following three visits by

Theatregoround to the North Havering College of Further Education, one attendee, Howard Gilbert, observed,

> The Royal Shakespeare Company's Theatregoround came three times within the week to Havering, and upwards of eight hundred people, young, old, and middle-aged, took part in the presentations. [...] In some strange way these 'bare board' presentations seem to stir people more than the most slick and polished of performances. One student said to me afterwards: 'With a company like that, who wouldn't go to see Shakespeare?' Another comment upon the same lines was: 'I didn't like those Pinter plays when they were broadcast, and I very nearly stayed away, but I'm glad I came'. By the same token, it seems to me that Shakespeare is toppled from his artificial, scholastic pedestal and Pinter from the aura of preciousness which is partly his popular image, both to be set upon real platforms as chroniclers of human stories.
>
> (1967)

Gilbert's claims resonate strongly with Kustow's earlier observation concerning the stripping away of the 'hifalutin philosophy' of Pinter's *The Birthday Party* and the company's juxtaposition of the play with melodrama. Gilbert's attention to the efficacy of the 'bare board' presentation style of Theatregoround versus the 'slick and polished' performances possible on the company's mainstages captures a sense of how the material conditions under which this mobile, touring work was produced significantly impacted both the aesthetics and reception of the work, in this case enabling audiences to comprehend, enjoy and perhaps learn from these productions.

The 'bare board' presentation Gilbert refers to is certainly evident in the archival documentation of Theatregoround's 1967 tour of the Midlands that included Pinter's *The Dumb Waiter*, directed by David Jones. Like Hall, Jones was a key figure in cultivating the company's repertoire beyond Shakespeare and a long-term collaborator of Pinter's, particularly for television and film. He would go on to direct, for example, Pinter's screenplay adaptation of Aidan Higgins's novel *Langrishe, Go Down* (1966) for BBC2 in 1978, the film version of *Betrayal* (1983) and Pinter's film adaptation of Franz Kafka's *The Trial* (1992). In 1985 Jones would direct Pinter himself as Deeley in *Old Times* (assuming the role from Michael Gambon for an American tour).[8]

Prior to these well-known examples of the pair's collaboration, however, was Theatregoround's *Dumb Waiter* starring Hugh Sullivan as Gus and Richard Moore as Ben. The season as a whole was, as appears to be typical for Theatregoround, ambitious in its range and pedagogy. It offered a mixture of classical and contemporary texts alongside devised work, condensed versions of Shakespeare by RSC director John Barton and instructive demonstrations from RSC directors and actors discussing their craft. These included, for example, sessions on 'The Actor/Director' and 'The Actor at Work' alongside plays such as *The Knack* (1962) by Ann Jellicoe; *The Hollow Crown*, an anthology of the kings and queens of England, devised by Barton which premiered at the Aldwych in 1965 before touring nationally until 1979; *The Proposal* (1890) by Anton Chekhov, directed by Hands; *Pleasure and Repentance*, devised and directed by Hands; and Dylan Thomas's *Under Milk Wood* (1954), also directed by Hands. Further refining the broad theatrical and historical scope of *How to Stop Worrying and Love the Theatre*, this programme offered a microcosm of the RSC's own wider programme and practices specifically.

Based on the selection of production images held in the RSC's archives, Jones's production of *The Dumb Waiter* bears a resemblance to the broadcast of *How to Stop Worrying and Love the Theatre*.[9] At the back of a small, heptagonal and raked wooden stage are three wooden flats with the eponymous dumb waiter in the centre. The venue itself (not credited on the images) is visible behind the stage. Two beds with metal frames on either side of the dumb waiter are the only other visible scenery. Collectively, these images evoke the same stripped-back, no-frills approach of the broadcast fragment of *The Birthday Party*; there is no attempt to disguise the utilitarian staging or the venue in question to make it appear like a conventional theatre space. The material conditions of its production are, if anything, central to its aesthetic and make Theatregoround's commitment to producing theatre at a low cost manifestly present.

If *The Homecoming* was able to adapt to and embrace the wide, expansive stage of the Aldwych, in this example Pinter's *Dumb Waiter* appears as if tailor-made for both the material circumstances and remit of Theatregoround. Set in a basement room, each aspect of Pinter's opening stage directions has been observed. Despite the small stage, there is a door stage right and what appears to be a recessed anti-room stage left, likely intended to provide the off-stage locations of the bathroom and kitchen which are integral features of the play script and action. The positioning of the beds, though not 'flat against the back wall' as Pinter's script indicates, follows the guidance noted in the 1961 Samuel French Acting edition used for this production, which 'follows a production in which the smallness of the stage determined the positions of the two beds'.[10]

Returning to the idea of the relative 'smallness' of Pinter's plays and the simultaneous artistic and pragmatic advantages they afford, we might consider these material economies of scale in relation to what Taylor-Batty has described as Pinter's 'efficient ideas':

The communicability of Pinter's 'efficient ideas' is immediate, in that he strives to convey human experience directly, without excessive symbolism and without overly manipulating his discoveries to make any direct statements. Having found a manner in which he can articulate certain aspects of human interaction, he allows his artistic discoveries to resonate in each of us as subtle recognition, not tacit knowledge.

(2001: 125)

What the examples explored in this chapter suggest is a particular cohesion between the artistic 'efficiency' or directness of Pinter's practice with the stripped-back staging conditions of these lesser-known small-scale productions. While Pinter's writing has the potential to communicate complex, intangible human experiences on a variety of stages and across multiple media, it is rarely considered in the context of small, fleeting or seemingly less auspicious production conditions. By focusing on these examples that took place early in Pinter's career and during the RSC's first decade, both writer and institution can be reappraised in terms of their work beyond the mainstage – work that was initiated by other key collaborators, in different, temporary spaces and aligned with more overtly politicized ambitions for engaging audiences in the practices and artistry of the company and its featured writers.

Conclusion

There are conflicting records of how many performances of *The Dumb Waiter* appeared in this Midlands season and another small-scale London season. According to the RSC's online performance database, there are three recorded instances of the play at the start of the Midlands tour.[11] However, a document entitled 'Data Concerning Theatregoround: The Period from June 22nd 1966 until September 30th 1970' notes five performances of *The Dumb Waiter* in Croydon, Romford and Stanmore as part of a London Season and twelve performances during the Midlands Season at Nuneaton, Worcester, Rugby, Manley in Arden and Ashby-de-la-Zouch (Ormand 1970). Whatever the case, neither this production nor the fleeting live and televised appearances of initiatives like *How to Stop Worrying and Love the Theatre* can compete with the production runs and subsequent tours of Pinter's works on the RSC's mainstages in terms of status or visibility. Nor do they need to. In accounting for these instances of Pinter in production at the RSC I do not wish to suggest an equivalency between the mainstage and these itinerant productions. I want, rather, to emphasize their striking differences in order to underscore the flexibly of Pinter's writing, its potential to adapt to different performance conditions and economies, and in the process to serve different company imperatives: in this case, attracting new audiences to the RSC but also to theatregoing in general. Looking beyond the mainstage successes of Pinter's work at the RSC and his collaboration with Hall, then, offers a more representative image of the range of his work undertaken by the company, a deeper understanding of the multiple contexts and platforms for new work at the RSC's inception and an explicit commitment to making these works accessible to a wider audience. By focusing on *How to Stop Worrying and Love the Theatre* and Theatregoround's *The Dumb Waiter* the complex position of Pinter at the RSC emerges; his association with the company gave rise to both award-winning mainstage productions that represent Britain's theatrical establishment *and* minimal, stripped-back, mobile stagings that actively sought to challenge the kind of wisdom that can work to enshrine and rarefy the work of writers like Pinter.

Notes

1   While the RSC's productions of *Silence* and *Old Times* represented the works' first appearance in any medium, *Landscape* officially premiered on the BBC's Radio Third Programme in 1968 prior to receiving its stage debut alongside *Silence* in 1969.
2   In addition to his productions for the RSC, following his appointment as artistic director of the National Theatre in 1973, Hall directed *No Man's Land* (1975), *Betrayal* (1978), and the triple-bill *Other Places*, which included *Family Voices*, *Victoria Station* and *A Kind of Alaska* (1982).
3   For Hall's own accounts see *Making and Exhibition of Myself* (particularly Chapter Eleven, 195–202), 'Directing the Plays of Harold Pinter' (2001) and 'Directing Pinter: Interview by Catherine Itzin and Simon Trussler' (1974).
4   Alongside Pinter's *The Birthday Party*, the season included Peter Weiss's *The Persecution and Assassination of Jean-Paul Marat as Performed by the Inmates of the Asylum of Charenton under the Direction of the Marquis de Sade* (or *Marat/Sade*) (1964), David Rudkin's *Afore Night Come* (1962) and Roger Vitrac's Dadaist work *Victor* (1928).
5   At the 1967 Tony Awards, for example, the Broadway Transfer of the RSC's production of *The Homecoming* won the awards for Best Supporting Actor (Ian Holm as Lenny) and Best Dramatic Actor (Paul Rogers as Max), Best Director (Peter Hall) and Best Play. The same year, it also won New York Drama Critics' Circle Award for Best Play.

6   For detailed accounts of Pinter's acting engagements and touring locations between 1953 and 1957, see William Baker's chapter 'Ireland, Precarious Existence and Marriage' (2008) or David T. Thompson's *Pinter – The Player's Playwright* (1985).
7   According to Chambers, this anonymous donation was made in April 1966 specifically for Theatregoround, with Hall 'advocating its activities to Stratford's educational authorities' (2004: 42).
8   For Jones's own account of working with Pinter and directing his work, see 'Staging Pauses and Silences' in *Viva Pinter: Harold Pinter's Spirit of Resistance* (2009).
9   Images for this production were taken by Reg Wilson and are currently held in the Reg Wilson Photographic Collection, 1962–97 at the Shakespeare Birthplace Trust Library and Archives (RL5/2/1165).
10 The Samuel French Acting edition appears as part of the Prompt Book for this production, held in the Shakespeare Birthplace Trust Library and Archives, Stratford-upon-Avon (RSC/SM/1/1967/DUW1).
11 According to records on the RSC's online Performance Database, *The Dumb Waiter* was the feature show on 19 May at Lordswood Boys' Technical School, Birmingham, 22 May at Henley in Arden High School, Warwickshire, and 25 May at the Ashby-de-la-Zouch Festival, Leicestershire (see http://collections.shakespeare.org.uk/search/rsc-performances/view_as/grid/search/-17 (accessed 19 June 2020)).

Works Cited

Andrews, J. (2012), 'Harold Pinter', in S. Nicholson (ed.), *Modern British Playwriting: The 1960s*, 161–89, London: Methuen.
Baker, W. (2008), *Harold Pinter*, London: Bloomsbury.
Batty, M. (2001), *Harold Pinter*, Liverpool: Liverpool University Press.
Batty, M. (2005), *About Pinter: The Playwright and the Work*, London: Faber and Faber.
Bignell, J., and W. Davies, eds (2020), 'Introduction: Harold Pinter's Transmedial Histories', *Historical Journal of Film, Radio and Television*, 40 (3): 481–98.
Billington, M. (1996), *The Life and Work of Harold Pinter*, London: Faber and Faber.
Chambers, C. (2004), *Inside the Royal Shakespeare Company: Creativity and the Institution*, London: Routledge.
The Dumb Waiter prompt book: Theatregoround (1967), in Royal Shakespeare Company 1961–, Shakespeare Birthplace Trust Library and Archives, Stratford-upon-Avon, RSC/SM/1/1967/DUW1.
Flourish (1965), 'Royal Shakespeare Theatre Club Human Trailer Project', no. 4, Theatregoround Archive 1970–2019, Shakespeare Birthplace Trust Library and Archives, TGR Box 1.

Flower, F. (1964), 'Policy of the Royal Shakespeare Company', in Sir Fordham Flower, Stratford-upon-Avon, September 1964–January 1966, Shakespeare Birthplace Trust Library and Archive, Stratford-upon-Avon, DR1108/2/1/1.

Gilbert, H. (1967), 'Theatregoround: Two Views', first printed in *Adult Education*, in Theatregoround Archive 1970–2019, Shakespeare Birthplace Trust Library and Archives, TGR Box 1.

Gussow, M. (2001), 'Acting Pinter', in L. Gordon (ed.), *Pinter at 70: A Casebook*, 257–62, London: Routledge.

Hall, P. (1974), 'Directing Pinter: Interview by Catherine Itzin and Simon Trussler', *Theatre Quarterly*, 4 (16): 4–17.

Hall, P. (2000), *Making and Exhibition of Myself: The Autobiography of Peter Hall*, 2nd edn, London: Oberon.

Hall, P. (2001), 'Directing the Plays of Harold Pinter', in P. Rabey (ed.), *The Cambridge Companion to Harold Pinter*, 145–54, Cambridge: Cambridge University Press.

Hall, S. (1960), 'Introducing *NRL*', *New Left Review*, 1 (1): 1–3.

Jones, D. (2009), 'Staging Pauses and Silences', in B. Gauthier (ed.), *Viva Pinter: Harold Pinter's Spirit of Resistance*, 43–65, Bern: Peter Lang.

Kemp, P. (1968), 'Report on Theatregoround – November 1st 1966 to November 1st 1968', in Theatregoround Archive 1970–2019, Shakespeare Birthplace Trust Library and Archives, TGR Box 1.

Lawson, S. (1975), 'The Old Vic to Vincennes: Interviews with Michael Kustow and Peter Brook', *Theatre*, 7 (1): 78–91.

Norman, B. (1964), 'Dirt! Emile Littler in Storm over Shakespeare Company Plays', *Daily Mail*, 25 August.

Ormand, P. (1970), 'Data Concerning Theatregoround: The Period from June 22nd 1966 until September 30th 1970', in Theatregoround Archive 1970–2019, Shakespeare Birthplace Trust Library and Archives, Stratford-upon-Avon, TGR Box 1.

Pinter, H. (1966), Letter to Sir Fordham Flower, in Sir Fordham Flower, Stratford-upon-Avon, 1964–6, Shakespeare Birthplace Trust Library and Archive, Stratford-upon-Avon, DR1108/2/1/13.

Pinter, H. (1996), '*The Birthday Party*', in *Harold Pinter: Plays 1*, 1–81, London: Faber and Faber.

Rutter, C. (2012), 'Becoming the RSC: Terry Hands in Conversation', *Shakespeare*, 8 (2): 202–18.

Strauss, M. (1964), Letter to Sir Fordham Flower, in Sir Fordham Flower, Stratford-upon-Avon, September 1964–January 1966, Shakespeare Birthplace Trust Library and Archive, Stratford-upon-Avon, DR1108/2/1/1.

Sunday Night: How to Stop Worrying and Love the Theatre (1966), BBC One, 20 February.

'Theatregoround' Publicity Flyer (n.d.), in Theatregoround Archive 1970–2019, Shakespeare Birthplace Trust Library and Archives, Stratford-upon-Avon, TGR Box 1.

Thompson, D. (1985), *Pinter – The Player's Playwright*, Basingstoke: Palgrave Macmillan.
Wilson, R. (1967), 'The Dumb Waiter, Reg Wilson Collection Photographs: Theatregoround', in The Reg Wilson Photographic Collection, 1962–97 at the Shakespeare Birthplace Trust Library and Archives, Stratford-upon-Avon, RL5/2/1165.
Wyver, J. (2019), *Screening the Royal Shakespeare Company: A Critical History*, London: Bloomsbury Arden.

8

Theatre's Dark Matter: Pinter's 'Staging' of Systemic Violence and Its Influence in Contemporary British Theatre

Alex Watson

On the stark stage of the Jerwood theatre, downstairs at London's Royal Court, two performers are engaged in a drawn-out linguistic battle – a family discussing which gesture is the least compromising when avoiding arrest:

Son So if I put my hands up –

Mom a threat, threatening.

Son Slowly?

Mom Provocative.

Son Showed my palms

Mum inflammatory. Could be.

As the debate drags on, it becomes obvious that this is a puzzle with no satisfactory answer. In another performance on the same stage, a different family are sheltered inside their home which is obviously in need of repair:

Anna What happened?

Maureen The window broke.

Anna How did the window break?

Maureen This is a temporary arrangement

Anna Did someone break the window or?

Maureen until a glazier arrives.

Anna Who broke the window?

Maureen It's very difficult at the weekend to find a glazier.

After years away, Anna has returned to the family home with a fiscally driven ulterior motive; Maureen is psychologically oppressed by her husband who himself is fixed upon a task that becomes clear he will never accomplish. All the while, a mob circles outside and threatens to invade the domestic space at any given moment. Neither of these plays were written by Harold Pinter, yet one could be forgiven for thinking they were.

These plays are, respectively, debbie tucker green's *ear for eye* (2018: 4) and Mark Ravenhill's *The Cane* (2018: 3). They share several characteristics with Pinter's theatre such as the evocation of domestic spaces, oppressive situations and a use of dialogue that Martin Esslin describes as transcribing 'everyday conversation in all its repetitiveness, incoherence, and lack of logic or grammar' (1991: 243). Such stylistic similarities complement mutual objectives in all three writers' work: to reveal how societal oppression and systemic violence can be established through language. tucker green and Ravenhill are by no means alone on the contemporary British stage in this concern, with newer writers such as Lucy Kirkwood, Cordelia Lynn and Alistair McDowall as well as more established playwrights such as Caryl Churchill and Dennis Kelly opting to represent violence and oppression through dialogue rather than physical acts.[1] It is my contention here that one major factor in this contemporary turn is the influence of Pinter.

This chapter examines the interrelation between three kinds of metaphorical 'dark matter' through which we can understand the effectiveness of Pinter's ability to dramatize issues of societal oppression. The first of these relates to the societal oppression mentioned above: the concept of systemic violence. Coined by the cultural theorist Slavoj Žižek, who describes it as 'the very zero-level standard against which we perceive something as subjectively violent' (2009: 2), systemic violence comprises the oppressions of a society or culture fundamental to its existence. It is maintained by and influences the innocuous, smooth functioning of conditioned actions, gestures, images and bodies that compose a society; therefore, Žižek illustrates it as 'something like the notorious "dark matter" of physics' (2).

The second kind of dark matter explored here takes up Andrew Sofer's use of the metaphor to refer 'to the invisible dimension of theater that escapes visual detection, even though its effects are felt everywhere in performance' (2013: 3). Sofer contends that it 'is dark matter that produces the difference between horror and terror, for example. Horror is what we see; terror is what we know is there though it remains unseen' (5). Indeed, Pinter tends to opt for the implied over the apparent – what was popularly characterized by Irving Wardle as 'menace,' with Walter Kerr even calling it 'the adjective most often used to describe the events in a Pinter play' (1967: 14). Pinter's dramaturgical techniques, then, appear to fit Sofer's categorization of theatrical dark matter.

The final interrelated metaphor I wish to discuss here is my own: that the influence of Pinter can be felt through British theatre like dark matter. It is sometimes not immediately apparent, but nonetheless present. This statement is arguably merited given Pinter's fame, the longevity of his work in production and the quantity of his output. The extent of Pinter's impact was recently showcased in director Jamie Lloyd's commercially and critically successful curated season of plays, *Pinter at the Pinter* (2018–19), in London's West End, and his influence has been directly cited by writers like David Edgar, who claimed that Pinter 'changed how dialogue was written in British theatre as definitively as Cézanne changed how paintings were painted in France' (2008: 2).

Unsurprisingly, it is Pinter's dramatic dialogue that contributes most to exposing oppressive power working through language. Pinter's unique brand of stage dialogue is a recurring subject of critical debate in Pinter studies and beyond.[2] In this chapter, I focus on its influence in contemporary theatre. Rather than situating Pinter's dramatic language solely within the context of the time he was writing, however, I consider it in terms of Pinter's engagement with societal oppression. Linking Pinter's work to other, especially contemporary, playwrights on this basis underscores the ongoing relevance of his legacy, which is often assumed more than it is actively contended.[3]

In identifying and drawing connections between these three kinds of dark matter, this chapter is divided into two parts. The first draws attention to corollaries between Pinter's work, contemporary British theatre and concepts related to systemic violence. The specific plays analysed here are *The Caretaker* (1960), one of Pinter's earliest and best-known plays, and tucker green's *ear for eye*, which presents similar issues of marginalization and societal inequality (albeit on a grander and more pertinent scale). The second part looks at how Pinter 'stages' systemic violence through dialogue, specifically in one of his later and lesser-known plays, *Party Time* (1991), which is compared with Ravenhill's *The Cane*. In using two markedly different plays by Pinter in terms of style, time and notoriety, as well as two established contemporary playwrights with their own varying backgrounds and techniques, this chapter highlights the underlying interest in systemic violence in much of Pinter's work, its effect on how contemporary writers present this issue and the widespread engagement with systemic violence on the contemporary British stage.

Staging Systemic Violence through Dialogue in *The Caretaker* and *ear for eye*

Of all forms of violence, 'systemic' violence is arguably the most difficult to theatricalize. This is because, by its very nature, it is *untheatrical*. It is a violence normalized or disguised in public perception: a sociocultural violence that many citizens are conditioned to believe is normal and therefore often innocently perpetuates in their language, gestures and actions. Existing in all social realms, it is inherent and banal – a violence that, through the lens of respective societies, is merely the status quo. Systemic violence, then, is markedly different from subjective violence, an example of which would be someone being punched, where a subject is directly enacting harm on another subject and other subjects may witness this act. On the other hand, systemic violence, like dark matter, can be 'seen' in its effects rather than its actions, such as prejudice and inequality. The 'act' causing these effects is ensconced in the very fabric of culture and society, often unwittingly built up in a myriad of ways by different individuals. Subjective violence can often result from systemic violence, when informed or even encouraged by societal prejudice, for example. However, since subjective violence is arguably easier to address because of its tangibility, its roots in systemic violence are often ignored despite being far more pervasive and harmful to society.

Systemic violence began to be theorized approximately ten years after Pinter's theatrical debut *The Room* (1957), with Johan Galtung's essay 'Violence, Peace, and Peace Research' (1969). Galtung uses the terms 'structural violence' and 'social injustice' to describe phenomena similar to what Žižek would call systemic violence around four decades later. As Galtung writes: 'Violence with a clear subject-object relation is manifest because it is visible as *action*. [...] Violence without this relation is structural, built into structure' (171; emphasis in original). Here we can see similarities to Žižek's distinctions in Galtung's thought, between violence as 'manifest action' (subjective) and violence as 'built into structure' (systemic).[4]

It is likely that Pinter had some idea of the issues Galtung would later theorize. As David Pattie writes, Britain going into the 1960s was experiencing newfound affluence that masked 'painful realities' such as prejudice against 'the status of women within British society, the racism encountered by immigrants from the West Indies and elsewhere, [...] homosexuality', and the attendant issues of an increasingly 'superficial consumer society' (2012: 18–19). Considering Pinter's outspokenness about violence and injustice later in his career, it is conceivable that he incorporated ideas related to structural inequality in his earlier plays, even if representing marginalized groups was not his primary focus. Concerns with wealth, class and race, for example, find their way into *The Caretaker*.

Written in 1959 and premiering at the Arts Theatre in Westminster the following year, *The Caretaker* shows how two members of the new 'consumer society' systemically marginalize a homeless man who they come to see as worthless. The two brothers, Mick and Aston, make many references to their own sense of entrepreneurialism – the former being 'in the building trade' and the latter doing odd jobs: 'I can work with my hands, you see' (Pinter 1996: 38). They are described by Graham Woodroffe as being emblematic of two generalized sides of British society at the time, with Aston having 'something of the old school Tory about him' – his hopes to tame his wild garden being representative of naive optimism in restoring 'the ruins of the Empire' – and Mick the Labour-supporting 'young generation, on the way up from the working class in an economic climate of increasing affluence' (1988: 507).

Much like post-war Britain under the 'care' of the Tories and Labour, the brothers' house is poorly maintained, with draughts and recurring leaks from 'cracks on the roof' (Pinter 1996: 35) reflecting a society in need of repair. Instead, Aston, who has most likely undergone traumatic electroconvulsive therapy ('he said, we're going to do something to your brain' (53)), ponders on less structural and more material decorations in his home: 'they've got these screens ... you know ... Oriental' (39). Likewise, Mick's ponderings on turning 'this place into a penthouse' (58) may reflect an acquisitive public, with illusions of prosperity distracting them from actually repairing the basic problems in their environment.

One of these basic problems, literally and figuratively, is the presence of Davies. Taken in by Aston after being fired and attacked by his employer ('he gave me the bullet [...] that Scotch git' (8)), Davies frequently lapses into racist tirades ('Blacks, Greeks, Poles [...] treating me like dirt' (6)). Yet, as a homeless person, he suffers prejudice and precarity himself. As Pinter stated in 1988, 'there's a similar attitude in the US and England about how to treat the poor, the homeless, the disabled, which is mainly to ignore them' (qtd. in Gussow 1994: 68). This precarity is referenced by Woodroffe, who notes, 'From the beginning to the end of the play, Davies never knows where he stands and what the brothers expect of him' (1988: 499). However, once Mick and Aston deem Davies unfit to be their caretaker, and therefore without worth, he is excluded from their society and property. The final lines of the play – Davies begging the brothers to reconsider – are met with a '[*l*]*ong silence*' and Aston literally turning his back on the once-again homeless man: 'ASTON *turns back to the window*' (Pinter 1996: 76).

Lucina Pacquet Gabbard has explored how many of Pinter's characters transform from victims into victimizers and vice versa.[5] Rather than transforming, Davies arguably victimizes those he perceives as others in response to himself being 'treated like dirt' – a phenomenon linked to structural inequality by Étienne Balibar. In his 1996 Wellek Library Lectures, Balibar theorized two classifications of violence: ultrasubjective and ultraobjective (again, similar definitions to what Žižek would later term the subjective and the systemic). In the acting of ultrasubjective violence, Balibar argues that 'a fantasy of animality' ensnares the perpetrated and the perpetrator which 'blurs the limits of the human' (2016: 70): the victim is perceived as less than human; the perpetrator forfeits humanity in the acting out of violence. Balibar sees ultrasubjective and ultraobjective violence as linked, however. As the name of the latter implies, it encourages the perception of others as objects – it is logical; it sees subjects as components of a system.

For Balibar, ultraobjective violence 'proceeds by way of an inversion of the utility principle and the transformation of human beings into not useful commodities but disposable waste' (61). Therefore, both kinds of violence are 'at once distinct and inseparable, of which one is something like the other's underside' (72); they inform one another in creating disposable humans. *The Caretaker* displays this figuring of humans as 'waste' both in Davies's racist remarks and in how the brothers treat Davies. Mick's veiled rant on negotiating a property contract with Davies is especially illustrative of Balibar's thought:

> You're an old barbarian. Honest. You got no business wandering about in an unfurnished flat. I could charge seven quid a week for this if I wanted to. Get a taker tomorrow. Three hundred and fifty a year exclusive. No argument. I mean, if that sort of money's in your range don't be afraid to say so. (Pinter 1996: 33)

Mick's relative wealth and social position foster a derisive vision of Davies that better allows Mick to perform subjective violence against him, seen earlier in his attack ('MICK *seizes his arm and forces it up his back*' (26)) and later in his eviction.

Jane Wong Yeang Chui argues that *The Caretaker* is a charter of Aston's return to the social: '[T]he friendship that Aston attempts to forge with Davies is an attempt at reconciliation with the past', to 'live as he did before the traumatic event – be *normal*' (2013: 37; emphasis in original). Yet this normality ultimately turns a blind eye to homelessness. Despite initially taking Davies in, Aston evicts him in solidarity with Mick and perpetuates his brother's language as he does so: 'You've been stinking the place out [...] You better go' (Pinter 1996: 67). Woodroffe deftly encapsulates both Davies's position in the brothers' home and, arguably, an individual subject in a society structured with systemic violence: 'This situation suggests an alternative understanding of "caretaker" where "take care of" is to be understood not in its altruistic sense, but as a euphemism for aggression' (1988: 500). Framed in this way, Davies is perhaps the 'everyman' of *The Caretaker*, responsible for perpetuating the mechanism of systemic violence in his attitudes and behaviour as much as he is oppressed by them. He is at once a 'caretaker' for social, systemic violence and 'taken care of' by social, systemic violence.

Over six decades after *The Caretaker*'s debut, the concerns of British theatre still include those pervading Pinter's writing. One example of this is the work of debbie tucker green, whose writing is palpable with fury at societal ills both local and global. Her work has engaged with issues such as mental health, racism and justice – all arguably feeding into a broader concern with systemic violence. Though Lynette Goddard cites tucker green's overt influences as poets and singers like Louise Bennett, Lauryn Hill and Jill Scott, Goddard argues the importance of tucker green's medium in that her plays 'bring audiences together in a shared space as witnesses to the effects of trauma, violence and loss and raise important questions about human rights' (2013: 191). These subjects naturally draw parallels to Pinter – especially later works such as *One for the Road* (1984), *Mountain Language* (1988), *Party Time*, *The New World Order* (1991) and *Ashes to Ashes* (1996) – with Vicky Angelaki writing that both playwrights share 'an affinity for staging the personal as political and vice versa; for stage action that is borne through language; for elliptical and yet imagery-rich work' (2017: 196).

Doubling down on the concerns and techniques identified by Goddard and Angelaki, *ear for eye* is arguably tucker green's most politically pertinent play to date. The three-part narrative represents the struggle for black rights against the inherent racism in the United States and the UK's police forces and more generally exposes the systemic violence that permits racism to thrive in these societies. The first act of the play comprises several sets of characters, some of them in mirrored situations, discussing the validity of protest ('[m]archin days is over man' (tucker green 2018: 78)), being abused by the police in custody ('I sat in that cell [...] tellin me the ... "suicide rates" of us in their "care"' (20)), and how to best negotiate a system designed against them.[6] The second act focuses on a younger, African American woman and an older, Caucasian American man arguing about the psychological profile of two young white supremacists who have committed a school shooting, while the final act is a series of filmed actors and non-actors from the United States and UK recounting slave codes and Jim Crow laws.

Though *ear for eye* takes a far wider view of societal injustices than that of *The Caretaker*, both plays use dialogue to reveal deeper layers of violence built into the structure of society. These kinds of violence can be identified through Žižek's classifications which, as seen above, are informed by Galtung and Balibar. Žižek conceives three general kinds of violence relating to one another like a pyramid-shaped iceberg, with subjective violence being the part 'above water': 'the most visible portion of a triumvirate that also includes two objective kinds of violence' (2009: 1). These objective types take their place in the triumvirate as the systemic and the 'symbolic', the latter being violence inherent in the symbolic world in which human cultures exist (1). For example, language that enables acts of violence to occur is symbolic violence. Each type of violence is illustrated in *ear for eye* and *The Caretaker*, both plays suggesting that these different types interact through dialogue. Though the plays are similar in this specific insight into systemic violence, it must be said that the plight of three white men (albeit analogues for class struggle) is not equivalent to the racial persecution of millions of people, and the direct address of *ear for eye*'s final act fittingly and unambiguously presents the widespread systemic violence of prejudice.

The figuring of other humans as non-subjects seen in *The Caretaker* is also far more explicit in *ear for eye*. This is evident in how the predominantly white police recurrently treat the black characters of the play – summarized when two parents attempt to explain the paradoxical value of their son's life to him:

Dad It means.

Of value. 'Of value'

Son I am –

Mom yes you are.

Son I/am.

Dad You are. You are to us Son.

Mom *Yes*.

Dad But you're not.

Mom … It means, of worth

Son same as value –

Dad not to them. (tucker green 2018: 44)

The dialogue, framed as one of the important 'talks' that parents have with their early adolescent children, deftly presents an example of Balibar's theory. Namely, young black men are framed as disposable by the police (and, often, by society more generally). In turn, violent actions informed by racism make the police less than human. The recurring linguistic game this family and their British counterparts engage in signals that this systemic process of disposability occurs through language.

This is most apparent in tucker green's use of language in act two's drawn-out duologue between a black female student and a white male academic. The student calls the perpetrators 'organised, militarised, uniformed, hierarchical, vitriolic, ritualistic, political-death-cult-European-Protestant-immigrant-psychopathic white-sheet-wearing cross-burning motherfuckers', while the academic describes them as 'Lone-Wolves, mentalists' (120–1). The implication is that white supremacists are not widely regarded as such in the media or by professional opinion, because it would admit the presence of structural racism in society. The duration of the argument signals to the audience that interpellation – the symbolic classification of individuals – is important to the extent that it may be linked to the abhorrent act being discussed. In *The Ticklish Subject* (1999), Žižek discusses the contemporary status of the individual between the real and the imaginary. He writes of the profiling done by corporations and governments, which even if inaccurate constitute 'me as a subject inherently related to and hassled by an elusive piece of database in which, beyond my reach, "my fate is writ large"' (260). This could not only be said to occur in such profiling, but in the very interpellation of an individual within society.

Such symbolic understanding reduces others to similar names and descriptions used by tucker green: 'FEMALE, *African American, twenties* | MALE, *Caucasian American, fifties*' (2018: 3). It is precisely the trap that both young sons of the two families in *ear for eye* cannot escape: they are 'of value'; their interpellated selves are not. *The Caretaker* also shows this process, with Davies becoming symbolically recognized by Mick (and eventually Aston) through repeated slurs. Both plays also use the recurrence and repetition of dialogue to establish an enclosed system, such as Davies's deferred quest for his papers (or identity) becoming emblematic of the 'disposable' and invisible homeless in society. In these cases, interpellation becomes symbolic violence as it recognizes an individual as part of a wider, prejudiced system. The description and naming of characters via dialogue, then, implicate them in the effects of systemic violence.

There is a pervasive sense that the situations represented by the characters' speech will never change. Unlike *The Caretaker*, *ear for eye* offers a reason as to why this might be. In the final act, where the written laws and codes of the United States and the UK's past are stated for the audience, tucker green excavates institutional racism and stages the historical and cultural core of this systemic violence. Just as the oppression of slavery and racial segregation has been inscribed in language, so does prejudice subsist in United States and UK cultures through the language of interpellation. *ear for eye* also shows that the laws of oppression still exist, especially by those who can best express them, such as the terminology of the older academic in act two or when a black woman is arrested in act one: the police stating that 'the four-a-them got more rights than me and they know 'em better than the few I got that he knew I didn't even know' (tucker green 2018: 18). In the plays discussed here and elsewhere in their work, both playwrights show that characters who have the best command of language have the most control over their situation, as in Pinter's *Mountain Language*, for example, or tucker green's *hang* (2015). *ear for eye*, then, fully explores an idea presented in *The Caretaker* (and developed by Pinter in his later work): that systemic violence is established through language, and language establishes subjects within violent systems.

To summarize, tucker green and Pinter both illustrate that language is the conduit through which systemic violence can frame individuals as disposable enough to attack or oppress, and its repetition and proliferation can preserve systems of power. Still, *ear for eye* does offer the prospect of change. tucker green's presentation of how systemic violence creates precarious conditions for oppressed individuals questions whether revolutionary, reactionary violence is the only solution against society's perceived oppressors. At the end of the play, three younger black characters – who have respectively questioned the effectiveness of non-violent protest, been subjected to abuse in police custody and tear-gassed during a demonstration – ask an older black character who advocates peaceful change, '[Go] on. […] Give me one reason to not' (tucker green 2018: 135). The troubling solution of violent revolution to eradicate systemic violence echoes Žižek: 'Sometimes, doing nothing is the most violent thing to do' (2009: 183). tucker green's approach then reflects the growing concern towards systemic violence in British society over the decades: it is no longer an ignorable issue, a slow-dripping crack in the roof, but an urgent flood for sustained resistance against.

Staging Systemic Violence through Absence in *Party Time* and *The Cane*

Pinter's dialogue, then, is central to the 'theatricalisation' of systemic violence onstage, by shaping theatrical dark matter or, as Sofer describes it, 'felt absences […]. Dark matter comprises *whatever is materially unrepresented onstage but un-ignorable*' (2013: 4; emphasis in original). Some examples offered by Sofer include 'offstage spaces and actions, absent characters, the narrated past, hallucination, blindness, obscenity, godhead, and so on'

(3). Pinter not only evokes systemic violence as a felt absence through his dialogue but routinely uses other absences such as offstage actions and characters to enhance the sense of systemic violence.

Creating felt absences through dialogue separates Pinter from most of his contemporaries, due to their more pronounced use of representations of subjective violence. Two such examples, written around the time of *The Caretaker*, include John Arden's *Live Like Pigs* (1958) and Edward Bond's *Saved* (1965), which respectively depict rehoused travellers and the unemployed. Though their dramatizations of structural inequality reinforce that these concerns were being theorized in the theatre before Galtung and Balibar, Pinter stands apart from them by relying on what is implied through dialogue to illustrate systemic violence, whereas Arden and Bond both use their characters' explicit actions to show entrapment in societal oppression: as in the traveller family's non-conformist behaviour in *Live Like Pigs* or the infamous stoning of the baby in *Saved*. Such representations display a marked concern in their work towards how acts of subjective violence help to reinforce inequality, rather than the systemic violence that Pinter summons into the background of his plays.[7]

Pinter's *Party Time* is a fitting example of how he forms theatrical dark matter onstage. First performed at London's Almeida Theatre in 1991, the short play focuses on a high-society party thrown by Gavin, who is being told about an extravagant member's club by his acquaintances Terry and Melissa ('I tell you, it's got everything' (Pinter 2011: 281)) as Charlotte and Liz suggestively catch up with their former flings Fred and Douglas ('He gave me a leg up in life' (299)). Throughout the play, however, Terry's young wife Dusty continually asks the other guests about her missing brother ('Did you hear what's happened to Jimmy?' (284)) and allusions are made to a crackdown on citizens' freedoms ('we want that peace to be cast-iron' (292)) as there may be a popular uprising in the vicinity ('we've had a bit of a round-up' (313)). At the play's end, a blinding light covers the stage, emitting from a door through which Jimmy appears, '*thinly dressed*' and stating, 'I had a name' (313). The skirting of Dusty's questions on his whereabouts throughout the play suggests that Jimmy has been executed or at least stripped of his identity by the ruling class whose members are gathered at the party. Systemic violence is brought to our attention first by the inferences of the characters' dialogue, only for its effects to become apparent in the ragged appearance of Jimmy. Sofer writes that Jimmy's entrance 'brings the repressed to (blinding) light; as in a Passion Play, the ocular proof of trauma is located on the victim's visible, tortured body' (2013: 119). Arguably then, the events taking place offstage appear to have more weight in *Party Time*'s fictional world than the action occurring onstage. This is likely influenced by Pinter's political views and contemporary events, given that the play was written at the time of the Gulf War.

Ibrahim Yerebakan emphasizes that 'Pinter became more outspoken and more provocative in his portrayal of human rights abuses and political states of affairs in his late work' (2014: 157). Indeed, the captured prisoners and abuses of power made by their torturers in *Mountain Language* and *The New World Order* seem to harbour the anger felt by Pinter at the time. Publicly denouncing the United States as 'a "rogue state" of colossal military and economic might' and 'Europe – especially the United Kingdom' as 'compliant and complicit', he perceived a lack of public interest in the military interventions of the United States and UK abroad and that 'this brutal and malignant world machine must be recognized for what it is and resisted' (Pinter 2001). Unlike *Mountain Language* and *The New World Order*'s representations of subjective violence, *Party Time* is arguably more subtle and scathing. It casts the audience, and by extension the British public, as the invited guests: by turns collaborative, concerned and (mostly) apathetic about the civil unrest their hosts refer to and the measures they appear to be implementing in response to it.

Like the dual meaning noted by Woodroffe in *The Caretaker*, the title *Party Time* relates not only to a social gathering, but a period dominated by a totalitarian party. By presenting upper-class characters in an informal social situation, *Party Time* reveals the complicity everyday life has with the systemic violence that informs even far-reaching events. This complicity is made apparent in the smoothness with which characters like Douglas go from flirting to '*clench[ing] his fist*' (Pinter 2011: 293) to allude to crushing dissenters, and how Terry's dialogue goes between recommending a members-only club and telling his wife Dusty to 'shut up and enjoy the hospitality and mind your own fucking business' (288).

Angelaki characterizes Pinter's *Party Time* as one of the best examples of his 'staging the personal as political and vice versa' (2017: 196). Another writer who can claim this characteristic is Mark Ravenhill, with his debut *Shopping and Fucking* (1996) darkly satirizing how consumer capitalism penetrates into all facets of its citizens' lives. Ravenhill emerged as part of what has been called 'in-yer-face' theatre – characterized as drawing attention to societal ills through explicit simulations of subjective violence – and so could be considered more 'Bond-like' than 'Pinteresque'.[8] Yet Ravenhill's plays have also demonstrated a consistent concern with systemic violence, and his output has increasingly relied on less obvious depictions of violence. 2018's *The Cane* is evidence of this and in its utilization of felt absences arguably draws on the influence of Pinter and *Party Time* in particular.

The Cane focuses on Anna (who helps to transition public schools into Academies) and her return to her estranged parents' home. However, 'there's a mob outside the front door' (Ravenhill 2018: 11), as it has been made public that Anna's father Edward, a former deputy headmaster, used the cane '[w]hen it was legal to cane boys' (12). Edward however is more concerned with completing a letter to Ofsted after the 'inspectors were very damning' of his school (19). Anna offers to help her father write the letter on his laptop, but her hostile mother, Maureen, is suspicious that Anna has only come home because 'your Academy was going to make a grab for the school to become part of its portfolio' (24). Later, Anna accuses her father of 'bullying' Maureen when it is revealed she accidentally let Edward's students find his old ledger recording those who had been caned (43-4) and then decides to sabotage her father by '*empt[ying] the pot of coffee into the lap top*' (57). Maureen then forces Edward to '[g]o up there and unwrap the blanket and look at your cane' (54); he retrieves the cane from the attic which, contrary to the import of the discourse surrounding it, is comically small and underwhelming. Anna, seeking vengeance against her father, allows him to cane her hand so she's 'got something to show the crowd' (78). The play ends as Anna '*opens the front door – a vast crowd can be seen and the noise deafens*' (80).

Both *The Cane* and *Party Time* construct the theatrical dark matter of an offstage crowd: a crowd that in turn creates the effect of a lingering threat that could invade the stage at any time. The mob of *The Cane,* like the civil dissent and totalitarian countermeasures of *Party Time*, also 'stand-in' (albeit through their absence) for the systemic violence referred to in each play, oppressing the borders of the onstage narrative. Specifically in *Party Time*, the chief concerns here are misogyny and authoritarianism, both of which become apparent through dialogue. When Terry suggests to Dusty that he could kill 'you and all your lot', it is not clear if he is referring to Dusty's 'lot' as being women or dissenters:

> We've got dozens of options. We could suffocate every single one of you at a given signal or we could shove a broomstick up each individual arse at another given signal or we could poison all the mother's milk in the world so that every baby would drop dead before it opened its perverted bloody mouth. (Pinter 2011: 302)

Terry's brutal language here is indicative of what Yerebakan sees as a common feature of Pinter's later plays, 'that obscene language is used here to a devastating effect, a very crude tool to oppress, to demolish the voice of the voiceless' (2014: 165). Pinter uses dialogue, rather than relying primarily on bodies, objects and lighting, to create an explicit stage picture of violence and does so in a way that leaves spectators, like Dusty, in 'anticipation' (Pinter 2011: 302), that is, oppressed by a violence that could easily be performed because of the world constructed by the party guests and the danger imagined just offstage. Once again, as in *The Caretaker* and *ear for eye*, command of language presupposes the ability to inflict violence.

Judith Saunders argues that Pinter shows how 'language can be used to inflict violence and how, in the process, language itself is abused [...] pos[ing] a threat to civil discourse and the democracy that depends on it' (2019: 14). The language of civil discourse and democracy also feeds systemic violence, demonstrated in *Party Time* by the intermingling of claims about governance through peace and security and the repetition of sexual slurs and demonstration of ignorance about wider events. *The Cane* too illustrates how systemic violence is transmitted by language, not only in the cyclical speech between Edward and the oppressed Maureen but in the quasi-authoritarian language from which he is 'excluded' by the school investigators, which Anna uses to outmanoeuvre him.

In a speech that resembles Mick's rattling through the details of a housing contract in order to humiliate Davies, Anna explains to Edward that

> All of our Academy schools operate an eyes forward policy. Students must keep their eyes to the front of the class at all times. At all times, staff must be able to see into student's eyes. [...] We also have a silence policy. Nobody speaks in the classroom unless they're invited by the teacher. The corridors are entirely silent spaces. Eyes forward, lips sealed and move to the next class. (Ravenhill 2018: 72–3)

This comes close to the end of the play and is striking in how it enables the audience to envisage the students under Anna's Academy system as more oppressed than the students caned by Edward decades ago – constantly watched by teachers and disciplined by their own internal 'second nature'.

Anna's dialogue evokes the theatrical dark matter of systemic violence, markedly different from the subjective violence of Edward's era. This is emphasized in the closing lines of the play where Edward proclaims, '[L]et all the fat bald men who were once boys who were caned accuse those men and let the caned decide what the punishment for those old men should be' (80). Edward's dialogue points out how what once functioned smoothly and was systemic may now, by contemporary standards, be regarded as subjective violence and how, by taking individuals such as himself to account for their actions, the surface-level of violence can only ever be addressed, rather than its deeper, systemic roots.

The felt absences of systemic violence in these plays, then, emerge through dialogue which functions to create a sense of oppression: both from the offstage and invisible (the crowd or protest) and the onstage (the misogyny of Terry in *Party Time*, the power struggle of Anna and her family in *The Cane*). This threat of oppression through dialogue – repudiating the more obvious means of representing subjective violence – signals that the most important thing going on might not be the action occurring in the respective rooms of *Party Time* and *The Cane*, but what is happening in the societies that the individuals in those rooms are indelibly a part of.

Conclusion

As more and more British playwrights opt to represent violence on stage without 'showing' it in any explicit way, the continuation of Pinter's legacy becomes more pronounced. As argued through the case studies above, Pinter's ability to convey and explore societal oppression through dialogue can be used for several, often intertwined purposes. As shown in *The Caretaker* and *ear for eye*, slurs, degrading comments and interpellated naming perpetuate a prejudice anchored in issues like wealth, class and race. Such dialogue can symbolically assign individuals as 'waste' and, as in Balibar's theory of violence, objectify them to the extent that harm can be done on them with impunity. Dialogue, essentially, shows the characters of these plays existing in a world of systemic violence.

Additionally, Pinter's language conveys felt absences: absences that construct permeating or pervasive threats to the characters and audience. Such felt absences, like missing people, offstage crowds, or acts of violence in indefinite suspense, paradoxically reveal the intangible and inescapable nature of systemic violence. It is telling that when physical manifestations of violence enter into the space of those felt absences created by Pinter's dialogue (Jimmy in *Party Time* and Ravenhill's comically small cane), they do not satisfy the expectations or answer the questions anticipated by the characters and/or audience. The systemic violence constructed by these absences is, simply, too all-encompassing to satisfactorily locate.

With such analyses, Pinter's narratives can seem bleak, illustrating a world enmeshed in inescapable and repetitive systems often propagated by the public's very relation to one another. Yet, just as he presents the perpetuators of systemic violence in his plays as the most effective communicators, so too does he prove that the power of systemic violence lies mainly in language. Just as it can be reinforced by proliferation, so can it be undermined by those same means. Both tucker green and Ravenhill appear to understand this facet of Pinter's writing, with both *ear for eye* and *The Cane* closing on verbal challenges to the system ostensibly directed at the audience. The influence of Pinter, then, has set a precedent for British playwrights to stage the systemic violence of our contemporary society, making this dark matter tangible through dialogue and revealing the unseen violence in urgent need of address.

Notes

1. To give some recent examples of these writers' output: Churchill's *Escaped Alone* (2016) dramatized the systemic issue of environmental disaster lurking beneath a tea party; Kelly's *Girls & Boys* (2018) is a one-woman monologue recounting an example of specifically male domestic violence; Kirkwood's *Chimerica* (2013) displays the evolution of governmental oppression in the United States and China; McDowall's *Pomona* (2015) literalizes how people trafficking lies underneath the modern city; and Lynn's *One For Sorrow* (2018) presents a white middle-class British family working through their suspicion and racism after a terrorist attack.
2. Notably in Marc Silverstein's *Harold Pinter and the Language of Cultural Power* (1993).
3. Two notable exceptions are Steve Waters's chapter 'The Pinter Paradigm: Pinter's Influence on Contemporary Playwriting' in *The Cambridge Companion to Harold Pinter* (2009), where Waters argues the continued relevance of Pinter's plays in comparison to the increasingly 'historical' plays of John Osborne and Arnold Wesker; and Andrew Wyllie's specific comparison between writers in 'The Politics of Violence after In-yer-face: Harold Pinter and Philip Ridley', in *Pinter Et Cetera* (2009).
4. The only major difference between Galtung's structural violence and Žižek's systemic violence appears to be in their titles, with *structural* implying that societies are built up like structures, independent to one another, while *systemic* suggests a more globalized perspective where issues of violence are more connective and invasive.
5. See Gabbard, 'The Pinter Surprise' (1986).
6. Though specific events are not named in *ear for eye*, there are many similarities to demonstrations organized under the Black Lives Matter movement and allusions to the extrajudicial murders of Michael Brown Jr., Eric Garner and Mark Duggan.
7. Pinter's restrained use of represented subjective violence too may account for why he was perceived as more 'absurdist' and less 'naturalistic' than his peers. As Esslin writes: 'It is the intriguing paradox of Pinter's position that he considers himself a more uncompromising, ruthless realist than the champions of "social realism" could ever be' (1991: 263). This may reflect a shift in British theatre from perceiving subjective violence as 'realist' in Pinter's time, to now, where systemic violence arguably appears as a more pronounced issue in society.
8. See Aleks Sierz, *In-yer-face Theatre: British Drama Today* (2001).

Works Cited

Angelaki, V. (2017), *Social and Political Theatre in 21st-Century Britain: Staging Crisis*, London: Bloomsbury.

Arden, J. (2014), *Plays: 1*, London: Methuen.

Balibar, É. (2016), *Violence and Civility: On the Limits of Political Philosophy*, G. M. Goshgarin (trans.), New York: Columbia University.

Bond, E. (1997), *Plays: 1*, London: Methuen.

Chui, J. W. Y. (2013), *Affirming the Absurd in Harold Pinter*, New York: Palgrave Macmillan.

Churchill, C. (2019), *Plays: 5*, London: Nick Hern.

Edgar, D. (2008), 'Pinter's Weasels', *The Guardian*, 29 December. Available online: https://www.theguardian.com/commentisfree/2008/dec/29/harold-pinter-politics (accessed 15 October 2018).

Esslin, M. (1991), *The Theatre of the Absurd*, 3rd edn, London: Penguin.

Gabbard, L. P. (1986), 'The Pinter Surprise', in S. H. Gale (ed.), *Harold Pinter: Critical Approaches*, London and Toronto: Associated University Presses.

Galtung, J. (1969), 'Violence, Peace, and Peace Research', *Journal of Peace Research*, 6 (3): 167–91.

Goddard, L. (2013), 'debbie tucker green', in D. Rebellato (ed.), *Modern British Playwriting: The 2000s: Voices, Documents, New Interpretations*, 190–212, London: Methuen.

Gussow, M. (1994), *Conversations with Pinter*, London: Nick Hern.

Kelly, D. (2018), *Girls & Boys*, London: Oberon.

Kerr, W. (1967), *Harold Pinter*, New York: Columbia University Press.

Kirkwood, L. (2016), *Plays: One*, London: Nick Hern.

Lynn, C. (2018), *One for Sorrow*, London: Nick Hern.

McDowall, A. (2015), *Pomona*, London: Methuen.

Pattie, D., ed. (2012), 'Introduction to the 1950s', in *Modern British Playwriting: The 1950s: Voices, Documents, New Interpretations*, 1–26, London: Methuen.

Pinter, H. (1996), '*The Caretaker*', in *Harold Pinter: Plays 2*, 1–76, London: Faber and Faber.

Pinter, H. (2001), 'Degree Speech to the University of Florence', 10 September. Available online: https://www.wussu.com/current/pinter3.htm (accessed 16 October 2018).

Pinter, H. (2011), '*Party Time*', in Harold *Pinter: Plays 4*, 279–314, London: Faber and Faber.

Ravenhill, M. (1996), *Shopping and Fucking*, London: Methuen.

Ravenhill, M. (2018), *The Cane*, London: Methuen.

Saunders, J. (2019), 'Language Performing Violence and Violence Performed on Language: A Political Lesson in Harold Pinter's *One for the Road, Mountain Language, The New World Order*, and *The Pres and an Officer*', *The Harold Pinter Review: Essays in Contemporary Drama*, 3 (1): 14–30.

Sierz, A. (2001), *In-yer-face Theatre: British Drama Today*, London: Faber and Faber.

Silverstein, M. (1993), *Harold Pinter and the Language of Cultural Power*, London and Toronto: Bucknell University Press.
Sofer, A. (2013), *Dark Matter: Invisibility in Drama, Theater, and Performance*, Ann Arbor: University of Michigan Press.
tucker green, d. (2015), *hang*, London: Nick Hern.
tucker green, d. (2018), *ear for eye*, London: Nick Hern.
Wardle, I. (1981), 'Comedy of Menace', in C. Marowitz, T. Milne and O. Hale (eds), *New Theatre Voice of the Fifties and Sixties: Selections from Encore Magazine 1956-1963*, London: Eyre Methuen.
Waters, S. (2009), 'The Pinter Paradigm: Pinter's Influence on Contemporary Playwriting', in P. Raby (ed.), *The Cambridge Companion to Harold Pinter*, 2nd edn, 297-309, Cambridge: Cambridge University Press.
Woodroffe, G. (1988), 'Taking Care of the "Coloureds": The Political Metaphor of Harold Pinter's "The Caretaker"', *Theatre Journal*, 40 (4): 498-508.
Wyllie, A. (2009), 'The Politics of Violence after In-yer-face: Harold Pinter and Philip Ridley', in C. Owens (ed.), *Pinter Et Cetera*, 63-77, Newcastle upon Tyne: Cambridge Scholars.
Yerebakan, I. (2014), 'Explicit Language, Radical Tone: Harold Pinter's Obscene Words Speak Louder than Action', *AAA: Arbeiten aus Anglistik und Amerikanistik*, 39 (2): 155-73.
Žižek, S. (1999), *The Ticklish Subject: The Absent Centre of Political Ontology*, London and New York: Verso.
Žižek, S. (2009), *Violence: Six Sideways Reflections*, London: Profile Books.

9

Faith, Telos and Failure: Pinter, Butterworth, Kelly

David Pattie

A man stands in an empty room; he hears the sound of people climbing the stairs, and he leaves before they enter. A man stands in a ruined cottage; when a low-flying aircraft passes overhead, he opens his mouth, preparing to scream. A couple, sharing a candle-lit dinner, are startled at the sudden arrival of a man in bloodstained clothing. These three opening images could possibly have originated in the imagination of one artist. They share a common dynamic: a setting that is a refuge and, at the same time, disturbingly open to the outside world; the intrusion of an outside force, an intrusion which demands a reaction and which will, in all three plays, act as a revelation of both the nature of the characters and of their relation to the space. It might be said that, since the early 1960s, there has been a term for plays that start by staging this particular dynamic. When there is a room, a character and a threat, critics and audiences can find themselves reaching for the term 'Pinteresque'; after all, Harold Pinter is the dramatist most closely associated with great threats in little rooms. Each one of these scenes shows the outside world forcing its way in to a space in which the characters are unguarded because they are unregarded. For a moment, they have the illusion that they have managed to escape the gaze of others, and almost as soon as that illusion is established, it is destroyed.

However, only one of these plays is by Pinter. The opening example is *The Caretaker* (1960), the second is from Jez Butterworth's *The Winterling* (2006) and the third from Dennis Kelly's *Orphans* (2009). It could be said that the similarity is unsurprising; both Butterworth and Kelly have spoken about Pinter's work and influence as being important to their development as dramatists. In an interview for *The Guardian*, Butterworth revealed that 'the three people I always used to send my plays and screenplays to first were Harold Pinter, Anthony Minghella and Sydney Pollack' (Lawson 2009) and Pinter himself was cast in the 1997 film adaptation of Butterworth's first full-length play *Mojo* (1995). Kelly recalled in the *Evening Standard* how he 'came across Pinter's plays at youth theatre, and although I wasn't particularly smart, when I read the stuff I knew it was good' (Kelly 2010).

As Steve Waters has noted, both Butterworth and Kelly are part of a generation of playwrights that owe a debt to Pinter's work (Waters 2009). Pinter might have faded from view somewhat during the 1970s, a period in which direct, clear social engagement was the prized quality for new, younger dramatists, but during the 1980s and 1990s, as the tide of socially engaged drama receded, dramatists found themselves in territory that Pinter had already mapped out. Sarah Kane, Mark Ravenhill, Martin Crimp and many of their contemporaries dealt with the power struggles behind even the most apparently banal dialogue; with the precarious nature of truth; and with the fragility of human relations, which could be disrupted by even the most trivial shift in power between characters. At the same time, Pinter's work appeared to move towards the concerns of younger dramatists; from *One for the Road* (1984) onward, his writing was more concerned with exposing the unacknowledged hypocrisy of the newly triumphant neoliberal West.

Waters argues that there were three new-writing strands in which Pinter's influence could be clearly discerned. Firstly, there was Pinter the comic dramatist, the writer whose ear for linguistic slippages, particularly in male speech, had influenced Butterworth, Patrick Marber and Joe Penhall. Secondly, there was Pinter the modernist, the inheritor of features of Kafka's and Beckett's work. This influence could be traced most clearly in the work of Ravenhill and Crimp. Lastly, there was Pinter the political dramatist, whose forensic examination of the operations of power was taken up by Kane early on and by Caryl Churchill later in her career. Waters's three-fold typology of influence does have much to recommend it, and it is true that the divergence between Pinter and new writing in the 1970s had turned to convergence in the 1990s. However, what is missing from his analysis is an account of a wider change in the nature of writing for the stage, a change later noted and discussed by Chris Megson in 2013:

> [Over] the past decade or so, there has been a perceptible shift in emphasis from the *objects and contents* of belief systems (especially ideological belief systems: their advocacy, contestation, the effects of their loss), to an exploration – often with metaphysical impetus of the *existential dynamics and viability* of belief as a foundational premise for personal identity and action in the world.
>
> (2013: 42; emphasis in original)

Megson traces this development in the work of Howard Brenton, Lucy Prebble, Ravenhill, Kane, David Greig and Kelly, arguing that this strand of playwriting emerges at a time when previously stable ideologies have crumbled. The end of the Cold War, however, doesn't simply push the question of belief to the forefront of people's minds; rather, Megson argues, it could be said that the entire span of post-war drama is marked by the persistent investigation of the idea of the individual's faith in culture, in political systems, in religion, and in social structures. What marks more recent drama from work done from the 1950s to the 1980s is that from the 1990s onwards the very idea of belief itself is in flux. Writers investigate not a belief in something but the mechanisms of belief itself, both as it declines and as writers and theatre makers try to establish the grounds on which an 'ethics of commitment' (45), as Megson puts it, can be created in a world without the structures of a defined faith.

Elsewhere, in 'Beyond Belief: British Theatre and the "re-enchantment of the world"' (2016), Megson argues that contemporary drama stages a double movement in relation to questions of faith. Faith is always directed outward; it is always vested in an other (whether that be an individual, a social structure, a belief system or an ethical framework). However, faith in external entities and structures is not in itself enough to guarantee that faith will be rewarded. Drawing on three contemporary dramas – *Bullet Catch* by Rob Drummond (2013), *Enron* by Lucy Prebble (2009), and *13* by Mike Bartlett (2011) – Megson argues,

> The three examples of dramatic writing discussed in this chapter put the emphasis, not so much on the propositional contents of belief systems nor the calibration of a thesis, but on the phenomenological experience that belief makes possible – for better or worse. If disenchantment marks the closure of a telos […] then the subject of belief reopens the telos by stoking the conversation about the kind of society we want to live in and the values that might shape it.
>
> (2016: 55)

In other words, faith always operates against the idea of disenchantment; a belief system that promises a final summary of individual and social existence (a telos, as Megson puts it) operates within a world that, according to Megson, is fundamentally disenchanted – a world that no longer sustains the idea that a telos is attainable. Moreover, the phenomenological experience of faith (that is, the experience of faith as something that fundamentally shapes our perception of the world) can in itself be misleading or damaging. For example, in one of Megson's case studies, *Enron*, a quasi-religious faith in the market leads most of the characters into financial ruin; it does so because the characters have managed to abstract an idea of capitalism as inherently moral and stable from the messy operations of the quotidian market. They construct a telos from their engagement with the world but that telos, necessarily, exists in a form that is abstracted from reality and, as such, is always haunted by the possibility of its collapse.

It is here that Pinter's work intersects with that of the writers who came to prominence in the 1990s and beyond. Pinter, from his earliest work through to *Celebration* (2000), created characters whose relation to the world they inhabit is based on a faith that there is a telos of some kind, accessible to them through their interaction with the world of the play. This faith could be in the oblique systems and institutions that govern their actions (as it is for Gus and Ben in *The Dumb Waiter* (1959), or Goldberg and McCann in *The Birthday Party* (1958)); it could be in another human being, as with Aston in *The Caretaker* (1960) who comes to have enough faith in Davies to inform him of the devastating medical treatment he received; or with political systems, which are invested with all the fervour of religious belief, as in *One for the Road*, *The New World Order* (1991) and *Party Time* (1991).

The precise focus of faith varies; what remains constant is the absolutist commitment of the person who has faith. When they must ground the telos of their faith in reality, characters like Goldberg frequently find that language fails them:

> **Goldberg** You know what? I've never lost a tooth. Not since the day I was born. Nothing's changed. (*He gets up.*) That's why I've reached my position, McCann. Because I've always been as fit as a fiddle. All my life I've said the same. Play up, play up, and play the game. Honour thy father and thy mother. All along the line. Follow the line, the line, McCann, and you can't go wrong. What do you think, I'm a self-made man? No! I sat where I was told to sit. I kept my eye on the ball. School? Don't talk to me about school. Top in all subjects. And for why? Because I'm telling you, I'm telling you, follow my line? Follow my mental? Learn by heart. Never write down a thing. And don't go too near the water. And you'll find—that what I say is true.
>
> Because I believe that the world ... (*Vacant.*) ....
>
> Because I believe that the world ... (*Desperate.*) ....
>
> BECAUSE I BELIEVE THAT THE WORLD ... (*Lost.*) (Pinter 1996: 71–2)

Goldberg's faith in an unspoken something might escape articulation, but this doesn't mean that it disappears. When Stanley comes downstairs, Goldberg acts as though he has not experienced a crisis in his ability to believe. However, even as an apparently decisive statement of belief disintegrates into cliché, uncertainty and silence, the underlying reason for Goldberg's declaration becomes clearer. He needs to believe; he needs to ground his belief in a telos that explains his reality. He might not be able to articulate the core nature of that belief, but the need to vest authority for his actions in some overarching system of which he is a part remains.

Goldberg might be able to move smoothly back from a moment of existential despair to business as usual. Other Pinter characters are not as fortunate; unlike Goldberg, when they encounter a moment of crisis they find that they cannot recover themselves. In *Tea Party* (1964), Disson, a small businessman, uses the occasion of a job interview for a new secretary to describe his job as a quasi-religious vocation:

> **Disson** We're the most advanced sanitary engineers in the country. I think I can say that quite confidently.
> **Wendy** Yes, I believe so.
> **Disson** Oh yes. We manufacture more bidets than anyone else in England. (*He laughs.*) It's almost by way of being a mission. (Pinter 1997a: 96)

Disson, for a man who likes to think of himself as rational, spends much of the first part of the play evincing and protesting faith in any number of things: his job, his new wife, his family, maleness, rationality, his own status and so on. When he begins to suspect that his faith is misplaced, he resorts to the kind of overstated assertiveness that Goldberg uses above, and, like Goldberg, he finds it impossible to sustain:

> **Disson** Drinking? You call this drinking? This? I used to down eleven or nine pints a night! Eleven or nine pints! Every night of the stinking week! Me and the boys! The boys! And me! I'd break any man's hand for ... for playing me false. That was before I became a skilled craftsman. That was before ... (126)

In *No Man's Land* (1975), the itinerant author Spooner's last offer to Hirst, his lauded, successful counterpart, is, in effect, also a profession of faith:

> Your face is so seldom seen, your words, known to so many, have been so seldom heard, in the absolute authority of your own rendering, that this event would qualify for that rarest of categories: the unique. I beg you to consider seriously the social implications of such an adventure. You would be there in body. (Pinter 1997b: 394)

Note the sentence 'You would be there in body'; momentarily, Hirst's attendance takes on the attributes of a religious manifestation – one could say that, for Spooner, Hirst's presence acts as a telos. Hirst, however, changes the subject; the offer of faithful service is rejected and the play ends with the characters locked in stasis.

Sometimes, and especially in Pinter's later work, a moral telos that cannot be articulated is held in place only through violence. In *Party Time*, for example, Melissa claims that the survival of the over-privileged club to which she belongs is down entirely to the code by which its members live:

> **Melissa** The clubs died, the swimming and the tennis clubs died because they were based on ideas which had no moral foundation whatsoever. But *our* club, *our* club – is a club which is activated, which is improved by a moral sense, a moral awareness, a set of moral values which is – I have to say – unshakeable, rigorous, fundamental, constant. (Pinter 2011: 311; emphasis in original)

As with Goldberg in *The Birthday Party*, Melissa is engaging in a form of moral grandstanding, professing faith in the rectitude of the power structures that sustain her in front of an audience, as though the only way to sustain such faith is to perform it. This encomium earns the praise of the other club members but, as another character, Gavin, confirms a moment later, the moral code can only be upheld through violent coercion and suppression:

> **Gavin** Now I believe one or two of our guests encountered traffic problems on their way here tonight. I apologise for that, but I would like to assure you. That all such problems and all related problems will be resolved very soon. Between ourselves, we've had a bit of a round-up this evening. This round-up is coming to an end. In fact normal services will be resumed shortly. (312–13)

The nature of the normal service that has been restored is left undefined (although one can guess that it works in favour of the members of the club). The moral code that justifies this, however, cannot be illuminated, and this suggests that the underlying structure of the society we see is as fragile as the characters seem to think. An unshakeable moral code would not need the support of the forces of the state.

In each of these plays, Pinter, it could be argued, dramatizes a failed attempt at the creation of a telos. The characters try to lift themselves beyond a quotidian reality which is variously dangerous, confused or imperfect; the ideal moment is in the past or in the future, or in some other part of the present. It is yearned for (and sometimes it seems it has been achieved) but it is never unqualified, and the quest for such moments comes at a cost. In each of these plays, and across Pinter's work as a whole, one can clearly discern a relation to faith that can be described as the repeated destruction of a phenomenological telos; characters attempt to craft an abstracted faith from the materials they have to hand, but these attempts are doomed to fail and in some cases the creation of that telos is itself destructive. Here, Pinter's work comes closest to that of Butterworth and Kelly, and it is to that relation that I will now turn.

The Still Point: Pinter and Butterworth

Jez Butterworth's *The River* (2012) carries an epigraph from T. S. Eliot's poem 'Burnt Norton' (1935), later published as part of *Four Quartets*:

> At the still point of the turning world. Neither flesh nor fleshless;
> Neither from nor towards; at the still point, where the dance is,
> But neither arrest nor movement. And do not call it fixity,
> Where past and future are gathered. Neither movement from nor towards,
> Neither ascent nor decline. Except for the point, the still point,
> There would be no dance, and there is only the dance.
>
> (qtd. in Butterworth 2012: ix)

For Eliot, the still point is a clear, if paradoxical, symbol of transcendence, a point at which, for a moment, the world is both completely at rest and perpetually in motion. It is freed from the one-directional temporal flow of conventional reality; it exists outside of time, and yet it contains time within itself. It is a moment of active tranquillity, in which both mind and body are simultaneously affirmed and denied. It is a moment that the characters in Butterworth's play would dearly like to reach. *The River* dramatizes the halting, uncertain relationship between an unnamed man and two women – women whom the man brought at different times to the cabin by the river in which the play is set. In each case, the man attempts to describe and re-enact a moment of harmony: a magical moment, in which the characters and the landscape merge into a perfect whole:

> **The Man** (*to himself*)   August. Low cloud. (*Aloud*) Blood red as far as the headland turning to lilac-blue wisps above the bluff. Trails of apricot, feathering out through blue, dark blue, and aquamarine to an iris ring of obsidian and above that the Evening Star. (*Finds it*) Yes. You little beauty. We're set.

> Beat.
>
> **The Woman**   That was a magical moment. That evening in the cabin. When they watched the sun set. Our sunset he called it. And she remembered the moment for ever. (Butterworth 2012: 8)

This exchange captures the play in miniature; a moment of connection, one in which a unique memory is caught at the instance of its formation, seems momentarily to promise both characters that they have reached a still point in their relationship. It is, to use Megson's term, as close as the characters get to the creation of a phenomenological telos. Note, for example, the fact that the sunset (which is presumably taking place when the man speaks) is converted into a past event by the woman. In their minds, the sunset is both present and past, and they are both in the present and the future. They and the world they inhabit move through time without moving. And at the heart of this idealized, timeless world is an encounter with nature which seems, as described by one of the characters, to be a clear moment of transcendent connection with the natural world:

> **The Man**   There's a long pool. Just past the bridge, just past the rapids where the path runs steep. The river suddenly plunges thirty-feet deep over black stones. I went out this morning. I climbed the cliff and looked down from the track above the pool. Deep in the river. Lined up in shoals. Like U-boats. Silver. Resting. Thirty or forty of them. The most beautiful, shyest, fiercest creatures … Huge. Waiting. Ready to run. And if you catch one … if you catch one, it's like catching a lightning bolt. It's like jamming your finger into a socket. Like a million sunsets rolled into a ball and shot straight into your veins. And you feel it. By God, you feel it. (14)

This speech echoes the lines from Eliot that Butterworth uses as the play's epigraph; the pool is still, in the midst of rushing, plunging water, and the fish is both resting and charged with movement. It is a lightning bolt: it is a drug that works instantaneously on the recipient. It is the incarnation of the transcendent moment as both still and in motion, as neither arrest nor movement, as the phrase from Eliot's 'Burnt Norton' would have it.

However, the play demonstrates that such a moment is unattainable; the characters might strive towards transcendence, but they will never reach it. The relation between the man and the women he brings back to the cottage is too unstable; they will never be fixed into a single moment that will encapsulate both the time they spend together and all the times they have spent and will spend together. The moment will always remain out of reach, and the play's three characters are haunted by the knowledge. In a long monologue near the play's end the other woman describes a moment in which transcendence is actively resisted. She and the man are making love; she looks into his eyes, and he looks away:

> **The Other Woman**   … I said your name. You screwed your eyes tight, and tensed your jaw, and flinched, and shuddered. And your skin went cold. Your breath turned sour. And your hands felt small… thirty seconds later it was over. And we lay there in silence. And you stood up, and came in here, and three minutes later you reappeared with two cups of strong tea, and you put them down on either side of the bed, and you asked me if the tea was okay. If that's how I liked it. I said it was perfect. It was just right. (41)

It is not simply that the characters fail to find a moment in which their relation is balanced; the man, when faced with the possibility of such a connection, both denies and displaces it – he looks away, and after the lovemaking is finished, he offers her a very pale substitute for the intensity of an event in which they might both have lost themselves. Throughout the play, similar moments are all displaced into the past, into events that are at best faint echoes of Eliot's still point, and, most damningly of all, on to other people.

This idea of a transcendent moment which is never quite there – which is in the past, or in a version of the characters' histories that can't be recreated because the characters can't agree on a shared sequence of events – is also explored in Pinter's drama, most clearly in *Landscape* and *Silence*, two plays first staged as a double bill by the Royal Shakespeare Company (RSC) in 1969. In *Landscape*, Beth is entirely consumed by the memory of a transcendent moment:

> **Beth**   He lay above me and looked down on me. He supported my shoulder. (*Pause*) So tender his touch on my neck. So softly his kiss on my cheek. (*Pause*) My hand on his rib. (*Pause*) So sweetly the sand over me. Tiny the sand on my skin. (*Pause*) So silent the sky in my eyes. Gently the sound of the tide. (*Pause*) Oh my true love I said. (Pinter 1997c: 197–8)

The moment she evokes at the play's end is one in which the boundaries between self and other, and between thought and feeling, have collapsed into one single, clear perception of a world both fixed and in motion. However, it takes place in the past and it cannot be shared with her husband, the only other character on stage. *Silence* takes Beth's desire for a transcendent relation as its main structuring principle. Ellen, Rumsey and Bates invoke memories that they try to elevate into the status of a telos:

Rumsey [...] I tell her my life's thoughts, clouds racing. She looks up at me or listens looking down. She stops in midsentence, my sentence, to look up at me.

[...]

Ellen I turn. I turn. I wheel. I glide. I wheel. In stunning light. The horizon moves from the sun. I am crushed by the light.

[...]

Bates Sometimes I press my hand on my forehead, calmingly, feel all the dust drain out, let it go, feel the grit slip away. Funny moment. That calm moment. (Pinter 1997d: 191, 198, 199)

As in *Landscape*, though, these moments are incommensurate; they can't be shared by the characters on stage.[1] For one thing, these moments are different in kind. Rumsey's is predicated on a connection with an unnamed woman (we assume this is Ellen, but the play doesn't make this clear), Ellen's is an idea of unending, annihilating freedom, and Bates's is simply a moment, which can be accepted as something that is by its nature transient (a moment is, after all, a fixed unit of time and will be replaced by the next moment, and the next). The characters' temporal relation to the moments they describe cannot be fixed; as Ellen puts it, 'I'm never sure that what I remember is of today or of yesterday or of a long time ago' (214). The dialogue between the three is structured as a series of denials; an action or connection is proposed only to be ruled out almost immediately. No wonder that, at the play's end, the characters are left with nothing more than fragments. The still point each one tries to reach will always be deferred, delayed, momentary or founded in a relation that is by its nature transient. A telos based on such a moment can, as in *The River*, be invoked; but, also as in *The River*, it is always placed just out of reach.

'I was so happy when you two got together': Pinter and Kelly

Dennis Kelly's *Orphans* starts with an archetypally Pinteresque image: a well-dressed couple, together in a location that suggests sanctuary, startled by the unexpected presence of an intruder. Pinteresque too is the characters' oblique, deceptively ordinary dialogue. Liam has entered wearing a t-shirt covered in blood, and one might expect that his arrival might be greeted with horror. Instead, Danny and Helen greet him with the kind of wary courtesy appropriate to an unexpected (but known) guest:

Liam Alright, Danny?

Danny Liam?

Liam Helen?

Helen Liam.

Pause

Liam How's it-

How's it all going, like, you alright?

Danny What? Yeah.

Pause

You?

Liam Yeah. You know. (Kelly 2013: 97)

The atmosphere of this opening scene, a mixture of tension and comic incongruity, can be matched to any number of Pinter plays. Vicky Angelaki, for example, notes that '[the] hovering sense of menace, claustrophobia within the confined spaces of oneself and one's surroundings' links plays like *Orphans* and *Love and Money* (2006) directly to Pinter's work (2017: 106). Kelly, in the first scene of *Orphans*, seems to be engaged in a self-conscious replication of the menacing comedy of *The Dumb Waiter* or *The Birthday Party*; Liam's awkwardness on stage replicates the kind of uncertainty Robert Gordon discerns in the early onstage activities of Goldberg and McCann (see Gordon 2013).

As the play develops, however, we move from the evocation of Pinteresque cliché to something rather more resonant. Liam initially tells the other two characters that he came across a youth bleeding on the street; as the play progresses, we learn that he has engaged in a racially motivated attack. Helen asks Danny to intimidate the victim, to protect her brother; however, Danny's complicity in Liam's violence serves to rupture the relation between him and Helen. During the course of the play, we learn that all three characters are in their various ways damaged and fearful; Liam intrudes, not because he wants to disrupt the relation between Danny and Helen, but because he wants to be as safe as they seem to be. Unlike Davies who, in *The Caretaker*, plays one brother against the other, Liam seems almost pathetically eager to declare that he is part of a community:

> **Liam** I was so happy when you two got together. I was over the moon when she told me you were getting married. I cried when she said she was carrying your child. I always knew she'd make a great mother, she could've abandoned me, could've let them split us up, that's what they wanted, they used to look at us and think we could really place that girl, but that boy… I know that, Helen doesn't know I know, but I know. And she never once allowed that, and more than that, Danny. Never even entertained the thought. (Kelly 2013: 119)

Liam, in other words, attempts to elevate a familial arrangement into an act of faith; he attempts to construct a telos from his relation to his sister. Helen, in the past, made an ultimate, unthinking commitment to him; so, in turn, Liam commits himself to Danny, Helen and their child. However, an attempt to build a transcendent relation – a relation that can exist beyond the stresses of the quotidian, which is not contingent on the shifting relations between the characters – is by its nature bound to come into conflict with the sheer mess of reality; so it proves in *Orphans*. To protect a relation that he sees as transcendent, Liam will attack those whom he fears are different and therefore dangerous:

> **Liam** I love being in this house, you two, Shane, walking in here is like walking in to, I dunno, perfume or like warm, a warm, I just love it actually. But going back out there is like walking into shit. Like walking into a soft wall of shit. Into fucking sewage. (160)

The threat that Liam first of all places outside of the sanctuary of his sister's home is gradually revealed as a threat which he carries, and it's a threat that both Helen and Danny carry in their turn. The characters in the room fear the outside world, but the outside world, it seems, has as much, if not more, to fear from them.

In *Orphans*, Liam tries to create a telos with Danny and Helen, founded on an abstracted idea of a community that transcends the everyday and which seeks to establish relations that are fundamental (based as they are on a familial relation that can be sustained independently of the world outside). However, the community he tries to create splinters, not because of an external threat, but because Liam is himself a threat to the community he wishes to create. This is a common dynamic in Kelly's work, apparent in earlier plays such as *Osama the Hero* (2005) and *Love and Money* and more recently in *Girls & Boys* (2018). Kelly's Channel 4 series *Utopia* (2013–14) employs the dynamic twice, both for the Network and for the loose group of conspiracy theorists that opposes it.

This pattern repeats, with variations, across Pinter's canon, from early works like *The Dumb Waiter*, *A Slight Ache* (1959), *The Caretaker* and *The Homecoming* (1965), to later plays such as *No Man's Land*, *Betrayal* (1978) and *Ashes to Ashes* (1996). In each one of these texts, attempts are made to form relationships that might transcend the effects of a disturbing and disruptive reality. In each, these relationships begin to take on the status of a telos – a moment of faith, vested in this case in the individual's relation to the other characters on stage. In each one, the threat – which plays out in various ways: through violence, rejection of the outsider, the disruption of relations that seem stable at the beginning of the text – is shown to have already been there. Pinter does deal, as the cliché goes, with people, a room and a threat, but, in both Pinter's and Kelly's work, often the threat comes from the people inside, not the people outside.

For example, *Old Times* (1971) starts with a stage image that *Orphans* mirrors. Two characters are together on stage; as far as they are concerned, they are alone, but we in the audience know that someone else is on stage. The initial image is held through the first dialogue exchange, which establishes both Deeley's nervous anticipation of the new arrival and the subdued tension of his relation to Kate:

Deeley […] Why isn't she married, I mean, why isn't she bringing her husband?

Kate Ask her.

Deeley Do I have to ask her everything?

Kate Do you want me to ask your questions for you?

Deeley No. Not at all. (Pinter 1997e: 250–1)

When Anna moves more squarely into the performance space, she does so with a speech that comprehensively stakes her claim to Kate: they shared a hectic, exciting life in London at some point in the unspecified past, one that Deeley, at first, seems to know nothing about. Deeley is, at least from his perspective, forced into the same position as Danny in *Orphans*; to protect the relation that defines him, he has to attack and neutralize the threat that Anna poses. Anna, on the other hand, is also in Danny's position; the threat is not to a defining relation in the present but to one in the past whose power has been effaced by Deeley. Deeley, to win, has to insinuate himself into the past; Anna has to bring the past into the present. Both have to create a relation with Kate that exists across time and, near the end of the play, Anna is the one who seems to have won:

Kate […] Is Charley coming?

Anna I can ring him if you like.

Kate What about McCabe?

Anna Do you really want to see anyone?

Kate I don't think I like McCabe.

Anna Nor do I. (300)

However, even here there are indications that her success is at best partial. Kate's answers are as oblique in the recreated past as they are in the play's present; the attempt to create a relation that transcends time is threatened in each case from within the relation itself.

This threat is finally manifested in Kate's monologue at the end of Act Two. Calmly, she describes remembering Anna lying dead in the room they shared; then, she describes bringing a man back to the same room:

Kate He liked your bed, and thought he was different in it because he was a man. But one night I said let me do something, a little thing, a little trick. He lay there in your bed. He looked up at me with great expectation. He was gratified. He thought I had profited from his teaching. He thought I was going to be sexually forthcoming, that I was about to take a long promised initiative. I dug about in the windowbox, where you had planted our pretty pansies, scooped, filled the bowl, and plastered his face with dirt. (310–11)

We can infer that the man is Deeley, but he is unnamed, and Kate talks of him as an ephemeral part of her life: 'He suggested a wedding instead, and a change of environment. (*pause*) Neither mattered' (311). Kate's final speech is an act of temporal violence; she invokes her past with both Anna and Deeley, only to deny and destroy it. In doing so, she shatters any possibility of a transcendent relation with either of them. Indeed, she shows clearly that such a relation always was unattainable; that any attempt to create a telos in which the individual's faith in the other is acknowledged, reciprocated and thereby vindicated was always doomed to fail. Symbolically, she kills Anna, and she effaces Deeley. At the play's end the characters are isolated, trapped under bright light, fixed in place, unable to communicate with each other – separated, all chance of a telos vested in the other is gone, as distant from the other characters as Liam, Danny and Helen.

Conclusion

Megson concludes his chapter on contemporary British theatre and the metaphysical imagination discussed above by quoting the Austrian filmmaker Michael Haneke:

> At a time when public confidence in ideological and religious belief-systems has become increasingly embattled, the 'metaphysical turn' in theatre speaks directly to Haneke's 'remnant desire for another world'.
>
> (2013: 52)

In other words, contemporary theatre, at least in some of its manifestations, evinces a strong desire for what Megson elsewhere describes as a phenomenological telos – a system of faith created through the individual's direct apprehension of other individuals, systems, histories, ideologies and traditions. Megson is correct to argue that this desire is both strongly felt and liable to fail; in Haneke's phrase, such a desire is a remnant, a holdover from a time in which, it might be presumed, systems that supported such faith were far more readily available. The collapse of ideological and religious belief systems has not lessened the individual's desire to create such a telos. However, it does mean that any such faith will be fragile because it is fundamentally unsupported by anything other than the individual's desire. If the other in which faith is vested denies that faith, or shows themselves unable to fulfil the terms of that faith, the telos collapses.

It is this movement – from the vesting of faith in the other to the moment where such faith decays – that is staged in the plays of Pinter, Butterworth and Kelly discussed above. In each, one or more of the characters attempts to establish a set of relations based on faith; in each, that set of relations is given the status of an all-encompassing telos. In each, the attempt fails and its failure traps the characters, isolating them from each other. It is in this, I would argue, that Pinter's presence in contemporary playwriting is most closely felt. His work can be thought of as an important precursor of the metaphysical turn that Megson identifies, in that it repeatedly demonstrates what I have described as a failure to achieve a workable, sustainable telos. It is here that Pinter's work has most in common with the generation of writers and theatre workers that includes Butterworth and Kelly. Time and again, Pinter's characters advertise their faith in each other, or in systems that supposedly sustain them, and time and again that faith crumbles, because it has no sure foundation.

Note

1 This notion has been a staple of Pinter criticism from its inception (see, for example, Esslin 1970). For a more recent discussion of the ways in which Pinter's characters use language to disguise themselves, see Hosokawa (2016).

Works Cited

Angelaki, V. (2017), *Social and Political Theatre in 21st Century Britain*, London: Palgrave.
Butterworth, J. (2012), *The River*, London: Nick Hern Books.
Esslin, M. (1970), *The Peopled Wound: The Plays of Harold Pinter*, London: Methuen.
Gordon, R. (2013), *Harold Pinter: The Theater of Power*, Ann Arbor: University of Michigan Press.
Hosokawa, M. (2016), *Harold Pinter and the Self: Modern Double Awareness and Disguise in the Shadow of Shakespeare*, Hiroshima: Keisuisha.
Kelly, D. (2013), 'Orphans', in *Dennis Kelly Plays Two*, 91–189, London: Oberon.
Kelly, D. (2010), 'Dennis Kelly: I Can't Imagine a More Violent Writer than Shakespeare', *Evening Standard*, 9 March. Available online: https://www.standard.co.uk/go/london/theatre/dennis-kelly-i-can-t-imagine-a-more-violent-writer-than-shakespeare-6736124.html (accessed 30 June 2020).
Lawson, M. (2009), 'The Grass Is Greener (interview with Jez Butterworth)', *The Guardian*, 24 March. Available online: https://www.theguardian.com/stage/2009/mar/24/jez-butterworth (accessed 30 June 2020).
Megson, C. (2013), '"And I was struck still by time": Contemporary British Theatre and the Metaphysical Imagination', in V. Angelaki (ed.), *Contemporary British Theatre: Breaking New Ground*, 32–56, London: Palgrave Macmillan.
Megson, C. (2016), 'Beyond Belief: British Theatre and the "re-enchantment of the world"', in S. Adiseshiah and L. LePage (eds), *Twenty-First Century Drama: What Happens Now*, 37–57, London: Palgrave Macmillan.
Pinter, H. (1996), '*The Birthday Party*', in *Harold Pinter: Plays 1*, 1–81, London: Faber and Faber.
Pinter, H. (1997a), '*Tea Party*', in *Harold Pinter: Plays 3*, 91–140, London: Faber and Faber.
Pinter, H. (1997b), '*No Man's Land*', in *Harold Pinter: Plays 3*, 315–399, London: Faber and Faber.
Pinter, H. (1997c), '*Landscape*', in *Harold Pinter: Plays 3*, 165–188, London: Faber and Faber.
Pinter, H. (1997d), '*Silence*', in *Harold Pinter: Plays 3*, 189–209, London: Faber and Faber.

Pinter, H. (1997e), '*Old Times*', in *Harold Pinter: Plays 3*, 243–313, London: Faber and Faber.

Pinter, H. (2011), '*Party Time*', in *Harold Pinter: Plays 4*, 279–314, London: Faber and Faber.

Waters, S. (2009), 'The Pinter Paradigm: Pinter's Influence on Contemporary Playwriting', in P. Raby (ed.), *The Cambridge Companion to Harold Pinter*, 2nd edn, 297–309, Cambridge: Cambridge University Press.

10

The Crimpesque: Pinter's Legacy in the Theatre of Martin Crimp

Maria Elena Capitani

Martin Crimp is a dramatist who is capable of merging his British *roots* with wider European *routes*. Tellingly, his multifaceted and challenging dramatic output, aimed at exploring the deepening crisis of subjectivity in a late capitalist world, has long been regarded with suspicion in Britain and, at the same time, widely appreciated on the Continent, earning him the title of 'one of British theatre's best-kept secrets' (Sierz 2012). However, 'as opposed to how it may have felt a few years ago', things are steadily changing for Crimp, and his 'recognition as one of the most important playwrights of our time' is 'on an upward curve' (Angelaki 2014: 309). Britain's public acknowledgement of Crimp's work is exemplified by the recent National Theatre's star-cast production of *When We Have Sufficiently Tortured Each Other* (2019), directed by Katie Mitchell and described by one reviewer as '[t]he most hyped play of the year' (Sierz 2019).

The complex palimpsestic and elusive quality of Crimp's work is in line with the versatility of this prolific author, who has experimented with different literary forms and artistic media and enjoyed a parallel career as a theatre translator and adaptor of theatre classics; he has shaped a singular dramatic territory or 'Crimpland'. This term was coined by the theatre director Dominic Dromgoole in his survey of contemporary British playwriting, *The Full Room* (2000):

> Martin Crimp is a truly European writer and, happily [*sic*] to subvert all my little Englander prejudices, a rather wonderful one. His work drips with a cool formal sense of theatrical possibility. [...] Crimp has carved out his own theatrical territory, Crimpland, full of hollow folk, all with offstage lives of loneliness and mystery, suddenly trapped together in a mutual obsession.
>
> (2000: 62)

Crimp's work combines various dramatic traditions and styles including absurdism, surrealism and, according to some critics, post-dramatic, which fruitfully intermingle. His dramatic corpus encompasses almost the entire range of textual transcendences mentioned by Gérard Genette in his *Palimpsestes* (1982): intertextuality, paratextuality and hypertextuality. Moreover, critics have noted a peculiar form of intratextuality in this simultaneously original and multi-layered output. Thus, 'Crimpland' becomes a slippery and liminal in-between space bridging British and continental theatre, in which, as Sierz suggests, 'influence takes the form of osmosis' (2013: 160). On the one hand, Crimp has influenced younger playwrights including Sarah Kane, Mark Ravenhill and, more recently, Simon Stephens, Martin McDonagh and the German dramatist Roland Schimmelpfennig. On the other hand, his stratified plays are pervaded by the legacy of various writers who 'have percolated slowly through his consciousness [...] into Crimp's theatre toolbox, which includes devices on loan from [Eugène] Ionesco, [Samuel] Beckett, Pinter, [David] Mamet and [Caryl] Churchill, and these have served him well for the past two decades and more' (ibid. 161).

Taking up Sierz's observation, this chapter explores the impact of Harold Pinter's legacy on Crimp's work specifically, which has been noted by many reviewers and scholars but not investigated at length.[1] After a brief overview which charts Pinter's influence on a selection of Crimp's early writings from the late 1980s and early 1990s, this study concentrates on the distinctive structural and linguistic features of *The Country* (2000), the play in which the echoes of Pinter are most evident. The chapter then considers more recent plays to show how the Pinteresque permeates, to varying extents, Crimp's entire output, despite his reluctance to recognize this influence.

Following Crimp's decision to direct a reading of Pinter's *Old Times* (1971) for the Royal Court's 1999 Playwrights' Playwrights season and the premiere of *The Country* at the same venue in 2000, many commentators stressed that Crimp owed a substantial debt to Pinter.[2] Strangely enough, while he has always cited the profound impact of Beckett on his writing, in a 2005 interview Crimp declared that he was not conscious of Pinter's imprint on his work:

> The Pinter connection took me utterly by surprise. The fact that I'd chosen to direct his play maybe put that into people's heads. When I was a teenager staging plays at school, I was interested in the absurdists, Ionesco and Beckett. I lived in a sleepy little backwater in the north of England and I didn't really come across the work of Pinter. So it's not a conscious influence.
>
> (qtd. in Aragay, Klein, Monforte and Zozaya 2007: 58)

Crimp added that he came to Pinter quite late and, although he frequently adopted some of the techniques developed by the distinguished dramatist, he felt that his and Pinter's aesthetic worlds and sexual politics were very different:

> Of course I have a toolbox as a writer and I happen to use some of the tools that Pinter invented. They are just there. That's not the same as appropriating somebody else's imaginative or aesthetic world. I feel that mine is very different from that of Harold Pinter's, particularly in terms of sexual politics, and of the weight of masculinity in his work.
>
> (ibid.)

Moreover, Crimp has always seen himself as someone who is utterly determined to experiment with the dramatic form and to push his writing in new directions. Although he considers Pinter one of Britain's greatest dramatists, Crimp seems to find his work quite repetitive from a stylistic point of view. According to Crimp, the only dramatist capable of constantly reinventing himself and rewriting theatrical rules was Beckett:

> Sometimes in Pinter's work you feel that he's doing more Pinter. He's a brilliant, fantastic writer. Some of his late work is really impressive, like *Ashes to Ashes*. But there's just a sense sometimes that he is copying or repeating himself. I want to avoid the trap of being just a satirist. I think that my work is characterized by diversity of output. There was a moment when that worried me slightly in terms of identity, but now I see that as being part of my identity. There is a danger of painting yourself into a corner with style. Samuel Beckett painted himself into a corner, but the harder he looked in it, the more he found.
>
> (ibid. 59)

These three excerpts offer significant insights into Crimp's ambivalent relationship to Pinter. If the first passage on his interests as a schoolboy genuinely evokes teenage memories, I would suggest that we should be wary about interpreting Crimp's words from the second and third passages. Here, Crimp seems to struggle to keep a safe distance from Pinter by generalizing and oversimplifying his work. While it is true that Crimp has created his own theatrical territory by sharpening some tools which Pinter initially created (as well as those invented by other playwrights) without appropriating the aesthetic worlds and sexual discourse of someone else, it is arguably simplistic to define the 2005 Nobel Laureate as a writer whose male characters tend to affirm existing patriarchal structures.

Similarly, Crimp describes Pinter's *oeuvre* as repetitive and homogeneous in contrast to Beckett's diverse output. However, like Crimp, Pinter is an eclectic writer, whose corpus spans different genres across media including poetry, a novel, television plays, radio dramas and screenplays. In contrast to Crimp's characterization, Pinter has been defined as 'a playwright who constantly reinvents himself' and 'remains so open to new forms, and voices' (Raby 2001: 2). Crimp's final reference to Beckett, a literary father that he and Pinter both acknowledge as a conscious influence, reinforces the similarities between the two rather than their dissimilarities; through a selection of Crimp's plays, this chapter will demonstrate that Pinter and Crimp have more in common than the latter admits.

Early Pinteresque Traces

Now an entry in several dictionaries and encyclopaedias, the word 'Pinteresque' first appeared in reviews from the early 1960s as an opaque attempt to describe Pinter's enigmatic plays. Drawing upon the work of Yael Zarhy-Levo (2001: 37), Marc Shaw offers a concise definition of this oblique expression, stating that it 'includes an atmosphere of menace, dialogic rhythms, the withholding of information, and the potential destruction of an individual' (2009: 215).

If the Pinteresque has become the playwright's signature style, another critical label, 'comedies of menace', is equally prominent in Pinter studies. It appeared in 1958 as the subtitle of David Campton's play *The Lunatic View* (1958), but it was theatre critic Irving Wardle who was the first to apply the term to Pinter's *The Birthday Party* (1958). Working from Wardle's implicit emphasis of menace over comedy, Basil Chiasson argues that 'comedy and menace are necessarily bound up, and are thus mutually empowering' (2009: 31). Reassessing the critical tendency to see the comedy and the menace as discrete, or to focus exclusively on menace, Chiasson also suggests that, despite being associated with Pinter's early plays, the phrase can be stretched to the dramatist's entire output: 'the comedy of menace aesthetic is dramatically crucial to the later political plays as well, albeit they have undergone a transmutation in the way of content, form, and effect' (31). My analysis will show how the 'Pinteresque' and 'comedy of menace' might be used to examine Crimp's *oeuvre*, a theatrical land characterized by – paraphrasing Shaw's definition – threatening domestic atmospheres, elusive and nervy dialogue, the lack of background information and the collapse of the self in late-capitalist society.

The first Pinteresque traces detectable in Crimpland date back to the late 1980s.[3] Crimp presented a trilogy entitled *Definitely the Bahamas* (comprising *A Kind of Arden*, *Spanish Girls* and *Definitely the Bahamas*), first performed in a production for BBC Radio 3 in 1987, where it won that year's *Radio Times* Drama Award. The trilogy's title play has subsequently been revived and directed by Crimp at the Orange Tree Theatre, a small fringe venue not far from his home in Richmond, in March 2012 in a double bill with *Play House*. In response to the play's 1987 broadcast, reviewers immediately stressed the debt Crimp owed to Pinter. Among them, the *Daily Telegraph*'s Charles Spencer's review, 'A New Pinter?', focused on the importance of dialogic minimalism and the sense of threat permeating the work of both writers:

> He probably won't welcome the comparison but there is much in his work that is reminiscent of Pinter, who also wrote for radio early in his career.
>
> Like Pinter, Crimp uses language with exhilarating economy – his dialogue doesn't appear to have a single superfluous word and seemingly mundane lines often achieve a startling dramatic resonance. Like Pinter, too, he creates an impression of fear and uncertainty just below the poised surface of his plays.
>
> (1987: 1253)

Sheridan Morley also noted the fact that both Crimp and Pinter worked for the radio early in their careers before suggesting that *Definitely the Bahamas* seemed to pay homage to Pinter:

> He gives at least one of his three new one-act plays (*A Kind of Arden*) a distinctly Pinteresque label, while the second (*Spanish Girls*) has a programme quote from Pinter, and the title piece seems strongly evocative of *A Slight Ache* as a suburban domestic haven is invaded by a mysterious stranger able silently to uncover its ghastly marital secrets.
>
> (1987: 1254)

Sierz points out that the programme quote was from Pinter's *One for the Road* (1984): 'You know, old chap, I do love other things, apart from death, so many things. Nature. Trees, things like that. A nice blue sky. Blossom' (2013: 22). He suggests that Crimp probably chose it to stress the contrast between the sunny images of exotic places such as the Caribbean, Spain or South Africa and the atrocities of illness, genocide and sexual violence. Comparisons to precursors such as Beckett and Ionesco were something that Pinter encountered at the beginning of his career when critics, struggling to categorize his plays, referred to similarities between Pinter and well-established writers. Like Crimp, Pinter admitted that he was a keen fan of Beckett but denied that Ionesco was an influence, as Crimp in turn did with respect to Pinter's work (see Pinter qtd. in Batty 2005: 108).

Among the various theatrical strategies shared by Crimp and Pinter, the notion of language as a tool to exert power takes thematic precedence. In *No One Sees the Video*, a piece first staged in 1990 at the Royal Court's Theatre Upstairs and based on his own experience as a transcriber of market-research interviews in the early 1980s, Crimp explores the linguistic structures and persuasive techniques used in marketing in order to, as director Lindsay Posner suggests, 'intrude into people's lives. The more you classify someone, the more you demean them' (qtd. in Sierz 2013: 189). When trying to convince the character of Liz to join the world of market research, the ruthless interviewer, Colin, claims that their job is not difficult at all: 'Skill doesn't come into it. Just acquaint yourself with the vocabulary, and the rest will follow' (Crimp 2005: 45). Thus, the play's focus on market-research strategies quickly turns into an exploration of the subtle mechanisms of language and power.

In Act Two, Colin explains the difference between a 'prompt' (when the interviewer leads the interviewee towards what he/she should say) and a 'probe' (an 'open' question that tends to become disturbingly intrusive): 'It's my job. Probing. Probing is a technical term. It means eliciting a response. […] You can probe or you can prompt. Trust the former, avoid the latter' (Crimp 2005: 57). This technique is exemplified by the mock interview conducted by Jo, Liz's teenage daughter:

Jo   How old are you?

Colin   Thirty.

,

I'm thirty-two.

Jo   I thought you were older.

Colin   I'm thirty-two years old.

Jo   Are you married?

Colin   Am I what?

Jo   I'm probing.

Colin   Very good.

Jo   Are you married?

Colin   Yes.

> **Jo**   What's your wife's name?
>
> **Colin**   (You're really probing.)
>
> **Jo**   Answer me. (59)

As Sierz observes, 'These question-and-answer techniques, so suggestive of police interrogation, give the play an air of manipulative power games with uncertain outcomes' (2013: 33–4), a comment that could have easily been made about the interrogation scenes in Pinter's *The Birthday Party*. As is well known, this play – in which the vulnerable Stanley Webber is visited in a seaside boarding house by two strangers, Goldberg and McCann, who proceed to verbally abuse, subjugate and finally remove him – revolves around the use of manipulative language (see Malkin 1992: 53–74 and Elyamany 2019: 1–22).

Crimp's early works play with uncertainty, creating Pinteresque atmospheres of growing tension which often derive from an impending danger that is left unspecified. For instance, in *Dealing with Clair* (Orange Tree Theatre 1988), the eponymous young estate agent mysteriously vanishes after meeting James, a wicked cash buyer in his fifties who probably killed her. In *Getting Attention* (West Yorkshire Playhouse 1991), a 4-year-old child, Sharon, who remains offstage, is secretly abused by her dysfunctional parents while the neighbours turn a blind eye. Paradoxically, as Aloysia Rousseau has observed, the curious character Milly perceives the child abuse exclusively through the filter of media coverage which screens her from next-door reality:

> Crimp's use of the newspaper as a shield blocking someone's view is also reminiscent of Pinter. Many of his plays open with a man sitting at a table and reading his newspaper while having breakfast, something that is rather typical of kitchen-sink drama. [...] They [the newspapers] act as walls separating the protagonists from their immediate surroundings.
>
> (2014: 346)

Since Crimp's cultivation of menace does not turn into an outbreak of in-yer-face violence, spectators are compelled to come up with their own image of Clair and Sharon's respective suffering in each play. In a 2006 interview, Crimp observed that the two pieces share the same technique: 'What these two plays have in common is a strategy that still makes me cheerful as a writer – the false happy ending. Both have a false happy ending. I don't often like my own writing, but I do like the last scene in *Getting Attention*. The brighter and more cheerful it is, the more it hurts' (qtd. in Sierz 2013: 96).

I would suggest that Crimp's final statement – echoing Beckett's famous claim that '[n]othing is funnier than unhappiness' (1964: 20) – is in line with Chiasson's (re)interpretation of Pinter's comedies of menace, in which comic and unsettling elements are fruitfully interwoven.

Crimp at His Most Pinteresque: *The Country*

After dismembering dramatic and theatrical conventions in his postmodern masterpiece *Attempts on Her Life* (1997), in which the different facets of an absent and protean character are conjured up by unnamed speakers, Crimp tried to reconstruct stage narrative in *The Country*, broadcast on BBC radio in 1997 before opening at the Royal Court Theatre on 11 May 2000 in a slightly modified version directed by Katie Mitchell. By refashioning what is conventionally described as a traditional five-act structure and examining a popular theme such as betrayal (one of Pinter's favourites), *The Country* challenges the spectator through dramatic ellipses, disturbing innuendos, subtle power games, evocative words and stage props.

Crimp's play explores the strained relationship between the character of Richard, a negligent GP and recovering drug addict, and his wife Corinne – a London couple, aged 40, who have recently moved to the country with their children to start a new and healthier life. One night, Richard brings home Rebecca, a 25-year-old American woman, saying he found her unconscious by the roadside. Corinne is highly suspicious of their guest from the beginning of the play and soon discovers that, overlooking his professional duty, her husband has induced Rebecca to overdose and has bought the stranger a gold watch. It transpires that this beautiful young historian, who has moved to the country to carry out a research project, is the primary reason why Richard left London. Moreover, during a tense telephone conversation with his senior partner, Morris, it emerges that Richard has neglected a dying patient to spend time with his lover Rebecca. In the middle of the night, a deeply upset Corinne flees from the house with the children. In the fifth act, two months later, Richard is celebrating Corinne's birthday: he promises to stay clean and gives his wife an expensive pair of shoes as a present. Despite this artificial reconciliation, there is no guarantee of future happiness for the couple.

The fact that the first draft of the play was originally broadcast on radio allowed Crimp more time to work on the stage version, specifically its structure and content. This was the first time that Crimp risked experimenting with retrospective narration: following Pinter's steps but at the same time refashioning the technique by tempering the forward movement characteristic of his playwrighting with storytelling that looks backward in time:

I was aware that certain writers, such as Beckett or Pinter, had taken a turn at one point late in their careers, and began writing plays which were all about looking back. Pinter tried to sustain it in a couple of pieces, *Landscape* and *Silence*. And I think that's dangerous. I have always taken particular care to propel things forward, that's my preferred method. Not looking back. So this is a play that pushes forward constantly and then hits retrospective narration – if you like – in a similar way to *Old Times*.

(Crimp qtd. in Sierz 2013: 104)

Unsurprisingly, the majority of theatre critics who saw the 2000 production concentrated on its Pinteresque echoes and the theme of marital infidelity: 'Pinter' appears at least once in all the reviews of the play. For instance, the *Mail on Sunday*'s Georgina Brown described Crimp's 'creepy, unsettling piece' as 'the most Pinteresque play I've ever seen', in which the writer 'detects the tumour of betrayal with a specialist surgeon's precision and accuracy' (2000: 616). Her assessment echoes Spencer's words in the *Daily Telegraph*, which highlighted the influence of Pinter on Crimp's work in general and in *The Country* specifically:

[H]e often appears to be up to his ears in debt to Harold Pinter. That debt is particularly burdensome in *The Country*, and at times the piece seems less like an original play than an immensely skilful parody of dear old Harold. The setting is one of those vaguely forbidding rooms that are such a feature of Pinter's work, and Crimp quickly wheels on the old device of the intimidating stranger who threatens another character's possession of the territory.

(2000: 616)

This excerpt is revealing in that it gives a sense of the burden that constant comparison to an acclaimed canonical writer places on Crimp – here described as someone who reproduces the style of Pinter in a skilful way – and, in a sense, justifies his attempts to distance himself from his precursor. Despite downplaying Crimp's originality, Spencer is right in identifying some of the effective (and affective) strategies adopted from Pinter, that is to say, the use of a seemingly familiar domestic setting and the disrupting figure of the intruder, who upsets the already precarious balance of the couple.

Significantly, like many of Pinter's plays, *The Country* starts *in medias res*. Drawing attention to Crimp's (and, by extension, to Pinter's) penchant for elusiveness and ambiguity, Michael Billington observed in his review that the dramatist 'artfully withholds information to generate suspense' (2000: 618). For David Nathan, Crimp 'is sparse with his information, clearly believing, as Pinter does, that we are not entitled to any more information than would normally be revealed in an overheard conversation between two people who have known each other for a long time' (2000: 617). Indeed, *The Country* opens with a Pinteresque domestic duologue between husband and wife, whose defamiliarizing ordinariness echoes Petey and Meg's opening conversation in *The Birthday Party*, Bert and Rose's in *The Room* (1957), and Jerry and Emma's in *Betrayal* (1978):

> What are you doing?
> I'm cutting.
> What are you cutting?
> I don't know ... I'm making something. Why are you looking at me like that?
> You don't normally cut. You don't normally make things. What are you making?
> — I just thought I'd cut out some pictures to go round the cot. I thought they'd be stimulating. (Crimp 2005: 291)

The first sinister reference to the mysterious intruder appears just after a few lines, when Corinne starts questioning Richard about their uninvited guest: 'This. ... person. Is she asleep? When will she wake up?' (292). Although Richard claims that he saved the young woman exclusively for medical reasons, Corinne becomes more suspicious and the atmosphere increasingly tense, in line with Pinter's well-established formula. Unlike Pinter, however, Crimp goes so far as to stage Corinne's emotional breakdown, provoked by the unexpected arrival of the American 'Other' whom she perceives as an insidious threat to the safety of her family. Although in the fifth act the reunited couple appear more relaxed on Corinne's birthday, with Corinne more at ease in her domestic territory, her final line 'What if I have to spend the rest of my life simulating love?' (366) and Richard's reluctance to kiss her suggest that they are still entrapped by their lies and emotional paralysis, but that the turmoil is starting to be managed, suppressed even – as one finds so often in Pinter's world.

The theme of marital infidelity has been developed in many of Pinter's plays including *The Collection* (1961), *The Lover* (1963), *The Homecoming* (1965), *Old Times*, *Betrayal* and *Ashes to Ashes* (1996). Among them, *Betrayal* – as its title makes clear – is more explicit in its anatomization of the discourse of extramarital desire. Divided into nine scenes, Pinter's drama unfolds backwards chronologically, while *The Country* – whose final act is set two months later – pushes forward while looking back. The two plays also differ in the composition of the marital triangle: Pinter presents two men (Robert and his friend, Jerry) and a woman (Emma, Robert's wife, who had an affair with Jerry), whereas Crimp stages a domestic battle between two very different women (Corinne and Rebecca) and a male character (Richard). This possibly explains Crimp's perception of the distance between his own gender politics and Pinter's: '[A] play like *The Country* has a strong female bias, whereas in Pinter's work you're always pulled towards the male pole' (Crimp qtd. in Aragay, Klein, Monforte and Zozaya 2007: 58). If Pinter's drama appears as more male-oriented, perhaps it is because Pinter is interested in investigating different kinds of betrayals over and above the one defining the heterosexual marriage: Emma's adultery as well as Jerry's betrayal of his friendship with Robert and his betrayal of Emma in the form of his dedication to and competition with Robert as a friend and colleague in the publishing industry. An unseen male character, the writer Roger Casey, complicates the inner dynamics of homosocial bonds further, with Casey revealed as the current lover of Emma as well as working with both Jerry and Robert, thus constituting the third vertex of the male triangle. In response to Crimp, one might say that Pinter does not concentrate exclusively on the male pole but rather he aims to explore both directions.

Things are further complicated if one reads the play as showing a more positive portrait of the woman, who 'moves away from emotional paralysis to competent independence, effectively moving towards creativity', than of the two men, who, 'betraying their literary ideals to market forces, move backwards and away from one another and her' (Batty 2005: 58). Beyond infidelities and absent or otherwise invisible characters, Pinter and Crimp share a characteristic approach to stage dialogue; their characters' speech is riddled with carefully constructed gaps, repetitions, non-sequiturs, pauses and silences. For instance, two of the duologues Crimp incorporates into *The Country* are strongly reminiscent of the semantic discussion between Ben and Gus in *The Dumb Waiter* (1959):

Ben   Go and light it.

Gus   Light what?

Ben   The kettle.

Gus   You mean the gas.

Ben   Who does?

Gus   You do.

[…] How can you light a kettle?

> Ben   It's a figure of speech! Light the kettle. It's a figure of speech!
>
> Gus   I've never heard it.
>
> Ben   Light the kettle! It's common usage! (Pinter 1996a: 125).

Similarly, in the opening act of *The Country* Corinne and Richard speculate on the correct use of the words *purse* and *bag* in British and American English:

> [...] So there wasn't a bag?
> A what?
> A bag. A purse. Didn't she have some kind of ...
> A purse?
> Yes. A purse. A bag. Whatever. Don't look so/blank.
> Why did you say that: purse?
> Why do I say it?
> Yes. Why do you say it when it's not English?
> What is not English?
> Purse is not English.
> I'm not speaking English?
> Of course you're speaking/English. (Crimp 2005: 297)

Crimp plays not only with words but also with onstage visibility and invisibility given how *The Country* revolves around two opposite yet complementary types of bodies: visible, palpable and prominent onstage figures – especially the sensual Rebecca, who appears inherently conscious of the magnetic potential of her body – that might be defined as bodies *in praesentia* and, simultaneously, bodies *in absentia*, that is elusive, (im)material traces left by unseen characters. While the protagonists of the love triangle maintain a tangible presence, other important characters are deliberately kept offstage in ways that contribute to the creation of the disturbing atmosphere of his own comedy of menace.

In fact, these absent figures interact with onstage characters through (im)material words and material props. For example, the unnamed children are mentioned many times throughout the play, but they never appear. Morris and Sophie manifest via a domestic object, an old telephone which disturbingly rings until the final scene of the play:

> [...] Kiss me.
> *The phone continues to ring.*
> I have kissed you.
> *Pause.*

I have kissed you.
Then kiss me again.
Neither moves. The phone continues to ring. (366)

The phone repeatedly interrupts Richard and Corinne's tense conversations, increasing the sense of menace for the audience and for stage characters themselves. Rousseau has noted that

> [i]t is to them a highly ominous sound […] The recurring ringing represents more generally everything that Richard would like to keep buried: his unfaithfulness to his wife but also his neglect of his patients and his on-going drug addiction.
>
> (2014: 347)

Crimp himself has always considered the telephone 'an instrument of doom' (qtd. in Sierz 2013: 105). As he declared, 'hav[ing] a life of their own' (ibid. 106) and being largely instrumental in constructing narratives, stage objects perform an essential role in plays, like Pinter's dumb waiter, described by David Pattie as 'an active participant' (2009: 55). Stanton B. Garner, Jr. draws a parallel between stage objects and the linguistic system: 'Like language, props extend the body's spatializing capacities and its projective operations' (1994: 89). So it is in *The Country* and in *The Dumb Waiter*: far from being lifeless objects, the phone and the dumb waiter erupt into (and disrupt) the domestic universe, voicing offstage characters by giving them a means of expression and 'projecting' them into the claustrophobic and gloomy space in which the two plays are set. Pinter's mysteriously comic dumb waiter serves a double function: its role is both ambiguous and enhances the generic intersection between farce and menace in the play. In a more straightforward sense, Crimp's old-fashioned phone provides the audience with a comic moment when Richard remains trapped in the wire: 'I'm just getting myself tangled, Morris, in this flex. The phone here is something out of a *museum* … you have to rotate the … That's right: the dial' (Crimp 2005: 310; emphasis in original). The disturbingly constant ringing of the phone – which 'reverberates in the auditorium [and] will probably linger in the audience's minds' (Rousseau 2014: 347) – is just one of the threatening sounds permeating Crimp's audioscapes. Characterized by minimalist aesthetics, Mitchell's 2000 production at the Royal Court made effective use of various aural inputs, affecting theatregoers through a vast range of sinister stimuli increasing the sense of discomfort and menace (see Angelaki 2012: 99).

Working as it does on different levels of perception, *The Country* should not be reduced to the status of derivative or a pale copy of some of Pinter's plays. Rather, it should be considered a challenging play in its own right which draws upon Pinter's techniques while adapting the tools he created. Crimp's comedy of menace invites the audience to explore the said and the unsaid, embodiment and disembodiment, materiality and immateriality, and presence and absence in new ways. In Crimp's stratified piece, which moves forward while looking backwards at key points, elusive dialogue and imposing objects and sounds are rich in ellipses; two opposite female worlds clash in a domestic battlefield where the seeming absence of certain characters and their words speaks as loudly as those which are present.

More Recent Instances of the Pinteresque

While *The Country* may be the most Pinteresque play in Crimp's output, he has continued to appropriate and adapt his predecessor's techniques in more recent pieces, such as *The City* and *In the Republic of Happiness*. First presented at the Royal Court in 2008, *The City* can be considered 'a companion piece to *The Country*' (Sierz 2013: 227). The play opens with a conventional end-of-the-day conversation between Chris, who works for a large corporation, and his wife Clair, a translator. This unhappy marriage is threatened by the sudden arrival of an intruder, their neighbour Jenny, a sinister nurse married to an army doctor, who visits the couple to complain about Chris and Clair's children playing in the garden and preventing her from sleeping. As Sierz suggests, the language in *The City* is even more defamiliarizing than in *The Country*: 'The dialogues are more awkward and there is a sense of disconnection: both Chris and Clair talk past each other. They utter monologues rather than have dialogues […]. When there is something like genuine communication, it usually results in a threat of violence or in physical revulsion' (228–9). This technique is similar to the one Pinter employs in *Landscape* (1968), a retrospective one-act play in which a middle-aged couple seated in the kitchen of a country house bring back past memories through interwoven monologues. In the opening stage directions, Pinter states that 'DUFF *refers normally to* BETH*, but does not appear to hear her voice*' and 'BETH *never looks at* DUFF*, and does not appear to hear his voice*' (Pinter 1997: 166), the information already, and perhaps unlike Pinter's other plays, stressing the failure of marital communication from the outset. The (inter)personal collapse staged by *The City* might also be reminiscent of the disrupted conversation between Rebecca and her husband Devlin in *Ashes to Ashes*. Rebecca evokes what appear to be disturbing memories about an abusive ex-lover overlapping with images of large-scale atrocities (the Holocaust, for example). This descriptive intermingling of micro- and macro-violence is something that Graham Saunders has identified in *The City*, where suburban anxieties overlap with verbally mediated horrific events and 'imaginative cityscapes that exist outside the seemingly familiar locale of Crimp's London' (2019: 17).

If *The City* can be reasonably considered as the urban counterpart of *The Country*, Crimp makes clear that *In the Republic of Happiness*, first performed at the Royal Court in 2012, 'follows on from […] *The City*, of which the last scene is a Christmas scene. So in a way I am revisiting that, and carrying on from where I left off' (qtd. in Sierz 2013: 233). In these two plays, Crimp opts for a seemingly conventional everyday language which simultaneously appears artificial: 'I wanted the naturalistic world to fall apart as we watch it' (ibid. 234).

Divided into three parts, the play opens with three generations of a family gathered around the table for a Christmas meal, suddenly interrupted by the unexpected arrival of Uncle Bob:

Mum What're you doing here, Robert?

Uncle Bob Well to be frank with you, I've really no idea. I thought I would just suddenly appear, so I did. I suddenly appeared. I craved your company – craved to be with you all – and here I am. I hope I'm not putting you out at all. (Crimp 2012: 19)

Crimp appears to be using some of the main ingredients of Pinter's comedies of menace, namely the intrusion of an outsider who undermines domestic (in)stability. Uncle Bob's denial of knowing his motivation for appearing, his offering up of a description of his emotional state in a way that is difficult for spectators to trust and his inquiry into whether or not he is imposing in a way that may or may not be in earnest are typical of Pinter's approach to plot, situation and character.

In both *In the Republic of Happiness* and *The City*, the unnaturalistic language of the speeches 'have a high sense of artificiality in which Crimp's characteristic linguistic markers and ticks are mixed with declamation and declaration, with a critical lyricism peculiarly his own' (Sierz 2013: 233–4). Yet, as the passage above makes clear, Pinter's influence on what is now characteristic and peculiar to Crimp is evident. Uncle Bob's use of language, for example, makes it difficult for spectators to ascertain precisely what he means or intends, underscoring Crimp's use of stage language as a filter, screening emotions. Decades earlier, in 1962, Pinter discussed this very technique in his speech for the National Student Drama Festival in Bristol:

The speech we hear is an indication of that which we don't hear. It is a necessary avoidance, a violent, sly, anguished or mocking smoke screen which keeps the other in its place. When true silence falls we are still left with echo but are nearer nakedness. One way of looking at speech is to say it is a constant stratagem to cover nakedness.

(1996b: xiii)

Furthermore, at the end of 'Destruction of the Family', the first (and most traditional) part of *In the Republic of Happiness*, the stage is plunged into darkness in a moment that is subtly reminiscent of *The Birthday Party*. The female characters, especially Mum, appear anxious about this:

Madeleine   Bit dark in here.

[…]

Mum   […] When did it get so dark?
[…]

D'you think we should put the lights on? Someone's going to hurt themselves.

Dad   We've got the tree.

Mum   The tree's not very bright, Tom. I think we should get the bulbs out. Please? Can we?

Dad   Okay. (Crimp 2012: 29–30)

Similarly, at the end of the second act of *The Birthday Party*, darkness constitutes a source of anxiety for the characters celebrating Stanley's 'birthday'. Unexpectedly, the party descends into a nightmarish moment in which the absence of light is laden with threatening echoes:

There is now no light at all through the window. The stage is in darkness.

Lulu   The lights!

Goldberg   What's happened?

Lulu   The lights!

[…]

Someone's touching me!

[...]

Meg   Why has the light gone out?

Goldberg   Where's your torch? [...]

McCann   My torch!

Lulu   Oh God! (Pinter 1996c: 58)

As is well exemplified here, in a falsely convivial atmosphere like that of *In the Republic of Happiness*, darkness and lack of sight (Goldberg and McCann have just taken Stanley's glasses) cause distress and danger, in particular to female figures such as Lulu, whose vulnerability is exacerbated by the impossibility to see clearly.

As the final section of this chapter has shown, Crimp's reworking of the Pinteresque and of some of the distinctive elements of the comedy of menace can be identified at key moments throughout his entire body of drama. While early traces can be detected in Crimp's plays from the late 1980s and early 1990s – and if *The Country* marks his Pinteresque climax in 2000 – Crimp's more recent dramas still adopt some of the Nobel Laureate's strategies, but with further reworking and personal touch.

Conclusion: The Anxiety of Influence and the Crimpesque

It is not hard to see why many scholars and reviewers, at least in passing, acknowledge Pinter's stylistic legacy in Crimpland, an unsettling theatrical territory where – as Rebecca claims in *The Country* – 'the more you talk, the less you say' (Crimp 2005: 328) and conventional genres are constantly blurred. Despite this stylistic overlap, in interviews Crimp appears to be deeply wary about the Pinter connection. Torn between two drives (the impulse to draw upon the toolbox of his – unacknowledged – progenitor and the desire to establish his own methods and uniqueness), Crimp appears to struggle with the burden of this literary debt. This 'anxiety of influence' (see Bloom 1997 [1973]) also emerges from his 1996 mordant rewriting of Molière's *Le Misanthrope* (1666), where Alceste's friend (renamed John) says: 'I liked the pause particularly' and the theatre critic Covington rebukes: 'You don't think it owes too much to Pinter?' (Crimp 2005: 122). Even if these couple of lines, like many others in the play, are evidently meant to be funny, 'owing too much to Pinter' appears to trouble Crimp on a personal level.

That being said, this chapter has also demonstrated that, throughout his career, Crimp has not sought to merely imitate Pinter but to appropriate his tools by adapting them to his own dramatic vision. Writing about Pinter's successors, Saunders argues that 'childe Harolds' can be divided into two groups of dramatists: 'one continuing to explore existential fears based on the Pinteresque with the other breaking away to expose and name new threats' (2019: 16). I share Saunders's assertion that Crimp can be placed in 'the middle ground between these two positions' (16), which prompted this chapter's title – the neologism 'the Crimpesque' – which encapsulates both debt and originality. If we can, on the one hand, argue that Crimp and Pinter comfortably fit into one sentence, then I suggest, on the other hand, the Crimpesque should not be diminished in value; it represents a distinctive aesthetics which borrows from the Pinteresque while refashioning this style in innovative and fascinating ways.

Notes

1. The only exception being Graham Saunders's recent article 'Masters (and Mistresses) of Menace', which devotes one section to Crimp (Saunders 2019: 16–18).
2. When asked about this choice Crimp declared, 'I was simply attracted to the writing. It has some really surprising phrases in it, such as "I remember you dead." And there's a couple of passages which describe a decadent party at which people are sitting on a sofa, arguing about China and death. The speeches have an enormous self-contained integrity and energy, they're dense but at the same time transparent, which is difficult to pull off, this thing of being simultaneously clear and complex' (qtd. in Sierz 2013: 104).
3. Sierz affirms that it is possible to find traces of Pinter in Crimp's first solo play *Living Remains* (1982), which has never been published: 'From the beginning, Crimp understood the uses of repetition. In *Living Remains*, Woman's opening lines are: "It's me! I remembered! I'm here!", followed by variations of "Surprise surprise! It's me!" and "surprise surprise, it's me, hello" (p. 1). Reminiscent of Meg's lines at the start of Pinter's *The Birthday Party*, their repetitive cheeriness is clearly a cover for guilt and anxiety. Crimp's Woman knows that her relationship with her husband is on the brink but she's hanging on to the illusion that things are hunky-dory. Her subsequent repeats of "Are you sure?" are riddled with pure anxiety' (Sierz 2013: 113).

Works Cited

Angelaki, V. (2012), *The Plays of Martin Crimp: Making Theatre Strange*, Basingstoke and New York: Palgrave Macmillan.
Angelaki, V. (2014), 'Introduction: Dealing with Martin Crimp', *Contemporary Theatre Review*, 24 (3): 309–14.
Aragay, M., H. Klein, E. Monforte and P. Zozaya, eds (2007), *British Theatre of the 1990s: Interviews with Directors, Playwrights, Critics and Academics*, Basingstoke and New York: Palgrave Macmillan.
Batty, M. (2005), *About Pinter: The Playwright and the Work*, London: Faber and Faber.
Beckett, S. (1964), *Endgame*, London: Faber and Faber.
Billington, M. (2000), *The Guardian*, 17 May, *Theatre Record*, 20 (10): 618.
Bloom, H. (1997 [1973]), *The Anxiety of Influence: A Theory of Poetry*, 2nd edn, Oxford: Oxford University Press.
Brown, G. (2000), *Mail on Sunday*, 21 May, *Theatre Record*, 20 (10): 616.
Capitani, M. E. (2017), '"Perhaps That Taste of Nothing Is What You Can Taste": Sensory Landscapes, Absence, and Objects in Martin Crimp's *The Country*', *Itinera*, 13: 299–310.
Chiasson, B. (2009), '(Re)Thinking Harold Pinter's Comedy of Menace', in M. F. Brewer (ed.), *Harold Pinter's The Dumb Waiter*, 31–54, Amsterdam and New York: Rodopi.
Crimp, M. (2000), *Plays One: Dealing with Clair, Play with Repeats, Getting Attention, The Treatment*, London: Faber and Faber.
Crimp, M. (2005), *Plays Two: No One Sees the Video, The Misanthrope, Attempts on Her Life, The Country*, London: Faber and Faber.
Crimp, M. (2008), *The City*, London: Faber and Faber.
Crimp, M. (2012), *In the Republic of Happiness*, London: Faber and Faber.
Dromgoole, D. (2000), *The Full Room: An A-Z of Contemporary Playwriting*, London: Methuen.
Elyamany, N. (2019), 'Pinteresque Dialogue in the Interrogation Scene of *The Birthday Party*', *Athens Journal of Philology*, 6 (1): 1–22.
Garner, S. B., Jr. (1994), *Bodied Spaces: Phenomenology and Performance in Contemporary Drama*, Ithaca: Cornell University Press.
Genette, G. (1982), *Palimpsestes. La littérature au second degré*, Paris: Seuil.
Malkin, J. R. (1992), *Verbal Violence in Contemporary Drama: From Handke to Shepard*, Cambridge: Cambridge University Press.
Milne, D. (2001), 'Pinter's Sexual Politics', in P. Raby (ed.), *The Cambridge Companion to Harold Pinter*, 195–211, Cambridge: Cambridge University Press.
Morley, S. (1987), *Punch*, 14 October; *London Theatre Record*, 7 (20): 1254.
Nathan, D. (2000), *Jewish Chronicle*, 19 May, *Theatre Record*, 20 (10): 617.
Pattie, D. (2009), 'Feeding Power: Pinter, Bakhtin, and Inverted Carnival', in M. F. Brewer (ed.), *Harold Pinter's* The Dumb Waiter, 55–69, Amsterdam and New York: Rodopi.

Pinter, H. (1996a), 'The Dumb Waiter', in *Harold Pinter: Plays 1*, 111–149, London: Faber and Faber.
Pinter, H (1996b), 'Introduction: Writing for the Theatre', in *Harold Pinter: Plays 1*, vii–xvi, London: Faber and Faber.
Pinter, H. (1996c), 'The Birthday Party', in *Harold Pinter: Plays 1*, 1–81, London: Faber and Faber.
Pinter, H. (1997), 'Landscape', in *Harold Pinter: Plays 3*, 165–188, London: Faber and Faber.
Pinter, H. (2011), 'Betrayal', in *Harold Pinter: Plays 4*, 1–117, London: Faber and Faber.
Raby, P., ed. (2001), 'Introduction', in *The Cambridge Companion to Harold Pinter*, 1–3, Cambridge: Cambridge University Press.
Rousseau, A. (2013), '"The Brighter and More Cheerful It Is, the More It Hurts": Martin Crimp's Darkly Disturbing Comedies', *Études britanniques contemporaines*, 44. Available online: https://journals.openedition.org/ebc/563 (accessed 10 July 2019).
Rousseau, A. (2014), '"Didn't See Anything, Love. Sorry": Martin Crimp's Theatre of Denial', *Contemporary Theatre Review*, 24 (3): 340–50.
Saunders, G. (2019), 'Masters (and Mistresses) of Menace', *Journal of Contemporary Drama in English*, 7 (1): 12–28.
Shaw, M. E. (2009), 'Unpacking the *Pinteresque* in *The Dumb Waiter* and Beyond', in M. F. Brewer (ed.), *Harold Pinter's* The Dumb Waiter, 211–29, Amsterdam and New York: Rodopi.
Sierz, A. (2012), 'theartsdesk Q&A: Playwright Martin Crimp'. Available online: https://theartsdesk.com/theatre/theartsdesk-qa-playwright-martin-crimp (accessed 10 March 2012).
Sierz, A. (2013), *The Theatre of Martin Crimp*, 2nd edn, London: Bloomsbury Methuen.
Sierz, A. (2019), 'Martin Crimp's *When We Have Sufficiently Tortured Each Other* at the National Theatre'. Available online: https://thetheatretimes.com/martin-crimps-when-we-have-sufficiently-tortured-each-other-at-the-national-theatre/ (accessed 30 January 2019).
Spencer, C. (1987), *Daily Telegraph*, 28 September, *London Theatre Record*, 7 (20): 1253.
Spencer, C. (2000), *Daily Telegraph*, 18 May, *Theatre Record*, 20 (10): 616.
Wyllie, A., and C. Rees (2017), *The Plays of Harold Pinter*, London and New York: Palgrave Macmillan.
Zarhy-Levo, Y. (2001), *The Theatrical Critic as Cultural Agent: Constructing Pinter, Orton and Stoppard as Absurdist Playwrights*, New York: Peter Lang.

Part Three

Conversations with Collaborators

Between 2017 and 2019, both editors worked as part of the research team on the Arts and Humanities Research Council-funded project, Harold Pinter: Histories and Legacies. During our time on the project we both had the pleasure of speaking to a range of Pinter's key collaborators, practitioners, friends, fans and critics. The following selection of conversations was chosen in line with our ambition for this collection to look ahead to the next stage of Pinter scholarship and performance. Collectively, these conversations capture recent and long-standing creative engagements with Pinter's work from the perspectives of actors, playwrights, directors and designers. In being attentive to the preconceptions and assumptions that practitioners, critics and audiences bring to Pinter's work in performance, the insights shared here reappraise and celebrate definitive features of Pinter's practice while also charting new and exciting interventions and approaches for future productions.

Chinonyerem Odimba

Chinonyerem Odimba is an award-winning playwright, poet and director working across theatre, film and radio. Her plays include *Princess & The Hustler* (Bristol Old Vic, Eclipse Theatre Company and Hull Truck Theatre co-production, 2019), *Unknown Rivers* (Hampstead Theatre, 2019), *The Seven Ages of Patience* (Kiln Theatre, 2019), *The Bird Woman of Lewisham* (Arcola, 2015), *Joanne* (Clean Break/Soho Theatre, 2015) and *His Name Is Ishmael* (Bristol Old Vic, 2013). In 2020 she was appointed Chair of Theatre Bristol. In 2017, Odimba was the assistant director on *The Caretaker* (directed by Christopher Haydon) at the Bristol Old Vic and Northampton Royal and Derngate Theatres. The following is excepted from an interview with Basil Chiasson on 18 October 2018.

Basil Chiasson (BC): What does Pinter mean to you as a writer?

Chinonyerem Odimba (CO): I was interested to take a classic play [*The Caretaker*] by a very well-known writer and look at it from a contemporary point of view. But I wouldn't list Pinter as a huge influence in my writing. There's definitely that aspect of the way he chooses to tell his stories that as a writer I still find quite fascinating. We're just two very different writers. You know he's not one of these writers who's particularly experimental with form, which is one of all the things as writer that I'm interested in. But I am fascinated by how we hold these writers up as the pinnacle of British playwriting and how that sits alongside our modern plays. [...] I think there are playwrights like Pinter who are slightly more problematic because there is something about the intention of their writing that we can uphold. But for me we can only uphold that if we absolutely acknowledge the unconscious bias that comes with that. As a classical piece of text, *The Caretaker* is admirable. I mean who writes a monologue as long as Aston's in that play and makes it convincing? You know, as a writer I think that's what's rich, that's quite admirable.

BC: In this production of *The Caretaker*, I felt like there were some key experimental and important choices, such as the heavily stylized set and the casting of three black actors. Did you find that you were really bringing something new to the play? Did you get inspired by what you felt was in the play already?

CO: I think that the direction and the way that Chris [Haydon] decided to approach the play was really different. There was a real sense of wanting to crack something in the play that maybe as an audience we haven't tried to get to those bits of the play before? There was a lot of thought about how we might bring that – I don't even want to use the word experimentation – that sense of cracking something open in the text at times that you wouldn't necessarily try and do if you didn't have a cast that represented all those versions of men of colour. That was always the starting point: we knew that we were going into bits of process that would be about trying to find that stuff in the play.

BC: What was your sense of the critics' reaction to the production? The precedent for having an all-black cast in that play is from 1981 [in a production for the National Theatre, directed by Kenneth Ives and starring Norman Beaton (Davies), Oscar James (Aston) and Troy Foster (Mick)] and I think you noted that production in the programme. Was there anything remarkable about the way the press responded to that casting choice?

CO: I mean, how the very text of the play is understood when those words are coming out of actors of colour is very different. We had a lot of issues partly because I don't think audiences are familiar enough with African dialect, whether that's diasporic or not, on British stages. There was a kind of weird assumption made by quite a lot of the press reviews that the actor [Patrice Naiambana as Davies] was Caribbean. The things that really made people very concerned were actually the things that we were baffled by. But that's a lack of familiarity with those voices on British stages; whereas there is more – but not near enough – familiarity with Caribbean and West Indian actors in popular culture. It was almost easy for these people to assume that that was the accent that the lead character [Davies] was assuming.

BC: Can you tell me about the rehearsal process? What are the moments that stand out as significant?

CO: The times where it felt like we'd come across something in the play text where – and it's obvious where Pinter's unconscious bias comes in – he wrote the play assuming that those roles would be played by white men. So, the context of their controversial conversation [the characters, namely Davies and Aston] was within that realm. Trying to understand how you get an audience to engage with a kind of nuance when those words are coming out of a man of colour. In the rehearsal process it felt like those were the most exciting moments because, as we'd come across them, it felt like we had to almost down tools and sort of sit there and work out as agreeable people what that actually meant. I mean, all rehearsal processes have big discussion but there was this really, really tricky and sensitive discussion that had to be had about what we were presenting to an audience and how they might understand that, and making sure we were really clear about what the intention is by casting it in that way and making those choices. Though I knew the play before the process, I think I certainly came to know the play in a completely different way after the process, because it requires so much 'under the skin', let's say, in order for us to present that version to an audience and for that audience to understand where we were coming from with it.

BC: It's an interesting idea when you're faced with having to reconfigure or reimagine these characters – who we all know or at least assume were intended to be cast as white – in order to be suitable for your purposes and what you're trying to achieve.

CO: It would never have occurred to Pinter necessarily to write a black character when actually your play is poking at race and class. You know, you can talk about those things in a way that doesn't require you to engage the people that you're talking about. It's a play of its time and all of that, but, as I say, from a process point of view – to read – it really demanded that kind of getting in to the play in order to even know what one was presenting an audience and then what that institution even becomes in the context of the play. What the writer did do – kindly but without maybe knowing it – was to leave enough room for someone to work out what the play means in a modern context. There are lots of plays that age that don't leave that room. I think finding those cracks in the play made me love the play more. His characters are extremely flawed. Again, there are versions of writers from that era with whom you sometimes feel like they were giving you cardboard cut-out versions. That's not something anyone can accuse Pinter of, especially in this play. Each and every one of those characters are so deeply flawed, so actually what we can understand fairly early on in the play is that what each of them is searching for may not be attainable because they get in their own way. I think certainly in terms of characterization with this play he does get something right in terms of keeping that sense of humanness.

BC: Along the way did you encounter any unwritten rules or assumptions about what 'should' and 'shouldn't' be done with a Pinter play?

CO: If you're doing a Pinter play then there's a kind of approach to it that might be influenced by what happens when you put writers on a pedestal? But I suppose the thing for this production was that we were coming with such a different approach in the first place that we couldn't buy into any of that. We had to interrogate the play in a way that was going to be true to our casting and that vision that Chris had about how he wanted to put the play on. So, I think in some ways we sidestepped a lot of that and didn't allow ourselves to go down that road, you know: 'it must be played by the big boys and that line must land because that line is ... '. We had to find completely new meanings – in every line! – in order to get an audience to go along that particular journey with us. But it's always when you're approaching these classics and you know that there are whole groups of people who think they should be done in a certain way and only in that way. Having written a modern version of *Medea* earlier that year, I was all too aware of the issues of approaching a classic bit of text. But ultimately as artists our job is to free ourselves from expectations, even if those expectations are coming from audiences. There is a sense that until an audience has seen something happen differently, they will always revert back to what they know or what they think they know. It's about not letting your artistic instincts get tainted by those 'shoulds' and 'has to bes' when you're creating anything.

Nancy Meckler

Nancy Meckler was the founder and director of Freehold Theatre Company (1969–73). Following her training in classical acting at the London Academy of Music and Dramatic Arts she studied experimental theatre at NYU and worked with the La MaMa Plexus company in New York. In 1981, Meckler was the first woman to direct for the National Theatre (Edward Albee's *Who's Afraid of Virginia Woolf*). She ran the Leicester Haymarket studio company prior to becoming artistic director of the touring company Shared Experience in 1987 where she worked for twenty-two years. In 1990, she directed Shared Experience's *The Birthday Party* which toured Britain and Ireland. The following is an excerpt from an interview with Basil Chiasson on 20 September 2019 as part of the Harold Pinter: Histories and Legacies conference, hosted at the University of Leeds.

>**Basil Chiasson (BC):** I'd like to begin by inviting you to talk about your practice and any highlights in your career that you'd like to talk about alongside your early experiences with Pinter.
>
>**Nancy Meckler (NM):** When I got involved with Shared Experience I thought this would be an opportunity to go back to working expressionistically, and a lot of the work that we did there had that commitment. We did many adaptations of novels, but we were often choosing novels where the characters were extremely repressed and where their inner lives were very hidden. So that was part of the reason that I adored the work of Pinter and Sam Shepard. Those two in particular because I always felt that, with their plays, what you were seeing wasn't what was *really* happening. What you were seeing and hearing was what was really going on inside them. I remember going to see *The Birthday Party* and *The Homecoming* and, having absolutely no idea what they were going to be, it was just overwhelmingly mind-blowing, indescribable. It was a physical experience, it felt like you'd been taken to another level of being or something. It was just so overwhelming. I was just enraptured and wanted to know how did they do it and what were they thinking and how did they rehearse it, and all of that.
>
>**BC:** When I think of Shared Experience I think of experimental work. I'm curious to hear if you think of Pinter's work as experimental?
>
>**NM:** Well, experimental if you think expressionism is experimental. In that sense I don't think there's anything real about the plays, except they

have a very real setting. You know particularly in *The Birthday Party* and *The Homecoming*. The setting is very, very real – super real. And somehow that allows you to explore the inner reality rather than the external reality. When I got to do *The Birthday Party* I knew Harold well enough to say, 'Harold, we want to do *The Birthday Party*, and we would be touring it, and we would only be bringing it to The Place, in London.' Because it wasn't that easy for us, Shared Experience, to find a place to do it in London. And he was, as usual, extremely generous, because he could have said, 'well look it's *The Birthday Party*, you can't bring *The Birthday Party* to London and only do it at The Place', which was actually a dance theatre at the time. And he was incredibly generous about it. The interesting thing was that when I was working with the designer on *The Birthday Party* I kept thinking 'Is there some way that we could stylize the set or take it out of this obvious thing of the hatch has to be here or the table has to be there and the doorway has to be there?' It seems so prescribed, you know? We spent hours trying to think there must be some way – what if you set it on a bed of roses? We just tried to think as widely as we possibly could, and I suddenly realized: well, you can't do that. I think with Pinter, with those early plays, you have to put it in a real place in order for the comedy to work. Because as soon as those weird, strange things are said and done in ordinary surroundings, people laugh from the absurdity. It's Theatre of the Absurd. It's like 'oh my god we're sitting in an ordinary kitchen and somebody's just said that to somebody else.' Whereas if you set it in an abstract setting, I have a feeling the meaning of the play would come across very powerfully but I think probably it wouldn't be funny because you wouldn't get the contrast of people saying absurd, outrageous things with very, very ordinary surroundings with ordinary tea towels and ordinary tables.

BC: I'm fascinated by the fact that you're focusing on the comedy because, for some scholars especially, there's an emphasis on the heaviness of the work, its gravitas. Perhaps, if I were to generalize, in Britain there's more of a tendency to appreciate the comedy in the work.

NM: You sort of have to ask yourself 'well what sort of comedy is it?' And I think it is an outrageous kind of comedy. It's not so much funny ha-ha as it is comedy of the unexpected. We laugh almost out of hysterical nervousness, rather than because it's really entertaining and funny. The few times that I actually saw Harold himself performing, what was so fantastic was that he was so terrifying and so funny at the same time. And you just think how is that possible? But he could really achieve that.

BC: It's amazing how much attention Pinter – as an actor and a writer – draws to the interiority of his characters while still keeping the cards 'close to the chest', like he doesn't reveal that much about their interiority, their needs and desires.

NM: What you do know is that their needs are so powerful. And we sort of think 'I don't know what they mean when they say that? What he's talking about, what she's talking about?' But the reason the plays feel so alive is because the characters have this huge need for something that we can connect to as human beings. 'Why am I so fascinated by these people, I don't even know what they're talking about? Why do they have so much attraction?' I think it's because they have these huge desires and needs, it's just that they're not articulating them with words.

Douglas Hodge

Douglas Hodge is an actor, director and composer. He is a key figure in the history of Pinter's life and career, with extensive experience acting in and directing Pinter's work. He performed alongside Pinter in the roles of Foster in David Leveaux's *No Man's Land* (Almeida and Comedy Theatres, 1992) and James in *The Collection* (dir. Joe Harmston, Donmar Warehouse, Richmond Theatre, Theatre Royal Bath, 1998) and created the role of Jake in *Moonlight* (dir. Leveaux, Almeida, 1993). He directed a film version of *Victoria Station* (2003), *The Dumb Waiter & Other Pieces* (Oxford Playhouse, 2004) and a revival of *Old Times* on Broadway (2015). In 2019 he directed and acted in a Platform Performance reading of *Mountain Language* at the Royal Court Theatre, with proceeds donated to the Barzani Charitable Foundation to support their humanitarian work with displaced peoples and refugees in Kurdish regions. The following is an excerpt from an interview conducted over email with Basil Chiasson on 18 October 2018.

Basil Chiasson (BC): Have you found that, within the industry, there are assumptions – even expectations – about Pinter's plays, particularly when it comes to how the plays should be staged?

Douglas Hodge (DH): Many assumptions, yes, and especially over-reverence and caution. From both audiences and performers. For example, audiences assuming it will be unintelligible, when in fact there is no need to decipher or decode it, it just is what it means to you. And from actors, tip toeing round real people written with the most exact ear, and playing a sort of style rather than the piece. I simply hate Pinter in black roll neck sweaters and leather jackets and fake cockney accents spouting ambiguities into a sort of black box vacuum.

BC: You've directed a triple bill of Pinter plays and then single plays. Can you speak a little about the challenges and freedoms of these two different contexts for staging Pinter?

DH: Harold once talked to me about riding the top decks through London when he was younger, on the night buses, and getting sometimes a peek into a room with some people in it. From these silhouettes he would extrapolate what might be going on. He glimpsed some people in a room and it wouldn't leave his imagination. He wrote *The Caretaker* when he glimpsed a man rummaging through some rammel through a slightly open door in a house in Chiswick. He saw a man standing over another man in the light and he wrote *The Room*. These rooms are strange, Hopper-like paintings, moments of power struggles and dreadful unknowns. For me, directing his plays is often about these rooms. Even when I directed *Victoria Station* on film I found the rooms that they were trapped in, the cells they inhabited, had to be clearly understood. For the more impressionistic memory plays like *Old Times* I felt the walls might just be sheets of mist, a very, very tender membrane where past and future and present could be passed through. Miriam Buether created a whole slice of a house for me when we did the sketches at the Oxford Playhouse and each room was a different arena in which the drama was held.

BC: It has been observed more than once how Pinter's plays appeal to actors. What about directors? Are there ways in which his plays offer directors an experience or ways of working that is unique or even unusual?

DH: My answer would be the same for the actor as for the director. It's the music. There is no doubt that the longer one works on the text – and everything begins and ends with the evidence of the text, and also because there can be zero changes to the text – it reveals its own exact musical qualities. The rhythms, the pauses, the silences start to suggest, somehow, a true way to say the text. You can still be utterly real within it, but it is a very exact science.

BC: In Britain, there seems to have been some apprehension over the years about being too experimental with Pinter's plays. Do you think that British productions of Pinter's work are pushing it in interesting and new directions, or as much as you'd like to see?

DH: I have, for a while, dreaded what would happen when he died and a certain licence which he would never allow started to infiltrate the stage with the usual directors whose vanity thinks they can improve or mend the piece or use it as a launch pad. I know Harold would welcome any such experimentation as long as the words are never, never changed or cut or rearranged.

BC: In other interviews you've observed how Pinter's plays are taking a page from previous playwrights, for example Noël Coward. Have you discerned any other influences? Do you think Pinter is evident in the work of any contemporary playwrights or even writers and work in other media, say, television or film?

DH: I think there's a lot of work that simply couldn't have happened, both in theatre and film, if Pinter hadn't existed. Pinter dramatised memory on stage – something no one to my mind had really truly achieved before. His free use of rooms and pithy phrases and his abrupt cuts in time and place are both filmic and also the essence of theatre. Movies like *Inception* [2010, dir. Christopher Nolan], plays by the likes of Marber and Penhall and Mamet all draw from the well of Harold's work. Looking backwards, I do believe there is a lineage – just as Olivier and Chaplin and Irving and Kean and Garrick all fed each other. I think Harold's early life on the proscenium arch stages of touring theatres, putting on weekly rep where the characters spouted epigrams and duelled with words and stances, all imbued Harold's framework. When I did *Betrayal* at the National, directed by Trevor Nunn, probably my favourite Pinter play, Trevor always argued that Harold was a direct descendant of Ibsen and Strindberg, but I always felt there was a deeper British connection; to music hall, to gritty movies and the novels of Beckett and of course Coward whose plays of manners resembled a lot the world of Harold's writing, where people say one thing while meaning another, where manners are a thin carapace for murderous feelings. Often in Pinter, as I've said elsewhere, you have to say the politest thing while secretly wanting to strangle the person you are addressing. For me these constraints run all through British theatre from Congreve and Sheridan and Wilde through Coward and into Pinter.

Jamie Lloyd

Jamie Lloyd is the founder and artistic director of The Jamie Lloyd Company. Prior to its establishment in 2012, he was associate director of the Donmar Warehouse (2008–11). His first main house production was Harold Pinter's *The Caretaker* at the Sheffield Crucible in 2006, and he has since directed many Pinter plays, including *The Lover* and *The Collection* at the Comedy

Theatre (2008), *The Hothouse* (2013) and *The Homecoming* (2015) at Trafalgar Studios, and the *Pinter at the Pinter* season and *Betrayal* at the Harold Pinter Theatre in London's West End (2018–19). The following is an excerpt from an interview with Catriona Fallow on 21 September 2019 as part of the Harold Pinter: Histories and Legacies conference, hosted at the University of Leeds.

Catriona Fallow (CF): Much of your work – and the work of The Jamie Lloyd Company – involves reconceiving major canonical works for contemporary audiences. What is it about these canonical texts that interests you and how does crafting them for a West End audience, for example, shape the way that you deal with those texts?

Jamie Lloyd (JL): I have an obsession with the past and the steps that have brought us here as a society, as the human race as a whole, and kind of excavating those decisions, analysing the choices that have been made in the past, the ripple effects of which are felt in the present. So considering those works and being able to re-approach them or re-invent them for a modern audience is fascinating and important. The plays teach us about our past behaviour and how we might have changed – or not – since. It's about stripping away the performance history – all the old-fashioned baggage, the traditional ways of approaching these famous plays – and discovering their absolute essence.

CF: What were your early experiences of working with Pinter like? What kind of collaborator was he and how did that shape working on the *Pinter at the Pinter* season, ten years after his death?

JL: On *The Lover* and *The Collection* in 2008 at the Comedy – which is of course now the Harold Pinter Theatre – we went through the entire process together. Obviously that was right at the end of his life so I was incredibly lucky to be able to spend a significant amount of time with him, talking about those plays and also talking more broadly about his work. I tried to ask as many questions about as many of the other plays as possible, many of which were in the *Pinter at the Pinter* season. From our production of *The Caretaker* onwards I became a Harold Pinter obsessive. So being able to spend that time with him was both initially daunting – was he going to be as ferocious as everyone said he was? – and also really nourishing. One of the things that struck me was talking specifically about actors, because of course he'd have complete casting approval. Talking about the available actors, people that may be appropriate or not for the roles and the qualities that they would bring, for example. He also showed real interest in the approach to the craft of the production and a fascination for how we were, for instance, going to light it and how we were embracing sound and music in a way that he probably hadn't expected. I guess a lot of people assumed that he was going to give very detailed, very specific notes about the language but it really was not the case in any way. It was nothing other than a very practical, no-nonsense approach.

CF: Working in a directorial capacity with him, what was that collaboration like for you?

JL: I've since heard that he was quite bemused about this young kid who was interested in his work. It was my second major production and it was in the West End, so I was incredibly lucky. I think from rehearsals and from the run-throughs he was interested in the fact that we were bringing out the humour of the plays. I remember him saying, 'all my plays are comedies, they're comedic, and I'm glad you're interested in that.' I think other people had been more reverential, not as interested in exploring the comedic rhythms of the plays, perhaps taking a more laboured approach with the text. That was at a point in time when young directors were not necessarily engaged with his work, so he was excited about that, a new generation exploring it, and therefore he was interested in a fresh approach to it. Certainly, since doing more and more of his work since he's not around – and then certainly doing the *Pinter at the Pinter* season – I can almost hear what he would approve of and what he would not approve of. Would I have even have dared to approach, for instance, *A Slight Ache* in the way that we did had he been around today? There was a conversation in my head throughout the entire process of the season: 'I know he'd love this – I got a very good measure of his taste from very thorough conversations – I know that he'd love this approach' and 'I'm not sure that he'd love this more radical approach but I'll give it go anyway'. There was sometimes an act of rebellion in it. Sometimes if you risk it, it can animate the text in a surprising, but no less honest, way.

CF: Over and above honouring Pinter, why was it important to have a season like *Pinter at the Pinter* and the subsequent production of *Betrayal*? Did we need a season that big to capture Pinter's legacy?

JL: The discovery of a wider body of work with which to reconsider the more famous plays was obviously a big mission. And as a kind of Pinter obsessive, to be able to be completely immersed in that work, in the 'Pinterverse', for many months was a real privilege; questioning exactly why he had such an impact on our culture and what we might learn from that. To be able to interrogate that, to be able to find the links between the pieces and the recurring motifs. To try to rediscover his work for a new generation and be brave with the approach, to test the theatrical form. We stick to every single word that he wrote and every punctuation mark and every pause and silence and pretty much every stage direction. There's a knowledge that there's a real rigour in the approach to the text which perhaps gives us the freedom to explore the visual language. His words are more important and visceral than ever. His passionate interrogation of the truth in politics and society, his call for honesty and authenticity, is a vital lesson for us all.

CF: Almost as though fidelity to text gives you gratis to unlock it aesthetically? If you wanted to really push Pinter to the next level aesthetically, would you have gone further with any of the choices that you made or was it far enough?

JL: It's difficult because inevitably there are some plays like *The Dumb Waiter* that carry the baggage of their performance history. What's really interesting about that particular piece is that it resists a different approach aesthetically. You could find a way of setting it in a contemporary world but then the food references are so particular to the period. I mean maybe that would take it out of time, maybe that would make the food requests even more baffling and weird and funny? But it's sort of like why, why would you do it? Would it damage the play rather than reanimate it? The problem then is that you essentially end up doing a relatively traditional reading of that play because it resists redefinition. So, I suppose in a way had I been truly brave I would have taken something like *The Dumb Waiter* and tried to find another route through it, a new meaning.

CF: Something that seems to have really resonated with audiences and critics in response to *Betrayal* and the Pinter season overall is the emotion underpinning Pinter's work – and that play in particular – and the importance of characters' desire for love. Can you elaborate on that? We talk a lot about power and violence in Pinter's plays, but the other side of that is perhaps love?

JL: That was a real discovery for me in the process of doing the season, the major insight that came as a result of being immersed in his work. I don't think you could really appreciate something like that without doing it day in, day out and moving swiftly from one piece to the next and understanding what all the characters share collectively underneath the surface of this entire body of work – which I think is this desperate need for connection. We're always talking about, as you say, the powerplay and this sort of interplay between a kind of threat and wit. I wish I could go back and look at some of the other plays now that I've done the season because there is this deep well of pain and loneliness, this real understanding that underneath all our power games, underneath our survival tactics, is this sort of terrible isolation. In a way people are so horrible to each other because they care about each other so much and want to affect each other in some meaningful way. The nastiness is a manifestation of deep insecurity and a longing for a different life or a return to a golden past. It was this discovery that gave the season its real purpose; Pinter understands the dark depths of our humanity – the truth – like almost no other playwright.

CF: You assembled an extraordinary cast of Pinter veterans and new talent for the *Pinter at the Pinter* season. What's your sense of the appeal of Pinter from an actor's perspective? What keeps them coming back or exploring his work for the first time?

JL: That is a real reason why I love working on his work: the opportunities and possibilities for actors. One of the great, exciting things about doing the season was that we knew we'd be working with the most astonishing group of actors because his work just always attracts the best. It's such a satisfying experience for them. It was a real luxury to transfer *Betrayal* and we didn't re-rehearse, but through the previews on Broadway we drilled further down, we had lots more discussions about specific moments and different approaches to minuscule thoughts. That's the thing (and the enjoyable bit!): you need to be as exact as possible, really dissect tiny thoughts, tiny looks, tiny moments. The most satisfying thing of course is the huge well of subtext that you can tap into. The characters use language to conceal what they really think or feel. The rehearsal process is about trying to discover what's really going on, not really through conversation – like, we don't really do any table work, sit around for weeks on end discussing it – but by getting up and just trying something. It's like drafting, like sketching. You know: you get up, you do your first sketch. The next one you might sort of shade that bit in there. Then you might add a bit of red paint on to that. You're constantly trying to discover it in the space, in the interplay between people in the space, rather than trying to approach it academically, I guess. It's that practical approach that I learned from Harold. And it's very, very nourishing. The plays just keep on giving. I sort of feel like there's no other playwright, genuinely, perhaps except Shakespeare, that you can learn so much about what makes us tick, what drives us, why we behave in these complex, sometimes confusing ways.

Soutra Gilmour

Soutra Gilmour is a stage designer. Following her training at Wimbledon School of Art, her work has appeared across the UK and internationally, but most notably on London's premiere stages such as the National Theatre, the Royal Opera House, The Old Vic, the Donmar Warehouse and multiple West End Theatres. In 2002 she designed the set for *The Birthday Party* at the Sheffield Crucible, directed by Erica Whyman. In addition to designing the full *Pinter at the Pinter* season and *Betrayal* in collaboration with the Jamie Lloyd Company (2018–19), Gilmour has also designed for Lloyd's productions of *The Caretaker* (2006) at the Sheffield Crucible/the Tricycle, *The Lover* and *The Collection* at the Comedy Theatre (2008) and *The Hothouse* (2013) and *The Homecoming* (2015) at Trafalgar Studios. The following is excerpted from an interview with Catriona Fallow on 7 June 2019.

Catriona Fallow (CF): Other than Eileen Diss, you have designed more Pinter stage works than anyone else. When did you first encounter Pinter's work as a designer?

Soutra Gilmour (SG): When I was at Wimbledon [School of Art] studying, one of the things I said I had no interest in doing, would never do, was designing Pinter plays because they were *definitely* boring. But, as you quite rightly pointed out, other than Eileen I have probably designed more Pinters than anybody else. There's a kind of irony in that but also an interesting lesson in that you always know less than you think you know. So, the first time I was asked to do a Pinter was with a director called Erica Whyman, who I did a lot of work with in the late 1990s and early 2000s, when she asked me to do *The Birthday Party* at Sheffield. I guess my thing is I've always come at things from quite a personal angle, I've not been particularly academic about it probably? It's very much a kind of: read the plays, feel the plays, make the plays. But actually, when I think about it, even in that very first production there was a sense of understanding somewhere that there was a play within a space and that Pinter was as aware of the space as he was the play. All the way through the designs for Pinter – and, as I say, I can see this in hindsight rather than something I was ahead of the game thinking about trying to do – was that there was always an element of the theatre environment being explored as well as the kind of scenic, described environment of the play. There's something see-through about the environments that mean that you do see bits of the theatre. Or you always have in all of mine, and that was a very *un*conscious decision. Like, there's always been this sense of somehow the back wall of the theatre or the threshold between the auditorium and the theatre being *exposed*. Because somewhere in the plays there's an inherent acceptance of the theatricality of them. That's just what I've felt as a designer. In a sense Pinter's always happy for you to see through the door to the wall of the theatre, however it is in different theatres depending on the configuration. And so that was something that happened really, really early on.

What was also extraordinary about that first moment with Pinter was that Ivan Kyncl took photographs of that production. He was a great collaborator with Harold, he photographed a huge amount of Harold's work, particularly the ones he directed – and he died not long after – and seeing his take on how to take the pictures. Because unlike any other production photographer he would be on stage, like in the furniture, under the glass table, behind the window, through the door. There was no boundary for him when he took those production shots. And I think that was also my reaction, that somehow the plays are not contained inside a little box or a little piece of scenery, that they seep out into the theatre. He just approached the photographing of them like that and was almost like another performer in the space. I've seen no other photographer photograph anything – let alone Pinter plays – like that. It's partly why he has such amazing shots but there was something about the need to get close, to feel uncomfortable, to feel the uncomfortableness. That's partly the thing about Pinter, isn't it? The uncomfortableness comes because they get a bit close, they become a bit sticky, somehow and I think that's because they don't stay on the stage, they seep off.

CF: Is that something that you think has endured in your designing of Pinter's plays over time or has it evolved to be something even more precise, or something that you're even more conscious of?

SG: I think I've definitely become conscious of it. And in the Pinter season we were constantly playing with: what was the theatre, what were the sets? How much set – whatever that means – how many scenic elements did you need to tell the story that the space somehow wasn't already giving you? The relationship between the industrial part of the theatre – the making place – and the threshold between that and the audience and the auditorium, the tensions between those things. I think particularly at a venue like the Harold Pinter Theatre, but of course was the Comedy, it's actually a really beautiful auditorium, it's like seeing the two parts of Pinter: like seeing the gritty, Hackney working class kind of thing *with* the Holland Park. There's this juxtaposition of this rough working space and this aesthetically beautiful, classy auditorium with its gilt and its posh plush seats and all of that. We had all this quite plush interior, very, very dark. But it felt really necessary to have part of the rough, working part of the theatre; it sort of became the street, and where the phone box was and all of those things. But it was *more* than that. It was really saying: 'never forget your inner theatre. Never forget this is a conversation. Don't just get dragged into some kind of fantasy moment. This is a conversation. You're here. You're an audience. These are performers.' And that feels really right and truthful and honest when you're doing a Pinter play.

CF: Because it keeps the audience implicated?

SG: It keeps the audience implicated. It keeps the space unreal in a really useful way, I think. Even if you have a level of naturalistic detail which of course was why, when I was nineteen, I thought he was boring. Because it was: there's the record player, and the hatch, and the apples in the basket, and the ashtray, and you've got to have the door in the right place otherwise you can't get to the ashtray and put on the record and get up the stairs in time. Because there are these very inherent locked in geographies in his plays. I mean objects have to have this very particular proximity otherwise you can't get between them and say the lines. But what I was missing at that point was the kind of depth of expression.

CF: And is that depth of expression something that you try and realize aesthetically in the choices that you make?

SG: For me he's like the Francis Bacon of writing. Part of British Expressionism. It couldn't be German, or American, or French, or Chinese. Do you know what I mean? There's an ugly heaviness about it that's quite emotionally charged. And I love Francis Bacon paintings, but they're not easy to look at: the screaming and the pain of humans and the brush marks and the strength of the colours, but they're so emotionally charged. And I think that Pinter for me is like the playwright version of Francis Bacon. The plays are kind of brutal. And kind of absurd. And people do very difficult things to each other. So, there's something about the kind of pain of being a human in there. But something about the smoggy, dirty, London, rough, black, messy way of expressing those things feels like what you get from those Pinter characters and what you get from Francis Bacon paintings, to me. They feel really sort of the same but expressed in different ways. I always see a lot of blackness in Pinter, and a lot of darkness, but there's also a lot of red. And red's not a colour I find that easy. But there's somehow always quite a charge of red, which again is a real Francis Bacon colour.

CF: And that appeared in something like your *Homecoming* that you designed.

SG: Yes, absolutely, and that kind of floor actually was a bit inspired by Francis Bacon, not an actual painting, but a sensation. Or even Rothko actually, which again is very visceral, very upset. Rothko paintings have a kind of sonic energy you feel when you're with them that goes way beyond the visual. You can feel this weird energy, like dark, upset energy coming off them, as you can with Bacon paintings. I feel like it's the same energy you get from a Pinter play, for me as a visual person. They're uncomfortable. If they're done well, they're a really uncomfortable experience. I think one of the things that probably has, weirdly and unbeknownst to me, matched me in quite a good way with Pinter is there's a kind of fine art, painterly sort of quality? I went to an art college that didn't have a drama department nor anything fashionable like fashion, it was all painting, sculpture, print making and theatre design. I went there because I wanted that kind of fine art background where you were making things that were personal and had a personal expression. So, something about being able to make objects that have a kind of emotional quality really suits me rather than one that's particularly flashy. That's really worked for the Pinter things, I think, in quite an interesting way.

CF: What was it like to try and have a vision for the Pinter season overall?

SG: It was an extraordinary gift, and also an extraordinary headache. I think in all my work, partly going back to this thing about emotional qualities to the objects on stage – because I don't like scenery, scenery is something I'm not very keen on which is odd as a person who designs scenery – there's something about trying to find the *essential*. So, even if I'm working on just one play, there's something about trying to find the essential quality that the design can bring to it that nothing else is already doing. I'm not very interested in the design somehow describing the narrative that's already being taken care of by the text or whatever. I like to find another thing, another essential line that only the design can do really. So, the season was a kind of uber version of that, like 'here's thirty-two plays and god knows how many readings'. Really early on I had this thought about this kind of Pinter-machine – which was like my spatial manifestation of Harold – which was him as a black cube. Because he always had the polo neck, the way he always dressed, and the fact that there's been a recurring theme (not actually in *Hothouse* but pretty much everything else) where this sort of black brick back wall comes back. So, this sense of if Harold was a set then he would be this black cube in space that could go any direction or do anything or manifest itself completely differently. I had this idea and I made this sketch of this little cube with these little bits sticking out of it like things might move in or move out or move down or move back. It wasn't a solid cube it was a linear cube that would sit in the space and it could turn so we could have every aspect of it. It was a funny process because I had the idea really quickly, I said to Jamie 'you know I think it's this skeletal cube, I think it gets filled, I think it has these things that do these things, I think it's a manifestation of Pinter', and that's why we had obviously the front wall with the name inscribed, 'PINTER'.

CF: Something that scholars and critics in particular endlessly debate is what genre Pinter's work fits into. Some would call it social realism; some would call it Theatre of the Absurd. Did you find yourself being influenced by a particular genre or style? Is that a way that you think when you approach a design?

SG: I probably wouldn't be able to relate to a sense of genre; social realism would feel far too naturalistic for me and Theatre of the Absurd would feel far too cartoon and cut out for me, too plastic in the sort of surface sense. The things I come back to are always art movements, not theatre movements. Architecture and fine arts are much more influential on me than theatre is. And that is both a great thing sometimes and not a great thing sometimes. It's a really interesting one because you know, of course, you're doing these productions in collaboration: you're doing it in collaboration with the play, collaboration with the director, collaboration with the place. So, there's all these other influences. In some sense it's not personal, it's a really collaborative thing. But really the only way of me operating, successfully, my best work, is the work that can then get siphoned through me and then somehow look like me – not visually like me but like my work. What I see in the work is a certain kind of muscularity, or a certain kind of power, or a certain kind of weight, or a certain kind of sensibility, or the things that I get drawn to visually in the world. What I don't really see is whether I use blue a lot or pink a lot or whether it's always white. It's more to do with objects in space, types of architecture in space. The way things sit in the room. I like to think that my work is about addressing the play in the moment that we are doing it in the place that we are doing it. So, everything I do is like a site-specific piece of work. The very *specific* spatial relationship you're making between the stage, the threshold and the auditorium is utterly at the basis of everything I do. Making sense of that place and that play and that time. Whether that's the Pinter cube or doing *Turn of the Screw* in Regents Park it's about it not looking like a set sitting on a stage but it looking like it's always been there. It's part of the room, it's part of the shared space of the audience and the actors and the play and the moment in time.

CF: Was there anything distinctive about the process for designing *Betrayal* as a stand-alone production following the season?

SG: We wanted to do something really lyrical, really fluid and something that really spatially describes the triangle of their lives, the passing places, the missed opportunities, the places where they cross each other and don't cross each other or are waiting or not waiting, and the places where somebody probably knew and somebody else thinks they don't. The thing of them all being the space felt really important and in order to do that there had to be a kind of lyrical abstraction to the space because otherwise it starts getting: 'what are they doing, sitting at a kitchen table?' You know, it had to be that they weren't really there, they were kind of just hovering in our mind or our thoughts or something. It just really had to all be about their relationships, and therefore the stuff, the bits weren't really relevant: 'what does the bed look like?' Who cares!

CF: What are some distinctive things that you – as a designer who has worked on so many Pinter productions – have taken from his work that might now be a part of your practice more generally or that you might have in mind in designing other work?

SG: I guess there's something to be said about not being so quick to assume you're not the person who should be doing those things. Be a little bit more open. I think it's really allowed me to investigate the things I'm quite passionate about. I'm passionate about space, people in space. I mean that's really the thing. I like the difficulty about the fact there's one set of people in a performing space and another set of people in an auditorium space and you need to find a way to bridge those things. The journey with Pinter has been part of that discussion. It's like you're almost conflating two things because you're conflating the described aesthetic of the play – and all of the actions and emotions therein – with the aesthetic of the stage and the aesthetic of the auditorium which are very often two different things. And I think a lot of that has come through the work with

Pinter, exposing the fact that the space is there. You're not in a bubble, you're not watching it on TV, or whatever. The space is there and the space is a massive part of the storytelling. It's my job to join all of that up and make it feel like it's utterly meant and one thing is not placed *on* the other. Some people love the idea that there's this little hole and that you put a totally magical world in the hole that's nothing like anything that's going on outside it, and some people are absolutely brilliant at that. And I'm absolutely terrible at that. All I can do is try and explode the hole and try and join them up. I guess that's what's really happened with all of this Pinter work and the necessity of audience being there. It's all about getting across any kind of sense of divide because that's clearly utterly necessary for him, that the audience is there.

Index

Abrams, Nathan 73
Absurdism 2, 71, 74, 154, 175
Agitprop Street Players 131
Ahmed, Samira 65
Alan Prince, Russ 36
Alderman, Geoffrey 73
Aldwych Theatre 121, 123–5, 133
Allen, Keith 108
Almeida Theatre 149
American Embassy in Ankara 99, 101
Amnesty International 97, 101
Anderson, Lindsay 45
Andrews, Jamie 125
Angelaki, Vicky 145, 150, 167
Angel-Perez, Elisabeth 80
Anholt, Christien 79
Anouilh, Jean 111
Aragay, Mireia 81, 92
Arden, John 68 n.2, 112, 149
   Live Like Pigs 149
Aristophanes 126, 131
Arts Theatre 41, 43, 143
Ashby-de-la-Zouch Festival 136
Ashton, Zawe 65–6
Associated-Rediffusion (television) 128
Atlee, Clement 110
Ayckbourn, Alan 65

Bachrach, Peter 55
Bacon, Francis 212–13
Baker, William 3, 38, 72, 76–7, 129, 136
Bakewell, Joan 21
Balibar, Étienne 8, 144, 146, 149, 153
Baratz, Morton 55
Barbican Theatre 49 n.6
Barker, George Granville 20, 31 n.3
Bartlett, Mike 159, *13*, 159
Barton, John 112, 124, 133

The Hollow Crown 133
Batten, Gerard 91
Baum, Devorah 75
BBC 96, 111
BBC Radio 42–3, 135, 178, 181
BBC Television 122, 127, 132
Beatles, the 109
Beaton, Norman 198
Beckett, Samuel 4, 15, 19–21, 31 n.4, 37–9, 41–7, 49, 64, 71, 75, 78, 111, 158, 175–9, 181–2, 205
   All That Fall 42
   Catastrophe 78
   Eh Joe 49 n.4
   Embers 42
   Film 44
   Murphy 20
   Waiting for Godot 41, 43
   Watt 20
Begley, Varun 64
Behan, Brendan 112
Bell, Mary Hayley 129
   The Uninvited Guest 129
Bennett, Louise 145
Bennett, Michael Y. 38
Bensky, Lawrence 76
Berger, John 45
Berkoff, Steven 73, 110
Bernhard, F. J. 21
Bibby, Adrianne 36
Bignell, Jonathan 49 n.3, 128
Billington, Michael 3, 20, 42, 44, 47, 49 n.6, 65–6, 71–3, 76–90, 107, 109, 112–13, 116, 129, 182
Birkett, Jennifer 42
Black Lives Matter 154
Blair, Tony 90
Blakemore, Michael 44
   Stage Blood 44

Blin, Roger 43
Bloom, Harold 15, 72, 75
Bogen, Nancy 31 n.1
Bolt, Robert 65
Bond, Edward 149–50
   Saved 149
Borowiec, Łukasz 3
Bourdieu, Pierre 6, 54, 57–60, 68
Bradley, David 108
Bray, Barbara 36, 42–3
Brearley, Joseph 62, 108
Brecht, Bertolt 45, 112–14
Brenton, Howard 113, 158
Breton, André 20
Brewer, Mary F. 10
Bristol Old Vic Theatre 9
British Film Institute (BFI) 1
British Foreign Office 97
British National Party (BNP) 91
Brook, Peter 112, 124
Brown, Georgina 182
Brown, Jr., Michael 154
Buether, Miriam 204
Bull, John 38
Buñuel, Luis 63
   Un Chien Andalou 63
Burge, Stuart 65
Burkman, Katherine 80
Burton, Harry 9
Butterworth, Jez 8, 157–8, 163–6, 171
   Mojo (film) 157
   The River 8, 163–6
   The Winterling 157

Calder, Angus 109
Campton, David 177
   The Lunatic View 177
Carné, Marcel 63
   Le jour se lève 63
Céline, Louis Ferdinand 20
Cézanne, Paul 141
Chambers, Colin 123, 136
Chaplin, Charles 205

Chekhov, Anton 4, 18, 28, 133
   The Proposal 133
Chesterfield, Lord 72
Cheyette, Bryan 72, 78
Chiasson, Basil 3, 6, 50 n.11 and 13, 60–2, 177, 181
Chomsky, Noam 102
Churchill, Caryl 140, 154, 158, 175
   Escaped Alone 154
Clayton, Jay 30
Campaign for Nuclear Disarmament (CND) 112
Codron, Michael 41, 44, 112
Cohen, Joshua 74
Comedy Theatre 205–6, 211–12
Complicité 48
Congreve, William 205
Conrad, Joseph 25–6
   The Secret Agent 26
   Under Western Eyes 26
Courtney, Tom 63
Coward, Noël 4, 112–13, 205
   Blithe Spirit 113
Craig, Ryan 78, 82
   Filthy Business 78, 82
   The Holy Rosenbergs 78, 82
Crimp, Martin 8, 158, 174–91
   A Kind of Arden 178
   Attempts on Her Life 181
   Dealing with Clair 180
   Definitely the Bahamas 178
   Getting Attention 180
   In the Republic of Happiness 187–90
   Living Remains 191
   No One Sees the Video 179
   Play House 178
   Spanish Girls 178
   The City 187–8
   The Country 8, 175–88, 190–1
   When We Have Sufficiently Tortured Each Other 174
cummings, e. e. 31 n.2
Cutforth, René 127

Daily Telegraph, 178, 182
Daldry, Stephen 112
Daly, Augustin 128
  Under the Gaslight 128
Dandaneau, Stephen P. 67
Davies, Will 55
Davies, William 128
De Jongh, Nicolas 21
Dennis, Nigel 111
Derbyshire, Harry 6, 66–7
Derrida, Jacques 75
Devine, George 45, 111
Dink, Hrant 102
Diss, Eileen 210
Dogan, Yalcin 99
Dos Passos, John 20
Dostoyevsky, Fyodor 63, 71
Dotrice, Michelle 126
Drama Critics' Circle Award 135
Dromgoole, Dominic 174
Drummond, Rob 159
  Bullet Catch 159
Dudley, William 108
Duggan, Mark 154
Duncan, Lindsay 108
Dyer, Rebecca 57

Edgar, David 141
Eliot, T. S. 4, 17–18, 20, 31 n.2, 66, 112, 163–4
  'Burnt Norton' 66, 163–4
  Four Quartets 66, 163–4
  'Tradition and the Individual Talent' 21
Eltis, Sos 43
Encounter (magazine) 46
English Stage Company 41, 111
Erbakan, Necmettin 94
Esslin, Martin 3, 31 n.4, 36–9, 40, 42–3, 47, 50 n.12, 55, 64, 71, 73, 75, 140, 154, 172
Evening Standard 22, 157
Evren, Kenan 101
Expressionism 2, 201, 212

Faber and Faber 1
Finburgh, Clare 38, 49 n.2
Finney, Albert 63
Fitzgerald, F. Scott 27, 118
  'The Rich Boy' 27
Flanagan, Pauline 78
Flourish (magazine) 126
Flower, Sir Fordham 121, 123–4
Foco Novo 131
Forbes (magazine) 36
Foster, Troy 198
Fox, Alex 23
Fraser, Lady Antonia (Pinter's widow) 3, 53, 68, 71–2, 74, 80, 90, 92
Freely, Maureen 101
French, Samuel 133, 136
Freud, Sigmund 75
Front Row (BBC Radio 4) 65

Galtung, Johan 142, 146, 149, 154
Gambon, Michael 132
Garner, Eric 154
Garner, Jr., Stanton B. 186
Garrick, David 205
Gauthier, Brigitte 10
Genet, Jean 43
Genette, Gérard 175
Giacometti, Alberto 20
Gielgud, John 118
Gilbert, Howard 132
Gilmour, Soutra 9, 210–16
Giroudoux, Jean 113
Goddard, Lynette 145
Goldstein, Michael 73
Golick, Peter S. 76
Graham, W. S. 20
Granger, Derek. 39
Gray, Simon 113
Greig, David 158
Grimes, Charles 3, 62
Grove Press 44, 68 n.1
Guardian 47, 157
Gulf War (1990s) 150

Gursel, Mustafa 98
Gussow, Mel 53, 110

Hackney (London) 71–2
Hackney Downs Grammar School 62, 73, 109
Hackney Public Library 74
Hall, Peter 7, 37, 43, 65, 108, 112–13, 121–6, 130, 132, 135–6
Hall, Stuart 130
Hamilton, Gabrielle 126
Hamlett, Dilys 111
Hands, Terry 129–30, 133
Haneke, Michel 171
Hardwick, Paul 126
Hardy, Thomas 31 n.2
Hare, David 109
Harold Pinter Estate 1
Harold Pinter Theatre 1, 206, 211–12
Harries, Davyd 126–7
Harris, David 31 n.2
Harwood, Ronald 79
Taking Sides 79
Haydon, Christopher 198, 200
Hemingway, Ernest 4, 16, 27
'Hills Like White Elephants' 28–9
'Soldier's Home' 27
Henley in Arden High School 136
Hern, Nick 47
Higgins, Aidan 132
Hikmet, Nâzım 102
Hill, Lauryn 145
Hinchliffe, Arnold P. 38, 43
Hobsbawm, Eric 109
Hobson, Harold 36, 41
Hodge, Douglas 8, 203–5
Holm, Ian 135
Hopper, Edward 204
Hosokawa, Makoto 172
Human Rights Watch 101
Hurriyet 96, 100
Hussein, Saddam 91

Ibsen, Henrik 205
Ilisu Dam Project 102
Ionesco, Eugène 15, 37–9, 42–6, 48–50, 64, 111, 175–6, 179
Exit the King 48
The Chairs 48
The Hard-Boiled Egg 44, 49 n.7
The Lesson 43
Irving, Henry 205
Itzin, Catherine 135
Ives, Kenneth 198

James, Oscar 198
Jamie Lloyd Company 1, 206
Happy Birthday, Harold 9
Pinter at the Pinter 1, 141, 205–16
Jays, David 73
Jayston, Michael 126–7
Jellicoe, Ann 45, 133
The Knack 133
Jewish Observer, the 15
Johnstone, Keith 45, 112
Joint Stock 113, 131
Jones, David 132, 136
Joyce, James 17–18, 20, 25, 63, 71, 113, 121
A Portrait of the Artist as a Young Man 18
Exiles 18
Ulysses 20, 25

Kafka, Franz 4, 15–16, 20, 31 n.4, 63, 71–2, 74, 81–2, 132, 158
The Trial (film) 74
The Trial (novel) 74
Kane, Sarah 4, 80, 158, 175
Blasted 80
Kean, Edmund 205
Keaton, Buster 44
Kelly, Dennis 8, 140, 154, 157–8, 163, 166–70
Boys & Girls 154, 168
Love and Money 167–8

Orphans 8, 157, 166–9
Osama the Hero 168
Utopia 168
Kelly, Sam 108
Kemp-Welch, Joan 128
Kerr, Walter 141
King's Theatre Hammersmith 129
Kirkwood, Lucy 140, 154
   Chimerica 154
Knowles, Ronald 17
Knowlson, James 44, 79
Koval, Ramona 90
Krausz, Ernest 82
Kristeva, Julia 21
Kustow, Michael 125–9, 131–2
Kyncl, Ivan 211

Laclau, Ernesto 61
Larkin, Philip 113
Lavery, Carl 38, 49 n.2, 50 n.15, 55
Law, B. J. 82
Lawrence, D. H. 20, 71
Le Pen, Marine 91
Leigh, Mike 73, 78
Leveaux, David 113–14
Littler, Emile 123–4
Littlewood, Joan 112
Lloyd, Jamie 9, 65, 141, 205–9, 214
Locke, John 72
Lordswood Boys' Technical School 136
Losey, Joseph 56–7, 64, 113
Lowell, Robert 20, 31 n.3
Lynn, Cordelia 140, 154
   One For Sorrow 154
Lyric Hammersmith Theatre 123

Maddox Ford, Ford 16, 25, 66
Mail on Sunday 182
Mamet, David 78, 81, 110, 113, 175, 205
   Catastrophe 78–9
Marat/Sade (Weiss) 135
Marber, Patrick 9, 81, 158, 205
Marks, Louis 75

Marowitz, Charles 15
Marsan, Eddie 108
Martin, Jean 43
Meckler, Nancy 8, 201–3
Merchant, Vivien 78
Mermaid Theatre 31 n.3
Merritt, Susan Hollis 65
McDonagh, Martin 175
McDowall, Alistair 140, 154
   Pomona 154
McMaster, Anew 111, 129
McWhinnie, Donald 36, 42–3, 45, 49 n.4
Megson, Chris 158–9, 164, 171
Mercer, David 108
Michell, Roger 108
Miller, Arthur 74, 81, 92–9, 102, 110
Miller, Henry 20
Miller, Jonathan 74
Milliyet (newspaper) 97
Milošević, Slobodan 99
Mills, C. W. 6, 54–6, 60, 67–8
Milne, Drew 3
Minghella, Anthony 157
Mitchell, Katie 174, 181, 186
Molière 126, 131, 190
   Le Misanthrope 190
Moore, Richard 126–7, 132
Moorsom, Sasha 42
Morley, Sheridan 178
Morris, William 130
Moskowitz, Judah (Pinter's maternal uncle) 78
Mosley, Oswald 76

Naiambana, Patrice 198
Nathan, David 183
Nathan, John 73
National Salvation Party 94
National Theatre (of Britain) 43–4, 48, 65, 68, 108, 113, 174, 198, 205
National Theatre (of Jerusalem) 74
NATO 98, 100–1
Naturalism 2, 117, 202

New Left Review 130
New York Times 53, 98–9
Nolan, Christopher 205
   Inception (film) 205
North Havering College of Further Education 132
Nunn, Trevor 124, 205

Observer, the 45
Odd Man Out (film) 117
Odimba, Chinonyerem 9, 197–200
   Medea 200
Old Vic 111
Olivier, Laurence 205
O'Neill, Eugene 4
Onič, Tomaž 3
Orange Tree Theatre 178, 180
Osborne, John 111–12, 154
   Look Back in Anger 38, 45, 111–12
Owen, Wilfred 31 n.2
Owens, Craig N. 10
Oxford Playhouse 204
Özal, Turgut 97

Pakula, Alan 81
   Sophie's Choice (film) 81
Pamuk, Orhan 94
Paquet Gabbard, Lucina 143
Pascal, Julia 78, 82
   Crossing Jerusalem 82
Pattie, David 142, 186
Peacock, D. Keith 58, 66
PEN International 92, 95, 97–8, 101
Penhall, Joe 158, 205
Percival, Ron 82
Pinter, Frances (Pinter's mother) 72
Pinter, Harold
   acting 78–9, 82, 122, 129, 132, 202, 204, 209
   allegory 117–19
   Angry Young Men 63
   Aristotelian form 113
   censorship 95–9
   characterization 17, 26–7, 75, 77, 114, 116, 117, 153, 176, 183–4, 188, 199–200, 202–3, 208–9
   class 6, 31, 45, 53–68, 72–3, 108, 111, 130, 142–3, 146, 149, 150, 153, 199–200, 212
   comedy 76, 108, 129, 158, 167, 177, 181, 188, 202, 207
   comedy of menace 2, 177, 188, 190
   directing 4, 44, 79, 113, 124, 136, 197–209
   elitism 6, 53–68
   feminism 116
   German Shakespeare Prize 114, 118
   Holocaust 72, 77, 79–81, 84, 110, 187
   homosociality 118, 184
   influence 2–8, 15–31, 37, 39, 44–6, 54–5, 60, 62, 64, 71–2, 76, 81, 84, 101–2, 113, 129, 139–54, 157–72, 174–91
   intertextuality 15–31, 30, 175
   Jewishness 6, 71–84, 110
   Kitchen Sink (drama) 63
   Middle East 7, 71, 74, 81, 88–103
   minimalism 17, 26–30, 114, 133–5
   misogyny 108, 116, 151, 153
   melodrama 126, 128–9, 132
   modernism 2, 6, 15–31, 64, 74, 81–2, 113, 115, 158
   National Student Drama Festival (Bristol) 115–16, 188
   Naturalism 24, 154, 212
   neoliberalism 59–61, 68, 158
   New Wave 63
   Nobel Prize 62, 67–8, 71, 89, 94, 96, 113, 176, 190
   originality 6, 15–18, 21–2, 25–6, 30, 64, 175, 182, 191
   'Pinteresque' 2, 8, 30, 46, 57, 64, 67, 150, 157, 166–7, 175, 177–91

politics 3–8, 16–17, 40, 45–50, 54–62, 67–8, 72, 88–103, 109, 130, 176, 184, 208
postmodernism 2 16, 81, 181
realism 2, 68, 154, 201–2, 212, 214
Royal Academy of Dramatic Art (RADA) 63, 111
space 21, 49, 72, 108, 116, 140, 145, 153, 157, 175, 186, 210–12, 214–16
Theatre of the Absurd 6, 23, 36–50, 55, 64, 75, 202, 214
transmutation 16, 21–2, 26, 28–30, 177
violence 8, 29, 55, 82, 88–90, 92–3, 102, 139–54, 162, 167, 169–70, 178, 180, 187–8, 208
Vital Theatre 63
Works By
   A Kind of Alaska 9, 107, 135
   A Night Out 42
   A Slight Ache 9, 42–3, 76, 169, 178, 207
   'American Football' 9, 88
   Apart from That 9
   Art, Truth and Politics 9, 62, 67, 89–90, 96
   'Arthur Miller's Socks' 99
   Ashes to Ashes 7, 9, 71, 78–80, 110, 145, 169, 176, 183, 187
   Betrayal (film) 132, 183
   Betrayal (play) 1, 6, 18, 20–1, 56, 59, 65–6, 109, 135, 169, 205, 207–9, 215
   Blithe Spirit 113
   Celebration 9, 20, 60, 68, 160
   'Death' 9
   'Democracy' 88
   Exiles 31 n.3, 121
   Family Voices 9, 135
   'Girls' 9
   God's District 9
   Langrishe, Go Down 132
   Landscape 9, 25–6, 64, 117, 121, 124, 135, 165–6, 182, 187
   Monologue 9, 20
   Moonlight 9
   Mountain Language 9, 88, 101–2, 145, 148, 150
   Night 9
   Night School 9
   No Man's Land 7, 20, 27, 57–9, 66, 107, 109, 116–19, 135, 161–2, 169
   Old Times 7, 20, 56, 107, 116–18, 121, 124, 132, 135, 169, 175, 182–3, 204
   One for the Road 6, 9, 47, 60–2, 78, 81, 88, 95, 145, 158, 160, 178
   Other Places 135
   Party Time 6, 8–9, 60–1, 95, 141, 145, 149–53, 160, 162
   Press Conference 9, 96
   Precisely 9, 95
   Remembrance of Things Past (stage production) 21
   Reunion 79
   Silence 25, 64, 117, 121, 124, 135, 165–6, 182
   Special Offer 9
   Tea Party 42, 161
   That's All 9
   That's Your Trouble 9
   The Basement 44
   The Birthday Party 7, 9, 15, 26–7, 39, 41–3, 45, 47–8, 50 n.13, 54–6, 71, 76–8, 80, 110, 112–13, 121–3, 126–9, 132–3, 135, 160–2, 167, 177, 180, 183, 189–91, 201–2, 210
   The Caretaker (film) 43, 49, 107
   The Caretaker (play) 8–9, 31 n.5, 43, 58, 65, 109, 112, 122, 141–50, 153, 157, 160, 167, 169, 198–200, 204, 206

The Collection 9, 44, 121, 124, 183, 206
The Dumb Waiter 9, 47, 50 n.13, 55–6, 122, 129, 132–6, 160, 167, 169, 184–6, 208
The Dwarfs (novel) 76–7
The Dwarfs (play) 42–3, 76
The Dwarfs (radio play) 76
The Examination 42
The Go-Between 56–7
The Homecoming 6–7, 9, 26–7, 29, 57–9, 71, 77–7, 81, 108–10, 112, 115–16, 121, 123–5, 133, 135, 169, 183, 201–2, 213
The Hothouse 9, 47, 60, 214
The Lover 9, 43, 56, 183, 206
The Man in the Glass Booth 79
The New World Order 9, 60–2, 88, 95, 145, 150, 160
The Pres and Officer 9
The Proust Screenplay 64
The Room 9, 24–5, 31 n.5, 41, 47, 55, 76–7, 109, 111, 114, 142, 183, 204
The Servant 56–7
The Trial 132
Trouble in the Works 9
Victoria Station 9, 135, 204
'Writing for Myself' 110
Pinter, Jack (Pinter's father) 72
Pirandello, Luigi 18
Pollack, Sydney 157
Portable Theatre 131
Postmodernism 2, 16, 81, 181
Potter, Dennis 108
Pound, Ezra 115
Prebble, Lucy 158
   Enron 159
Prentice, Penelope 62–3
Proust, Marcel 4, 21–2
   Remembrance of Things Past (novel) 21
   Remembrance of Things Past (stage production) 21

Queen Elizabeth II 124
Queen Elizabeth Hall 102
Quigley, Austin E. 76

Raby, Peter 2
Radio Times Drama Award 178
Rahman Khan, Shamus 54
Raine, Nina 78, 82
   Tribes 82
Rattigan, Terence 112
Ravenhill, Mark 8, 140–1, 150, 153, 158, 175
   Shopping and Fucking 150
   The Cane 8, 140–1, 150–3
Rebellato, Dan 38, 111
Red Ladder 131
Rees, Catherine 49 n.1, 72
Richardson, Dorothy 23
   Pilgrimage 23
Richardson, Ralph 118
Ridley, Philip 4, 154
Rimbaud, Artur 71
Robards, Jason 79
Rogers, Paul 135
Romanticism 17
Roof, Judith 18
Rosset, Barney 44
Roth, Philip 75
Rothko, Mark 213
Rothstein, Eric 30
Rousseau, Aloysia 180, 186
Royal Court Theatre 63, 65, 80, 111–12, 139, 175, 179, 181, 186–8
Royal and Derngate theatre 9
Royal Shakespeare Company 7, 43–4, 68, 112, 121–36, 165
   Actors Commando 122, 125–6, 130
   'Dirty Plays' scandal 123
   How to Stop Worrying and Love the Theatre 122, 129, 131, 133–5
   Theatregoround 122, 125–6, 129–32, 134–6
Rozik, Eli 73
Rudkin, David 135
   Afore Night Come 135

Rutherford School, Paddington 126
Rylance, Mark 9

Saint-Denis, Michel 111, 124
Sakellaridou, Elizabeth 3
Salem, Daniel 75–6
Saunders, Graham 188, 191
Saunders, Judith 152
Schatzberg, Jerry 79
Schimmelpfennig, Roland 175
Scolnicov, Hanna 80
Scott, Jill 145
Sereny, Gitta 79–80
Shaffer, Peter 74
Shaftsbury, Lord 72
Shakespeare Birthplace Trust 136
Shakespeare, William 4, 20, 107, 123, 125–6, 131–3, 209
Shared Experience 201–2
Shaw, George Bernard 4
Shaw, Marc 177
Shaw, Robert 79
Sheen, Michael 108
Shepard, Sam 201
Sheridan, Richard Brinsley 205
Shutt, Christopher 108
Sicher, Efraim 75
Sierz, Aleks 154, 175, 180, 191
Silverstein, Marc 76–7, 154
Simpson, N. F. 43, 45, 111
Smith, Ian 3
Smith, Stevie 31 n.2
Sofer, Andrew 140–1, 148
Sophocles 126, 131
Speer, Albert 79–80
Spencer, Charles 178, 182
Spender, Stephen 20, 31 n.3
Spielberg, Steven 81
    Schindler's List (film) 81
St. Vincent Millay, Edna 31 n.2
Stafford-Clark, Max 113
Stambollouian, Ed 9
Stein, Peter 115
Stephens, Simon 175
Stevens, Wallace 115

Stevenson, Randall 16
Story, David 108
Stoppard, Tom 38, 53, 65, 73, 77
    Rosencrantz and Guildenstern Are Dead 38
Stratford-upon-Avon 122, 125, 131, 136
Strausz-Hupé, Robert 100
Strindberg, August 4, 18, 205
Sullivan, Hugh 132
Sunday Night (BBC Television) 126
Sunday Times, the 41, 48
Surrealism 2
Sykes, Arlene 18

Tabachnik, Ely 72, 76–7
Taylor-Batty, Mark 3, 50 n.15, 55, 59–60, 73, 77, 81, 124, 133
Thatcher, Margaret 59–60
Théâtre National Populaire 126
The Place 202
Theatre Royal Stratford East 63
Thomas, Dylan 20, 133
    Under Milkwood 133
Thompson, David T. 136
Three (triple-bill) 43
Tony Awards 135
Trevis, Di 21
Trump, Donald 53, 91
Trussler, Simon 135
Tucker, David 49 n.8
tucker green, debbie 8, 140–1, 145
    ear for eye 8, 140–1, 145–8, 152–3
    hang 148
Turkish Embassy London 102
Turkish Peace Association 93, 96, 101
Turner, Lyndsey 9
Tynan, Kenneth 41, 44–6, 49–50 n.10, 68 n.2
Tzara, Tristan 20

Uhlman, Fred 79
    Reunion 79
United Kingdom Independence Party (UKIP) 91

United States Congress 97
United States Department of State 97
Vassaf, Gunduz 94
Vitrac, Roger 135
   Victor 135

Wainwright, Hilary 67
Wardle, Irving 42, 45, 141, 177
Washington Post 53, 97–9
West Yorkshire Playhouse 180
Waters, Steve 7, 154, 158
Webster, John 20, 63, 107
Wellwarth, George E. 108, 116
Welles, Orson 20, 45, 117
Wernick, Morris 73, 78, 82
Wesker, Arnold 74, 78, 110, 154
West, Samuel 79
Whyman, Erica 210
Wilde, Oscar 205
Williams, Clifford 124
Williams, Lia 9

Williams, William Carlos 115
Wilson, Angus 111
Wilson, Harold 109
Wilson, Reg 136
Wimbledon School of Art 210
Wolfit, Donald 111, 129
Women's Street Theatre 131
Wong Yeang Chui, Jane 144
Wood, Peter 56, 110
Woodroffe, Graham 143, 150
Woolf, Henry 3, 20, 41, 73, 82, 111
Woolf, Virginia 20, 71
Wordsworth, William 66
Wyllie, Andrew 72, 154
Wyver, John 126

Yeats, W. B. 20, 31 n.2, 66, 71
Yerebakan, Ibrahim 150–1

Zarhy-Levo, Yael 39, 42, 46, 54, 64, 177
Žižek, Slavoj 8, 140–1, 144, 146–8, 154

www.ingramcontent.com/pod-product-compliance
Lightning Source LLC
Chambersburg PA
CBHW072107010526
44111CB00037B/2018